CREATING AN
"OPEN BOOK"
ORGANIZATION

...WHERE EMPLOYEES THINK & ACT LIKE BUSINESS PARTNERS

CREATING AN
"OPEN BOOK"
ORGANIZATION

...WHERE EMPLOYEES THINK & ACT LIKE BUSINESS PARTNERS

THOMAS J. MCCOY

amacom
American Management Association

New York • Atlanta • Boston • Chicago • Kansas City • San Francisco • Washington, D.C.
Brussels • Mexico City • Tokyo • Toronto

This publication is designed to provide accurate and authoritative
information in regard to the subject matter covered. It is sold with the
understanding that the publisher is not engaged in rendering legal,
accounting, or other professional service. If legal advice or other expert
assistance is required, the services of a competent professional person should
be sought.

Library of Congress Cataloging-in-Publication Data

McCoy, Thomas J.
    Creating an "open book" organization— where employees think & act like
business partners / Thomas J. McCoy.
        p.   cm.
    Includes bibliographical references and index.
    ISBN 0–8144–0293–3
    1. Employee empowerment.   2. Employee motivation.   3. Expectation
(Psychology)   4. Compensation management.   I. Title.
HD50.5.M36   1996
658.3'14—dc20   95–52017
                                                                      CIP

Printing number

10 9 8 7 6 5 4 3 2

To
my wife
Cathy
Her understanding, support, and encouragement
are the reasons this material found its way into print.
Thanks, Cathy. I love you.

Contents

List of Figures

Acknowledgments

The information provided in this book is the result of collaboration and research with organizations such as The American Compensation Association, the Department of Labor—Office of the American Workplace, the Foundation for Enterprise Development, the National Center for Employee Ownership, and dozens of practicing companies.

In addition, I would like to thank my friends who provided insight as I travelled on the path. Special thanks to John Schuster and Jill Carpenter, with whom I have worked closely on several open-book projects; Ray Holton, a financial analyst who really understands how the numbers tell a story; Andy Huckaba, Chris Johnson, Trevor Ralston, John Savageau, Chuck Lindberg, Mike Niedenthal, Roland Raeker, and others mentioned and quoted throughout this book. These are just a few of the colleagues with whom I have discussed these concepts and came away better for it.

CREATING AN "OPEN BOOK" ORGANIZATION

...WHERE EMPLOYEES THINK & ACT LIKE BUSINESS PARTNERS

Introduction: The Open Organization

Employees are the key to success in a changing, competitive economy. A company's employees are the only resource that cannot be duplicated. The closer each employee performs to his or her true potential as an individual, the closer the company comes to being unbeatable in the marketplace. However, employees are also the most difficult resource to utilize effectively.

Forward-thinking companies recognize the value of their human resources and for over a decade have initiated involvement efforts to more fully engage them in the business process. Quality circles, management by objective (MBO), total quality management (TQM), business process re-engineering, and perhaps a dozen other techniques have been implemented. Yet the efforts always seem to fall short of the expectations.

In today's new economy, employees have become a strategic competitive advantage—one that can determine success or failure. Such weighty outcomes beg the questions: Are your current employee-involvement initiatives meeting your expectations? Are your most valuable assets—your employees—providing the best return they can? For that matter, do they really view themselves as members of your team?

Ask these questions to the general employee population and you probably will find they are not nearly as interested and enthusiastic about current employee involvement initiatives as senior management thinks they are.

In this new economy, it is critical to maximize the effectiveness of each and every employee. With that as an imperative, why aren't these initiatives performing up to their level of promise? The theories supporting these efforts are sound and effective . . . to a limited degree.

Perhaps that is the problem. Taken by themselves, each technique addresses a specific set of circumstances and performance issues. Each of these initiatives is really a stand-alone program, isolated from the other initiatives by its technology. The result is a series of parts that are less than the sum that they create. What is needed is an approach that incorporates key employee involvement and participation technologies in a holistic approach that addresses the cause rather than the symptoms.

It is possible to create a work environment in which each employee can make an impact on the company's profitability. Such an approach has been taken by a few leading-edge companies with dramatically successful results. Their success stems from creating a partnership with all employees. This partnership is developed through the application of a combination of proven and innovative human-resources initiatives that are based on trust and sharing and free from the concept of exploitation.

For example, your company most likely has implemented one or more of the following processes: reengineering of the organization, empowerment of all employees, and even the provision of several processes such as TQM and statistical process control that enable employees to participate and become involved. But are these efforts integrated? Have the employees been *educated* in the factors of the business? Do they understand how the company makes a profit and the importance of generating (and preserving) cash? Have they been *engaged* in the business with reward systems that provide satisfaction based on participation, performance, and results?

You may have enabled and empowered your employees, but have you educated and engaged them? The material in this book represents an integrated approach that applies multiple human-resources initiatives in a coordinated manner to create a partnership among all employees.

We will examine in detail the relationships between these initiatives and identify their synergy. In doing so, we will provide answers to questions that have plagued human resources professionals and managers of all levels as they attempt to more fully engage their workforce.

The E_4-R_4 Partnership Checklist — A Checklist for Success

Who could compete with an organization in which every employee is educated, enabled, empowered, and engaged? How flexible and responsive to the customer would an organization be if all employees understood their roles, knew and were comfortable with their rights, were committed to their responsibilities, and shared in the risks and rewards of their company?

The management technology exists today to achieve this organizational state. Various elements of this technology have been proven in literally hundreds of small and large companies already. Several of the more leading-edge organizations have included all the key elements in their change process.

The experiences of these companies tell us that to achieve this dynamic partnership, organizations must:

- Clearly understand the expectations of employees as they pertain to partnership.
- Assume certain practices that will link the fulfillment of these expectations to the achievement of key business objectives.

And employees must:

- Clearly understand management's perspective as it pertains to business objectives and profitability.
- Become completely engaged in the efforts to achieve the business objectives.

In this book, we will build the E_4-R_4 Partnership Checklist (see Exhibit I-1). This tool is a checklist of four management practices (E_4) and four employee expectations (R_4) necessary for the development of an open, partner-oriented, high-performance/high-involvement company. It will place in perspective a list of management practices and employee actions necessary for success.

The E_4-R_4 Partnership Checklist is a change-management architecture that increases customer satisfaction, employee satisfaction, and shareholder value. It is a set of management practices and employee responses that transforms employees into partners. It is a work system in which people and processes maintain a high sustained level of performance. It is a process that creates a company culture in which all employees work for the benefit of themselves, for each other, and for the stockholders as partners in the endeavor.

Applying the practices and perspectives provided in this checklist will develop a sustainable competitive advantage that can increase operating income, increase personal income, and increase job availability through growth.

Figure I-1. E$_4$-R$_4$ Partnership Checklist.

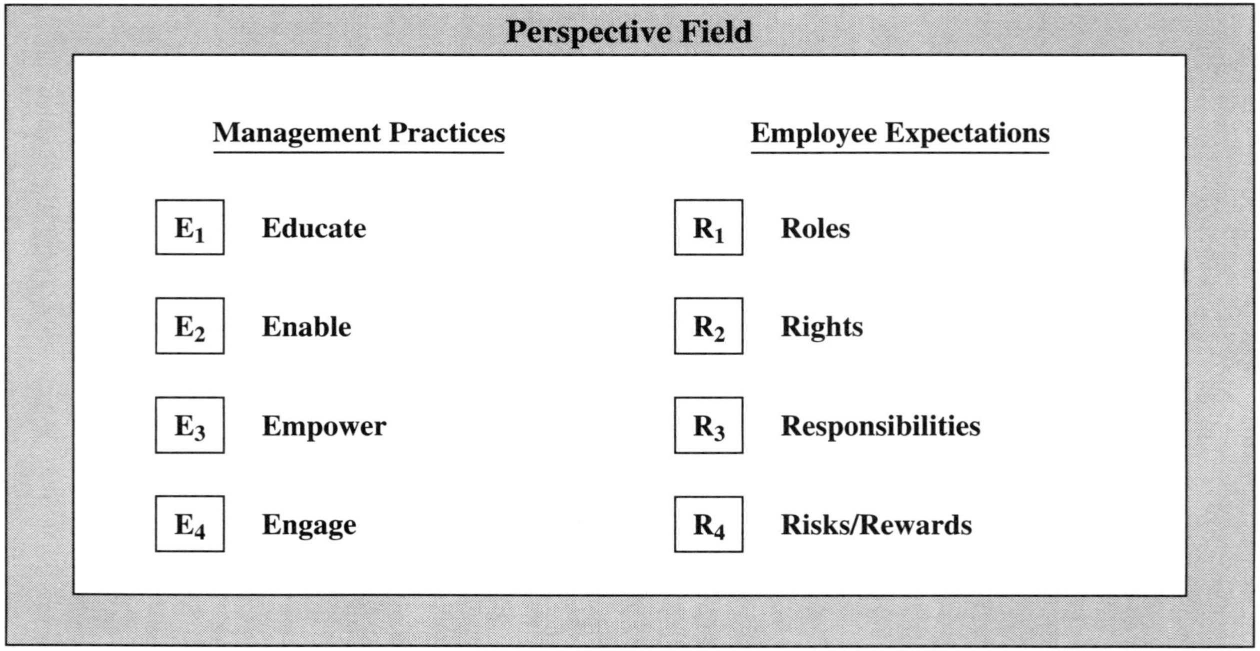

Perspective Field

Management Practices

E$_1$	Educate
E$_2$	Enable
E$_3$	Empower
E$_4$	Engage

Employee Expectations

R$_1$	Roles
R$_2$	Rights
R$_3$	Responsibilities
R$_4$	Risks/Rewards

A Unique Perspective

This book is unique because it examines the impact of management practices on employee expectations. This unique perspective provides important understanding of the forces that make the E4-R4 tool so effective and create such powerful results. The details and relationships of each practice and expectation are thoroughly examined. Wherever possible, graphics have been added for clarity and ease of use.

This emerging work culture is often referred to as an open-book organization by those who have successfully applied this integrated technology. In order to create an environment in which all employees view themselves as partners, it is necessary to open the organization. It is necessary to release the old styles of command and control and embrace the concepts of sharing: sharing information, sharing education, sharing responsibility, and sharing rewards associated with results. The outcome is an open, educated, partner-oriented, high-involvement/high-performance company.

This book includes theory and application techniques you can use to create a work environment in which employees become partners who possess the desire and capacity to contribute to the success of the business. It provides the information, models, templates, and working documents necessary to transform the relationship between employer and employee into a partnership capable of sustaining and building on change.

The Business Benefits of Using This Information

In this book, we review the conditions necessary to compete in the new economy. You will see how to prepare and align the organization to maximize the flow of information and work. We redefine how employees participate in the work process. Through a detailed examination of four key management practices and four key employee expectations, you will learn how to create a company staffed with employee partners.

Take the following self-test. If you answer yes to any of the categories listed below, then you will benefit from the theory and tactical applications contained in this book.

Does your organization need to improve in any of the following areas?

- Attaining higher quality
- Making fewer mistakes
- Implementing profit orientation
- Lowering costs

- Attaining greater loyalty
- Attaining a common business focus
- Attaining expansive creative thinking
- Attaining greater flexibility
- Attaining higher customer satisfaction
- Attaining higher employee satisfaction
- Attaining higher stockholder satisfaction

Fundamental to this concept is a comprehensive system of social, psychological, and material rewards that support and encourage employee involvement and participation in an environment based on equality.

Throughout my years of work with reward systems, I have observed that one of the greatest challenges to the compensation professional is in the area of incentive compensation, specifically, how to educate the general employee population so they understand and see the connection between their actions, company profitability, and incentive pay. In Chapter 7, you will gain access to perhaps the most sought-after employee-involvement tool for linking performance to pay and results—the Line-Of-Sight Linkage Tree™.

In Chapters 9 and 10, we use the Reward System Selector™ process that examines in detail how to choose the appropriate self-funding incentive compensation plan that will cement partnership commitment and drive performance to new levels.

The Personal and Social Benefits of Using This Information

One of the social outcomes of this book is that it helps working people help each other. Applying the principles described in this book will develop an open environment in which employers and employees work together for individual benefit, group benefit, stockholder benefit, and the benefit of the community. The processes explained here are based on the value of the individual and, when applied, they improve the quality of work life for all.

1

Successfully Competing in the New Economy

Publications such as *Business Week* magazine and *Harvard Business Review* have been reporting on how nations and industries will compete in the emerging "new" economy. The new economy is indeed new. It is an economy based on global competition, high technology, and instant access to information. It promises high-quality, custom-tailored products and services at mass-produced prices. It is an economy in which productive skills are the key to economic success.

To continue to exist, all companies will be required to pass from the old economy into the new. However, the barriers to entry into this new economy are high. They are nothing less than the fundamental restructuring of how work is organized and how people will participate in the work process. At question are the basic relationships between those who do the work, those who manage the work, and those who own the resources and capital.

The Downward Trend

We have already begun to experience the negative effects of these barriers to entry. Since World War II through the early 1980s, the growth of the "old" economy was driven by productivity improvements acquired through technology. As this growth-and-profit strategy reached the point of diminishing returns, it was replaced in the mid-eighties by a strategy of cost reduction, with labor cost as a key element.

By now we all know someone who has been affected by the reduction of low- and middle-income jobs. The Bureau of Labor Statistics reports that the average U.S. wage has been falling since 1973. Over the past twenty years, average wage earners have seen their real income drop 20 percent, from $315 per week to about $250 per week in 1994. Limited job availability has reduced or held down wage levels. How significant is this trend?

The Dire Consequences

The U.S. Secretary of Labor in the Clinton administration, Robert Reich, thinks this trend is extremely significant. In a recent public address he stated, "We depend on upward mobility and the work ethic as the moral centers of this economy. If we lose our middle class, we invite the worst forms of demagoguery." The Secretary of Labor is concerned because he has access to information that shows him, in great detail, the effects on society of the new economy we have entered. The overall effect is a widening gap between the rich and the poor as middle-income jobs disappear in record numbers. Interestingly, if we ever do reach the ambitious potentials of the information age, there may be very few consumers with the wherewithal to participate.

We hear of a continuing decline of jobs in the manufacturing sector, and then are told that service jobs will take the place of this decline. That may be true on a job-for-job basis. But if we allow the economy to continue down that path, the result will not be pleasant.

The Economic Policy Institute in Washington, D.C. reports:

> Manufacturing produces more and better jobs than the service sector. The average manufacturing job generates four and one-half times as many secondary jobs as the average retail job. Even industries on the low end of the industrial scale, such as textiles and apparel, have employment multipliers that are double those of the fastest growing parts of the service sector.[1]

Succeed and Grow Or . . .

On a national scale, the challenge is to restore and expand middle-class prosperity. From a business perspective, the challenge is to successfully compete and grow in both manufacturing and service industries. From an individual employee's perspective, the short-term challenge is survival: to keep a job and maintain a cash flow that is adequate to support a lifestyle. How can these objectives be achieved?

Productivity, a key element of successful competition, is also a key element in determining a nation's standard of living. An increase in productivity can lead to an increase in net earnings and/or growth for companies and can result in higher wages and greater job availability for employees. Middle-income jobs will only be made available through successful competition and growth.

Changes in Technology

One of the first effects of the new economy was the decline in middle-class blue-collar jobs. In 1950, 33 percent of all employment was in high-paying manufacturing jobs. In 1994, manufacturing jobs were 17 percent of all employment. This situation was caused by competition from low-cost foreign labor and the subsequent U.S. workplace productivity improvement efforts that were initiated as a response. For the past fifteen years, labor cost-reduction has been an element in any effort to improve productivity.

Changes in Corporate Culture

More recently, in the ongoing response to ever-increasing competitive pressure, middle-income jobs have been reduced through the process of downsizing, reengineering, and the advent of team-based work environments. In the last five years, over three million middle-management jobs have been eliminated—more than one-half million in 1994. This recent approach may be effective in keeping the wolf from the door *but only as a stop-gap, emergency measure.* And even then, it may be strategic folly.

Yes, many of the current functions and activities that middle managers perform can be conducted by employees who have a lower base-salary, and, therefore, labor costs can be reduced by eliminating middle-management positions. But that may be missing the point.

The point is that the role of the middle manager is changing. In the new business environment described in this book, managers become facilitators, mentors, and coaches. In order to effectively do that, they need people skills and a perspective that is best developed when the proper training is combined with years of experience managing people.

This experience is the true, unrealized value of middle management today. The years of on-the-job experience they have in dealing with a myriad of people issues provides real management depth to an organization. An MBA from Harvard can provide a certain intellectual capability. However, this intellectual capability is of little use in dealing with the interpersonal issues that are so much a part of a team environment.

The management techniques described in this book will awaken an understanding that, rather than dismissing this vast pool of unrecognized and unvalued talent, a very real competitive advantage can be obtained by redefining the roles and responsibilities. The Introduction presented the E_4R_4 Partnership Checklist as a model of management practices and employee expectation. These and other fundamental changes must be implemented in order for a company or organization to compete and grow successfully.

Mutual Perspective

From management's perspective, success in the new economy starts when the company develops the capability to compete: to grow in profit, revenue, and market share, and to identify and seize opportunities to diversify.

From the employee's perspective, success starts with job availability and income growth. Stated in this way, it is obvious the two perspectives are mutually supportive. They are focused on a single objective that provides something for each group. Success in the new economy provides multiple outcomes and addresses multiple needs. Herein lies the answer. They key to successful competition is to understand the strengths that exist in mutually supportive perspectives and to leverage this understanding as a key business strategy. The models, discussions, and observations presented in this book emphasize the application of this mutual perspective.

The age of the individual is over. In the new economy, success comes to those who can develop the most effective partnerships. Successful partnering results in united commitment toward a common goal. Partnering is the art of negotiating a win-win, where each party believes it will benefit from the relationship. And a fundamental element of successful negotiation is the practice of mutual perspective—seeing the proffered outcome from the other person's point of view. Perspectives and partnership: These are fundamental business techniques of the new economy.

The Individual's Responsibility

"A great skill shortage is going to occur that will eat away at our competitiveness," says John L. Clendenin, Chief Executive Officer of BellSouth Corp.[2]

On an individual level the prerequisite to rising wages and benefits is to assume responsibility for rising education and skill levels. Employees need to make themselves more valuable to their employers. At the 1994 World Congress on Personnel Management, Edward

E. Lawler III, Ph.D., spoke on how organizations can make more effective use of their people. He said, "Restructuring will lead to more downsizing, and configurations of organizations will continue to change, requiring new sets of skills from employees. The result is that people will have multiple careers, lateral careers. People will have to focus more on individual competencies than on relationships with their employers."

Being staffed strategically is no longer an option. Each employee must be able to answer the question "What have you done for your company . . . today." And the answer will need to be in terms of quantifiable impact on revenue. Only then will employees be in a position to act as partners of the business and expect that partnership to be reflected in their compensation. The link between education and reward systems has been forged.

Management's Responsibility

Management's responsibility is to develop an organization whose focus, systems, procedures, policies, and resources are integrated to compete successfully, to grow in profit, revenue, and market share, and to identify and seize opportunities to diversify. Lots of work to do here. Where does one start?

In recent years, the approach to improving internal organization and operation has been pursued in great detail. What has surfaced as a result is a universal observation that an organization's employees play a key role in issues of competition and growth.

Following this approach, several internally focused strategies have been developed to respond to the new economy. These employee-oriented approaches are processes with names such as TQM and self-managed work teams.

Each process has its own unique approach to addressing a specific issue. TQM involves employees in the problem-solving process and self-management work teams empower employees to make decisions that affect work design and product cost.

Unfortunately, an estimated 65 percent of these efforts fail. Why is there such an unacceptably high failure rate? The premise has been proven sound. There are plenty of success stories of companies who have come back from the brink of failure through the efforts of their employees. However, based on the data, these are in the minority of all organizations making the attempt. Perhaps the cause of this high failure rate can be found in the following observation by Albert Einstein: "The significant problems we face cannot be solved at the same level of thinking we were at when we created them."

Open Thinking May Be The Answer

Mr. Einstein's observation implies that effective strategies for success in a global economy will require a dramatic departure from traditional thinking about work structures and the relationship between labor, management, owners, and society. One such dramatic departure is the concept of an open work environment. At the center of this concept is the relationship of the individual employee to the organization's success.

An open environment implies access—access to information, to skill development, to social interaction, to authority, and to the rewards of success. An open environment results from the application of mutual perspective in the policy-making process. It is the basis of an egalitarian management philosophy.

There are indications that this philosophy is rising spontaneously in response to the intensely competitive new economy. It can be found in most companies that successfully implement employee involvement processes, like the food processing company with the employee principle that states: "We declare that this company is a vehicle for its people to get what they want." Now THAT is a strong use of mutual perspective.

In this book we examine companies that utilize an open environment as the foundation of their management philosophy. We investigate the effect that an open environment has on revenue, growth, employee income, and job availability. We also identify and analyze the other management practices and employee expectations that are necessary to successfully build on this approach.

Openness and Ownership

Openness is ownership—ownership of information, of responsibility, of results, and much more. An open environment provides all participants with an understanding of the intent of their organization. It provides all participants with the capacity to comply with the intent of their organization and the opportunity to develop agreement with the intent of their organization. An open environment results in an understanding that change is normal and it cultivates an attitude of accountability. (After all, when you understand, agree with, and have the capacity to comply with the intent of the organization, it's pretty hard not to assume accountability.) And, of course, the reward systems of such an organization contain elements of ownership that supports openness.

Reward systems appear to be a major driving force in an open environment. In 1992, I wrote *Compensation and Motivation: Maximiz-*

ing Employee Performance with Behavior-Based Incentive Plans. In it, I stated that "Redesigning compensation to align it more closely with performance and the gains of improvement is arguably the strongest and most far-reaching of all human resources tools currently available or on the horizon."[3] Well, the horizon has just expanded. The geography hasn't changed, but the development of the open organization has greatly enhanced the view. The more progressive organizations have used their reward systems to lead the changed toward open environments.

Open environments provide all the peripheral support necessary for employees to succeed in any well-designed incentive compensation plan. From the employees' perspective, an incentive plan provides the reason ("why") they should participate. An open environment provides the information and processes that answer the question "how" to participate successfully.

Many companies do not effectively communicate information to their employees on decisions such as pay ranges, merit increase budgets, and performance measurement. How logical is it to expect employees to trust that an equitable reward system exists without providing evidence that it does?

Contrast that to the software development company that offers all new recruits three salary options ranging from all salary and little stock to little salary and a lot of stock. Now THAT is a progressive pay philosophy, existing in an open environment and developed through the use of mutual perspective.

The Benefits

By design, an open environment results in flexibility, increased innovation, and fast response time. These capabilities enable a company to:

- Change product cost structure to maintain a competitive lead
- Set performance benchmark standards rather than trying to match those of others
- Capture and monopolize market share by being first into it

The information available in an open environment enables all employees to calculate which of their actions will improve profits and which will not. Teamwork is strengthened through the development of interpersonal relationships. Morale and attitudes are improved as the result of increased understanding. And do these results support the business objectives of improving revenue, growth, profit, cash, employee income, and job availability? You bet!

Educated Empowerment

One of the primary elements of an open environment is an advanced level of understanding. Assume you have empowered your employees to think, perform, and make decisions as if they were owners. For them to be successful, they need access to information. And they need to be able to understand this information. They must be educated in its meaning.

Properly administered, an open environment results not just in empowered employees, but in a company culture of educated empowerment. Empowerment by itself encounters serious problems during the decision-making process. These problems are normally associated with a lack of focus. Educated empowerment adds the elements of focus and organizational unity that enables employees to make clear and accurate decisions.

Educated Empowerment, Reward Systems, High Involvement, and High Performance

Open environments are nice, and we all want to live and work in a nice environment. But as individuals, the real reason we need to develop an open environment is because it results in a high-performance business unit that provides good-paying jobs.

Educated empowerment provides employees with skills, information, and decision-making responsibility. Add to that some form of incentive reward system, and the combination creates a high level of employee involvement. The result is performance and innovation on an individual level and on an organizational level.

"The preliminary anecdotal and imperial evidence suggests a strong relationship between these practices and corporate performance," according to Jonathan Low, director of the performance measurement project being conducted by the Department of Labor's Office of the American Workplace.[4]

Long Time Coming

Is this new thinking? Hardly. Because most growth is evolutionary, the roots of development run deep. *Harvard Business Review* hinted at things to come in 1966 when it published "The Change Seekers," an article by Patrick H. Irwin and Frank W. Langham, Jr. In it they espoused the concept of an open environment.

> Top management will strive to develop the talents and conceptual skills of the members of the workforce to a point where

they become involved increasingly in the total corporate situation in concert with management. In order to promote freedom of thought and a feeling of participation, the leader should try to establish a climate that permits an egalitarian network of communication and action among group members rather than act in an authoritarian way.[5]

Pretty progressive thinking for 1966. Now its time for senior management and human resources professionals to turn words into action.

Notes

1. Thea Lee and Dean Baker, "Employment Multipliers in the U.S. Economy," Economic Policy Institute, Washington, D.C., 1995.
2. "Inequality: How the Gap Between Rich and Poor Hurts the Economy," *BusinessWeek*, August 15, 1994.
3. Thomas J. McCoy, *Compensation and Motivation: Maximizing Employee Performance With Behavior-Based Incentive Plans*, (New York: AMACOM, 1992).
4. Office of the American Workplace, *High Performance Work Practices and Firm Performance*, U.S. Department of Labor, Washington, D.C., August 1993, p. i.
5. Patrick H. Irwin and Frank W. Langham, Jr., "The Change Seekers," *Harvard Business Review*, February 1966, pp. 75–86.

2

Fundamental Alignments Necessary for an Open Organization

"Excellence is not enough to know, we must try to have and use it."

—Aristotle

Chapter One has positioned the reasons for and the benefits of developing an open organization. Quite simply, it is to take full advantage of all available resources to compete effectively and win in the new economy. An open organization results in a high involvement/high performance workplace and there is a body of evidence that relates a high performance workplace to increased productivity and long-term financial performance.[1]

The results of an open organization are achieved through the development of an educated, enabled, empowered, and engaged workforce that has a firm belief in the purpose of the business and, to an individual, is committed to achieving it.

An open organization refers to the state an organization is in when:

- Each employee understands what the organization must do to be successful.
- Each employee understands their role in achieving those financial and operational objectives.
- All employees are involved in the goal-setting process.
- Problem solving and decision making are conducted by those closest to the issues.

- Success is celebrated and rewards shared by all who participate.

Aligning The Foundation First

The first step necessary to becoming an open organization is to properly align the primary elements of the business. A sort of housecleaning before the party if you will. Throughout this chapter we discuss a model that demonstrates how four key business elements—strategy, marketing, operations, and human resources—are aligned to work in concert with each other and prepare the way for transition to an open organization.

To emphasize the significance of the alignment process I often use two powerful questions related to the development of an open organization. These questions are posed on a first-person basis and provide deep insight into the ability of a company to achieve its business objectives. The first question is, What is your job? I sometimes phrase this question in the more open manner of, Why are you here? The second question is, What have you done for your company today?

Both questions could be perceived by the respondent as aggressive and threatening because they require a justification of one's employment. I take care to position the questions in a neutral light because the intent is to determine the current status of the organization's focus and the level of communication that exists. This information tells us quite a bit about the degree of alignment of the key elements. We will examine the dynamics of the first question now and examine the second question in Chapter Seven.

The Intent Is the Issue

The purpose of the question Why are you here? is to identify the level of understanding the employee has concerning the overall intent of the company. If the company's reason for being in business is clearly known and understood by the employee, the response will refer to his or her role in achieving the intent of the company. All too often the intent of an organization is undefined or, if defined, poorly communicated to all levels of employees.

A good example of this is my experience with an international energy firm that asked me to help them improve performance in one of their high-pressure, low-density (HPLD) polyethylene processing facilities. The objective of the assignment was to reduce the amount of time the facility was off-line because of maintenance. The approach was to develop management techniques that would encourage employees to become more involved in the business and therefore perform in a more proactive, empowered manner.

An HPLD processing facility can be an extremely dangerous place. Ethylene gas is placed under tremendous pressure in huge compressors and injected with catalysts that initiate a chemical reaction. This reaction links the gas molecules into chains that form polyethylene. The polyethylene forms a thick liquid mass that is then extruded from the "reactor." The catalytic process generates significant amounts of heat and, if it gets out of control in the reactor, can cause an explosion. Naturally, in such an environment there was a high emphasis on working safely and maintaining the process within safe operating guidelines.

During my initial fact finding, I interviewed a cross section of the employee population. I wanted to determine to what degree the culture of the facility was conducive to participation and involvement. I included, as a key question in each interview, Why are you here? The responses were quite illuminating.

Conflicting Signals

What was the intent of the organization? According to the management it was to produce a profit for the company through the production and distribution of polyethylene product. Profit and cost were the focus of discussion by most of the management in the administration building. (For safety purposes the administration building was located outside the reactor compound.)

Inside the reactor compound the intent of the organization was perceived differently. When I asked the question Why are you here?, the response by the majority of the processing employees was "to work safely." This was certainly a prerequisite to employment, but it was not the primary business intent of the organization. When an employee was hired he or she was told the purpose of the facility and what it produced. However, over the years management had placed an emphasis on safety and operational issues and had not maintained an emphasis on the fact that the facility existed to provide a return on investment to the corporation.

Intuitively simple you say? The employees knew, or should have known the intent. Yes, it is obvious, and that was the initial response of the management. But the reality was that the operations employees were focusing on safety and other day-to-day issues. They were not focusing their efforts on cost and productivity issues to the extent they could have because management hadn't focused them in this direction.

Management wanted every employee to perform as if they owned the facility. Management even referred to it as "your plant." While receptive to the idea, the employees didn't understand the concept behind the words.

In order to achieve this understanding, it was necessary to develop a communication and education process that provided all employees with a big picture perspective and management's expectation of their role in achieving the business objectives.

The Challenge

Why is it important for employees to understand the intent of their organization? In a public address, U.S. Secretary of Labor Robert Reich stated it is important because "a skilled, flexible workforce can offer an enduring competitive advantage. Employees can be a strategic trump card." The point is that, first and foremost, in order for all employees to participate and contribute to the achievement of the business objectives, they must be able to clearly express these objectives. They must be intimately familiar with the intent of the organization.

Understanding the intent of an organization provides the foundation from which all employees can fulfill customer expectations. It provides them with the basis from which to make decisions that reduce variations, yield loss, and customer dissatisfaction. It provides them with the reason to take actions and track improvements. To compete and win in the new economy all employees must be able to effectively answer the question, Why are you here?

The Customer Is King

Here is a good question on which to build this thought process. Envision the recipients of your company's product or service. In your mind's eye view them receiving and utilizing the product or service. Now ask yourself, Will the value they are receiving create a long-term competitive advantage for the company? Implicit in this question are issues about the level of quality, of customer service, price, and features. Does the product or service reflect technological leadership? Did the transaction create, in the mind of the customer, a sense that the company has a willingness and flexibility to address their needs above all else?

Why are these things important? Because in the new economy, the customer is king and competition for customers is greater than ever. Ultimately, only the customer can provide the profit and cash needed for an organization to stay in business. And who can provide this sense of service and partnership to the client? Ultimately, only the employees.

The wake-up call has already been heard by most organizations. There are significant trends in the business environment to lower costs, increase customer satisfaction, continuously improve the process, and more fully involve and engage all employees. These efforts, when conducted successfully, prove effective in increasing net earnings. A good example is the automotive market supplier whose process improvement efforts resulted in a 41 percent reduction in shipping errors, a 90 percent decrease in billing errors, and a 35 percent reduction in inventory.

Competitive Issues and Answers

The new economy has resulted in a changing nature of work and a change to the environment in which work is performed. Advanced technology has created a long-term effect on all aspects of products and services. Significant and far-reaching changes have been made in materials, manufacturing processes, distribution methods, quality, product life cycle, and the quality and quantity of communication. To remain competitive an organization is now required to address such issues as:

- Product/service characteristics
- Functionality
- Cost
- Quality
- Innovation
- Time to market
- Flexibility
- Service

Solutions to these competitive pressures are to be found in two fundamentals:

1. In the way organizations are structured
2. In the way people are managed

These two fundamentals are the foundation for a high-involvement/ high-performance workplace. Companies will need to realign their organizations and rethink the way people are utilized.

In Preparation for Success

The large-scale changes that the new economy has brought about require organizations to formulate new strategic directions. Once done, they often embark on a variety of change efforts to realign their work processes to support these strategies. These realignment efforts range from wholesale downsizing to detailed process reengineering.

Unfortunately, in many cases the efforts are disjointed. Rather than taking a holistic approach to renewal, the organization initiates a "program" or a group of programs conducted by separate entities within the organization. Often the focus tends to be on relatively short-term bottom-line results. While "staying alive" is certainly a key objective, these programs often fail to take a fresh look at the alignment of job duties, procedures, methods of operation, and the volume of work that accompany these changes.

Organizations that evolve to compete successfully in the new economy do so by using a process that leverages improvements throughout the entire organization. They challenge the very purpose of their business and undertake the change process with a clear understanding of the effort required for successful implementation. They work from a comprehensive outline. The basis of the outline is to identify the key business process each employee must be aware of and which must work in concert with each other.

Synchronization and Sharing

Organizations that successfully compete in the new economy have discovered the necessity to synchronize the operational and support functions with the marketing and sales functions and to focus every employee on the customer. These companies integrate, link, and streamline the process flow, and they communicate across all functional boundaries.[2] This alignment prepares the way for a company environment of openness where business plans, operating results, financial data, and other key performance indicators are shared with and used by all employees.

The Alignment Model

Figure 2-1, the Alignment Model, embodies the concepts of integration, alliance, innovative thinking, big picture perspective, and communication. The model aligns each business element in support of a common objective, the customer. To achieve successful synergy between the elements, each element must first be aligned internally and then aligned with the other elements. This alignment is the first step to achieving a competitive edge. It is based on the elimination of functional silos, where information flows up and down, but rarely across departmental boundaries. It lays the foundation of an open environment from start to finish.

Figure 2-1. The Alignment Model.

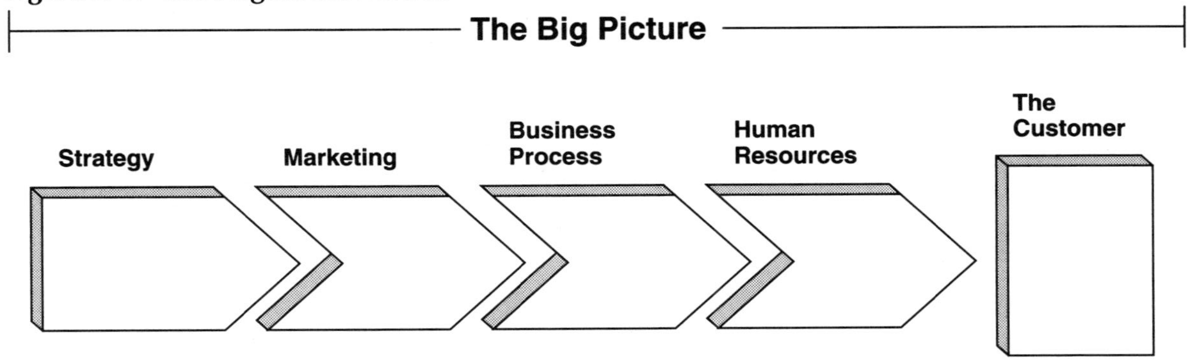

The Big Picture

Strategy Marketing Business Process Human Resources The Customer

Volumes have been written on each element of the alignment model and we do not attempt to duplicate that information here. Instead, our focus is on the human resources element of the model. However, this is a book about open environments and the principles surrounding the concept of educated empowerment. By definition, all elements of the Alignment Model are involved. Therefore, we will spend some time in an enlightening overview of the model as we define the key issues that must be present in each element and develop insight into the relationships between strategy, marketing, the business process, and the human resources.

Aligning The Strategic Element

Developing a successful competitive strategy starts by developing a clear understanding of what the new economy means to the organization. Questions about customers, competitors, suppliers, product life span, technology, new products, and cost trends must be formulated and then explored. Answers to these questions help redefine the organization's purpose and with proper analysis, lead to the identification of a new competitive strategy.

Proper situation analysis starts with a good process. Many organizations turn to the services of a skilled facilitator. In addition to technical expertise, a skilled facilitator brings a degree of objectivity necessary to develop breakthrough thinking. Although the development of a detailed strategy can be laborious and data intensive, the fundamentals are relatively straightforward.

It's as simple as getting from here to there. First, find out where you are, then determine where you want to go. Next, identify the difference between the two sets of data and, finally, generate a plan to close the gap and get where you want to be.

Keeping It Simple

The situation analysis process starts with the selection of a group of employees who will be responsible for developing a strategy that will result in a profitable and sustainable position. In an open organization the group will include a cross section of employees. All employees will be responsible for achieving the objectives defined by the strategy. Therefore it only makes sense to solicit their input in some manner during this stage.

This cross section will provide a perspective that is not available in the traditional top down approach and the result will be a sharper view of reality than could otherwise be obtained. The objective is to get new answers to the questions. (If you want the same answers, keep asking the same people.)

Once the group has been identified and engaged, the next step is to establish a baseline perspective. I usually achieve this through an informal interview with each member of the group. During the interview I ask some form of the question, What do you see as the current business strategy. The response to this question provides a baseline from which to build. I try to determine whether the response is based on the understanding of an explicit strategy, existing in some formal manner, or an implicit strategy, formulated out of the personal observations.

After the individual interviews have been completed the members are brought together as a team to evaluate the results of the interviews. Summaries of the responses are listed and the group identifies areas of common agreement and areas of difference. At this point we have aligned the collective thinking of the group. This alignment provides the perspective from which to build the new strategy.

Critical Elements

Competitive advantage is at the heart of any strategy. A company must make choices about the type of competitive advantage it wants to achieve and incorporate these choices as elements of strategy. The next step is to define and gain agreement on the elements that will be included in the strategy.

As recently as 1985 the leading-edge thinking on strategic design encouraged a company to place emphasis on one of three key strategic elements: cost leadership, differentiation, or focus.[3] However, today this approach goes awry because it fails to appreciate the underlying business realities of the new economy. It is a static approach in an economy that requires dynamic responsiveness in order to achieve a sustainable competitive advantage.

In an open organization, one with high involvement, these three key strategic elements are combined with a fourth element—the ability of employees to make a difference in business outcomes. The addition of the employee element results in a strategy with a dynamic level of flexibility. Why? Because when you include employees in your strategy you include their built-in capability for flexibility.

This flexibility enables an organization to place strong emphasis on multiple strategic elements concurrently. As an example, instead of just being a low-cost provider of a commodity product through an established distribution network, a company can become the low-cost, high-quality provider of innovative consumer products, first into the market and closest to the customer. Why? Because all employees are focused on the business objectives and they are exercising their individual initiative on a daily basis to achieve them—not exactly something an organization tied to central planning can accomplish.

The Strategic Employee Element

The strategic employee element is based on people-oriented issues, such as values, vision, and mission. From the organization's perspective, a statement of values helps define the behavior the organization will sanction and encourage. It also helps bind the employees to the organizational goals.

Values are a critical part of the human condition and, as such, form the foundation of an open organization. Open organizations exist for the purpose of employee involvement and participation. While not normally voiced, two questions are mentally asked by an individual anytime they are invited to become involved in a group. The first is, What is in it for me?

This is not a selfish question. Rather, as Abraham Maslow's work points out, it is a valid response to the drive to fulfill personal needs. The answer to this question determines whether or not the individual will become engaged in the process. We examine this question in great detail in Chapters 9 and 10. (For a more detailed explanation of the relationship between need fulfillment and contribution see the section about Abraham Maslow in *Compensation and Motivation*.[4]

The second question is less well defined but generally deals with the concerns (or fears) about the type of people they will become engaged with. For example, concerns about compatibility, trust, and other personal safety issues are the focus of the second question.

From the employee's perspective, when a group puts forth a statement of values, it provides answers to this question. A statement of organizational values that closely matches the individual's values goes a long way toward neutralizing the apprehension that could preclude their participation.

In an open organization, decision making is established at the level closest to the issue. Psychologists have determined that, during the decision-making process, values are the sounding board against which decision options are matched. These values establish moral conditions and determine why we make the decisions that we do.

The adage "Be careful what you ask for, you just might get it" certainly applies here. Great care must be taken in developing values that encourage behavior that is aligned toward the chosen competitive advantage. Values such as integrity, loyalty, and company pride are culturally oriented and support the development of interpersonal relationships.

Values such as time compression are performance related and support the development of a results orientation. Because it considers employees to be a critical strategic asset, the open organization naturally includes both interpersonal and performance-oriented values as core to its business strategy.

Management Concerns and Reassurances

It is natural for senior management to be concerned about the effects of moving to an open organization. Open organizations require the sharing of information between systems and functions and among people. In the past, information has been associated with power, and sharing it can be perceived as losing power. In actuality, sharing information makes the organization and the individuals in it more powerful.

Open organizations can be perceived as relinquishing authority when the decision-making process is moved to the level nearest the issue. In actuality, authority is not relinquished. Instead it changes from a dictatorial form to a leadership form. Open organizations can be perceived as losing control. In actuality, control of the business is increased. An autocratic style of management has the least amount of control because of the misunderstanding and time gaps that exist between executive decisions and the customer.

A clearly defined and accurately aligned set of values is necessary to provide management with assurance that, in general, educated and empowered employees will make high-quality decisions, quickly, at the right level. Only when they have this assurance will management proceed in the development of an open organization.

Partnerships — the Best Competitive Advantage

Open organizations are finding that the best competitive advantage is achieved through partnerships. Common sense and personal experience have shown us that teams are more effective than individuals in reaching organizational goals. The reason is that teams are a network of partnerships in which each member gives and receives in a win-win situation. Open organizations build a network of partnerships among employees. These employee-to-employee, labor-to-management, and employee-to-organization partnerships are part of the organization's culture.

Afraid of sharing sensitive information? Open organizations routinely include access to information as part of the process. Unless a partnership is established, this access to information could prove fatal. By establishing a partnership, all parties are working together for their own welfare and the welfare of the whole, making the issue of "sensitive" information no longer a concern. Partnership is discussed in greater detail in Chapter 3.

The Value of the Vision Thing

Let's say the group's values match the employee's values closely enough for them to see the opportunity for a rewarding partnership. The next question is, Where are we going, partner? That's where the vision thing comes in. A vision is a mental image of a future world. Again we look to the psychologists whose clinical analysis has shown that successful achievement of goals has a great deal to do with whether the participants "envision" themselves succeeding. A clear mental picture of the outcome or goal acts as a magnet to pull performance and decisions in that direction. For that reason it is important to have a statement of vision that is easily understood by all employee partners. I emphasize the term "easily understood" because I have seen statements that are all-encompassing, as if by leaving any element unmentioned, the author feared it would not be included in the employee behavior. This type of vision statement is not created in the spirit of trust, partnering, and respect.

Visions in an open organization are created with the understanding that the entire organizational system provides the information and resources that enable each employee to understand the vision statement. This educational process is examined in greater detail in Chapters 3 and 5.

The vision statement is a statement of intent. As such it is critical to align it with the organization's competitive advantage. Employee partners will be making decisions and taking actions based on their understanding of the intent of "their" organization. An example is the company whose intent is to place customer satisfaction above all else. The result is a customer service employee who finds ways to help customers achieve a competitive advantage. Not exactly in the typical job description for the position of customer service representative, but certainly in support of the intent of the company.

A vision statement that is accurately aligned with the organization's stated competitive advantage will enable employees to make decisions and take actions that propel the company forward.

The Mission

In support of the vision statement, many organizations develop a mission statement as part of their strategy. The mission statement outlines in general terms what must be done to achieve the vision.

This statement provides helpful action guidelines around which each employee partner can build his/her own decision-making judgments.

An "Open Strategy" Example

Eastman Chemical Company provides us with a good example of strategic human resources elements in support of an open organization. Eastman started quality initiatives in the early 1980s in response to a declining market share. When polled, their customers indicated the competition had surpassed them in quality. By the mid-1980s Eastman had established problem-solving teams in their operations.

Their vision statement is "To be the world's preferred chemical company." It's clear, concise, and aligned on a competitive advantage—the strategic element of differentiation, of being preferred.

Their mission statement is "To create superior value for customers, employees, stockholders, the community, and suppliers." As an empowered employee at Eastman, this would provide me with a good framework from which to exercise my job knowledge and decision-making abilities.

Lots of good value statements are implied in the mission statement too. Everyone that is affected by the organization is included as a partner and, as a result, they will be in support of the business objectives. Is this a solid approach? The results speak for themselves. In 1993 Eastman Chemical Company earned a Malcolm Baldrige National Quality Award.

An Open Strategy

The outcome of an open strategy is clear. It must focus on developing a sustainable competitive advantage through the use of people.

The strategy is a plan. The employees are the organization. They are the means by which the plan will be carried out and the objectives achieved. The old thinking was that employees had to align with the strategy. Figure 2-2 illustrates the new thinking. This thinking is more toward a middle ground where a competitive advantage can be achieved only when the strategy is in supportive alignment with the workforce.

Aligning The Marketing Element

Almost all of the performance improvement and quality issues that are being talked about today are focused on the operational aspects

Figure 2-2. Strategy: Internal and External Alignments.

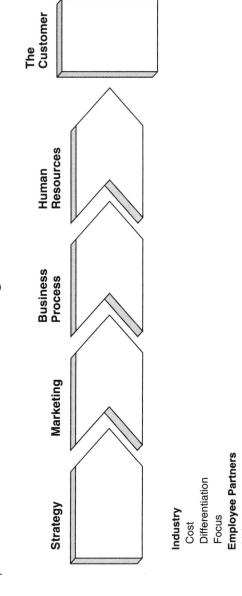

of a company. I have come across very little literature that includes the discipline of marketing in the continuous improvement effort. On a personal level, I know of only a handful of companies that have done this. At times, the separation between marketing and operations appears greater than the constitutional separation of church and state.

Consider the following scenario: Sparing no creative effort (and sparing very little expense) the marketing department establishes specific product and service expectations in the mind of the customer. All energy and effort are focused outward as Marketing makes promises that the company is committed to fulfill.

Yet how can the employees, who deliver the products and services, fulfill the customer expectations about which they have very little knowledge? The industry literature about quality and customer service issues is loaded with examples of companies who struggle to fulfill customer expectations based on promises put forth by the marketing department.

In a traditional organization, the marketing effort is aligned with the strategy and the customer, but is not aligned as well as it could be with the workforce or the operations processes. This misalignment causes disruption within the organization and externally, results in customer dissatisfaction.

The Marketing Partnership

Consider another scenario: Millions of dollars of capital are deployed in multiple facilities that employ thousands of skilled people. And yet, nothing happens until someone sells something. Prior to receiving the sales order, all that capital investment is just so much potential.

Odd, isn't it? Marketing drives the business but traditionally has played a very poor role as partner to the endeavor. Perhaps it is due to the nature of the personality types that inhabit the world of sales and marketing. Perhaps it is caused by the difficulty inherent in forecasting the workload for the organization. After all, predicting the amount of purchases a client will make is still an art form for most sales organizations. Perhaps it is because Marketing has traditionally aligned exclusively with strategy and the business plan. Whatever the reason, this lack of partnership causes friction between the marketing and operations functions that reduces the effectiveness of the organization.

Marketing has the complicated task of forecasting the future. This task is made more difficult because the forecast must, in some way, support the business plan for revenues. Sales must then be achieved that realize the forecast. Unfortunately, because of the nature of selling, there can be wide fluctuations between forecast and actual sales.

Operations, on the other hand, is focused on running the process as efficiently as possible based on the sales forecast. However, efficiency is difficult if not impossible to achieve when the only input from Marketing is the actual sales orders that rarely match the forecast in timing or volume.

A Classic Marketing Example

Open organizations that align their marketing function with the strategy, the customer, and with the operations function find that a partnership develops that enhances the flexibility of the organization. I had the opportunity to observe a manufacturing firm in the Midwest that had just such a problem.

The company, which employed about 200 people, produced semi-disposable consumer products. It was involved in the process of educating and empowering its employees. During the empowerment process it became clear that the operations function should assume responsibility for scheduling. The production schedule had always been created and maintained by the scheduling department based on the sales forecast. Upon closer investigation, it was discovered that a key function of the department was to adjust the daily schedule based on the input of actual sales orders from the marketing department.

Often scheduled production runs were interrupted with "hot" orders. These orders needed to be produced immediately to support the delivery commitments made by the sales force. (The sales employees thought they were exhibiting the highly desirable trait of flexibility to their customers.)

As a result, scheduling had become a major source of punishment for the operations department. The constant interruption to the production lines with hot orders caused a domino effect that slowed production and increased the incidence of late shipments. On-time shipments were a performance indicator for which the operations department was held accountable. The employees in the operations department took pride in their ability to perform and, in addition to being extra work, hot orders made them look bad.

Invoking the empowerment concept and applying the involvement process, a team from Operations was assigned to thoroughly investigate the production scheduling issue. At this point for this team, empowerment became educated empowerment.

With the help of the finance group, the team evaluated all aspects of hot orders from the perspective of cost and profitability. It became clear that hot orders were very expensive to the company. In fact, if all costs associated with labor, lost production, scrap, poor quality, and missed shipments were included, some hot orders were a net loss to the company.

Members of the team were now both empowered and educated. Strengthened by their deeper level of understanding, the operations group agreed to assume the scheduling function but only if they could gain partnership with the marketing department. They were sure that once the marketing management was educated in costs, hot orders would no longer be permitted. This would substantially improve the performance indicators by which the operations group was measured.

With assistance from the financial group, the operations team met with representatives from the marketing function and conducted a half-day workshop on the costs associated with hot orders. Because the organization was on the path toward an open organization there was a genuine spirit of partnering and cooperation during the workshop.

The marketing team was surprised and alarmed to find that some hot orders were resulting in a net loss. This was a competitive market and everyone was concerned about profitability. Not knowing the impact of hot orders on the operations process, marketing had developed a pattern of using delivery time as a primary tool for obtaining sales orders.

The operations employees were beginning to think they had seen the last of the hot orders until Marketing pointed out the company's competitive edge depended on the ability to meet customer needs and that often meant short delivery times.

Through a facilitated process of analysis and discussion, the two groups developed a plan to resolve the conflict. Marketing, with the help of Finance, agreed to educate the sales force as to the financial costs associated with interruptions to the production schedule. The sales employees would be keenly interested in this information because their compensation plan was being modified to emphasize profitability.

Marketing, finance, and operations also developed a plan to train the sales force in consultative selling. The sales employees would be educated to think of the customer as more of a partner and their focus would be to develop a keener understanding of how the company could fill customer needs. In doing this, they would have a greater ability to reduce last minute orders and perhaps capture business they would otherwise be unaware of.

Marketing also agreed that it was important for the operations group to attend meetings in which the sales forecast was developed. Operations would contribute insight into the development of a schedule that would be an acceptable compromise between the sales forecast and the best use of production resources.

They would work together, proactively, to reduce hot orders. Elements of the sales forecast that conflicted with maximizing the production resources would be discussed and the resolution would be based not on emotion or political power, but would be determined based on the impact on company profitability and customer satisfaction.

Moving from empowerment to educated empowerment advanced the development of an open organization at this company. Each group developed a greater perspective of the overall picture and their role in the strategy and business results. The employees in Marketing were educated as to their impact on operational costs. The employees in Operations were educated in the process of sales forecasting and the issues associated with customer acquisition and retention. Marketing and Operations aligned their efforts and, as a result, were able to develop a process that stabilized the sales forecast, reduced costs, and improved their competitive position. Figure 2-3 illustrates the new thinking that an open organization brings to the marketing and sales process.

Aligning the Business Process Element

A company achieves its strategic objectives through the business process. Ideally, the core processes of a business are defined and the organization's structure is then designed around these core processes—ideally. However, the new economy has redefined the customer, the customer's expectations, quality levels, and product and services offerings. With changes like that, "business as usual" is a formula for extinction.

In response, companies are changing their processes. The more progressive companies, such as Hallmark Cards, Hewlett-Packard, General Electric, and Ford Motor Company, are reengineering their business processes. They have found that changing the business process often results in a need to change the organization's structure.

For open organizations the important observations about reengineering are not concerned with the technical aspects. Rather, the key value that results from the reengineering effort is an understanding of the linkage this realignment process creates with the ability to educate, enable, empower, and engage employees.

The Link

The business process forms a vital link between empowered employees and the organization at large. Companies that reengineer their

Figure 2-3. Marketing: internal and external alignment.

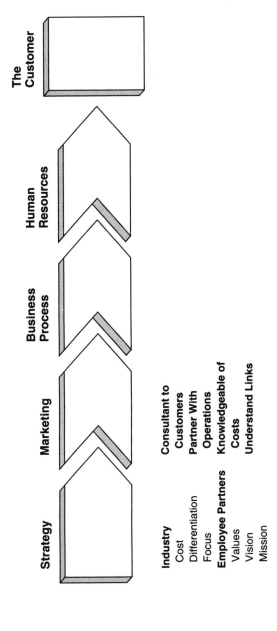

The Big Picture

Strategy

Marketing

Business Process

Human Resources

The Customer

Industry
Cost
Differentiation
Focus
Employee Partners
Values
Vision
Mission

Consultant to Customers
Partner With Operations
Knowledgeable of Costs
Understand Links

processes find that their organization's structure becomes flatter. As the non-value-added activities are removed from the process, the redundant hierarchy becomes obvious and is eliminated. This elimination of hierarchy presents certain communication challenges. In fact, it requires a major shift in communications philosophy.

In a traditional hierarchy, information is power and information flows in controlled amounts, from the top down. A flat organizational structure no longer has the elaborate capacity for control and distribution of information. As a result, a flat organizational structure establishes the need for networking and the need for a broader distribution of, and access to, information.

Open organizations use these needs as a platform for creating alliances that result in greater breadth of knowledge and a greatly improved understanding of the intent of the company. In flat organizational structures employees learn skills from each other as the result of enhanced interaction and as the result of expanded duties. In doing so, they gain a closer linkage to the business strategy and a bigger picture of the customer expectations established by the marketing function.

Trust is a value that can be enhanced as a result of the reengineering process. Lack of trust is not necessarily based on the perception of "evil intent." Hierarchical structures tend to fragment and isolate the employee population, creating distrust between functions if for no other reason than inaccurate information exchange. A common indicator of this lack of trust can be found in almost any hierarchical organization. It is manifested in the data verification activities that take place when one function passes information or product to another.

My experience as a manager in a Fortune 500 company presents a good case in point. I would receive performance data on a periodic basis from a source outside my functional silo. Part of my responsibility was to process the data, evaluate it, draw conclusions, and make recommendations based on the trends I identified.

Shortly after I assumed responsibility for this activity, I found the first order of work was to verify the data each time it arrived. Often the data would be inaccurate for the needs of the time period under analysis, but not necessarily because the provider's systems were inaccurate. Many times the conditions and requirements surrounding the performance period had changed.

These conditions and requirements could be affected by several departments and often the communication of changes did not keep up with the changes themselves. Lack of timely information about changes made to the systems and processes created mistrust. Although I had an excellent relationship with the data provider, I mistrusted the data.

Understanding the Value and the Power

Reengineering is an introspective process that is a key part of the alignment process an organization goes through as it moves from a closed environment to an open environment. That being the case, it will be valuable to briefly overview the mechanics of the process.

This overview is important because business process reengineering is not the same type of reengineering that is applied to a tool or product. Reengineering the business process has a direct impact on employees and their ability to participate in the organization. Understanding the basics of the technique will give insights into the alignment of work practices and work culture that can create an open environment.

Understanding the reengineering process will also help you, as a manager, respond to employee concerns about the process. *Business Week* published an article on reengineering that said, "Reengineering is the hot management buzzword. Of the largest industrial corporations, 83% say they have re-engineered their workplaces." 70 percent of the corporations claimed greater productivity as a result. But a poll by Pitney Bowes Management Services shows that 69 percent of the employees surveyed thought reengineering was an excuse for a layoff. 75 percent said they fear their own job loss and 55 percent say they are overburdened by work.[5]

Business process reengineering is not about downsizing. Downsizing may occur as a result, but high-involvement/high-performance companies place special emphasis on programs that minimize the impact of this on the employee population. They make exceptional efforts to walk the talk of treating their educated and empowered employees like valued assets.

Reengineering can range from the simplification and strengthening of processes to a complete redesign for the overall process. On the surface, the goal is to streamline planning and execution to a minimum and eliminate paperwork and delay. The benefits of improving the time and cost elements are important contributors to improved net earnings. However, for an open organization the key benefit that develops from reengineering is the understanding of the interdependencies between processes. This is where the real opportunities to develop a sustainable competitive advantage can be found.

Interdependence

As indicated by the alignment model in Figure 2-4, an open organization utilizes a people-oriented method of reengineering. This method applies the understanding of interdependencies between processes to align strategy, marketing, operations, and people in an organization that is totally focused on the customer.

Peter DiNicola, organization development director for Nabisco, understands these interdependencies. After extensive experience and success with reengineering, he applied the process jointly to logistics and field sales. He obviously recognized that by leveraging their interdependence it would be possible to create a synergy between the two that would result in increased customer satisfaction. The understanding of these interdependencies is true profound knowledge, a topic that is discussed extensively in Chapter 5.

What Does a People-Oriented Process of Reengineering Look Like?

In an open organization it is important to understand the process used to identify interdependencies. This process should be used as a tool by all employees to enhance their understanding and facilitate their empowerment. A brief overview of the six key phases of process reengineering will show how the interdependencies are identified.

The six key phases are:

1. Leadership
2. Planning
3. Research
4. Mapping
5. Analysis
6. Implementation

Leadership

Andy Huckaba is a friend and colleague with whom I have had many interesting discussions concerning process reengineering. He has over five years experience working on reengineering projects with companies such as Hallmark Cards, Yellow Freight, and a host of smaller organizations. Based on his experience, he is convinced that a critical element necessary for a successful reengineering process is strong, visionary senior management. He says, "Senior management must have the fortitude to stay fully engaged in the reengineering effort throughout its completion. Change can bring

Figure 2-4. Business process reengineering: internal and external alignment.

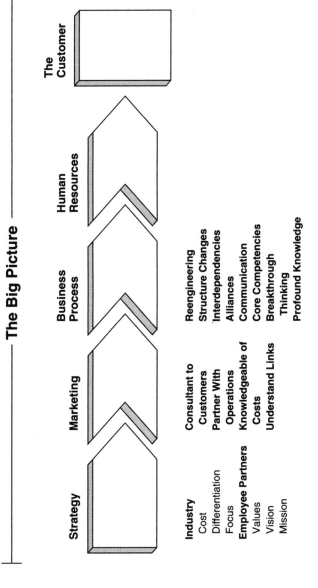

The Big Picture

| Strategy | Marketing | Business Process | Human Resources | The Customer |

Industry
Cost
Differentiation
Focus
Employee Partners
Values
Vision
Mission

Consultant to Customers
Partner With Operations
Knowledgeable of Costs
Understand Links

Reengineering
Structure Changes
Interdependencies
Alliances
Communication
Core Competencies
Breakthrough Thinking
Profound Knowledge

uncertainty, loss of focus and momentum, and confusion. Strong and ongoing leadership is absolutely necessary to achieve success with the reengineering process."

Planning and Research

The purpose for reengineering is to bring the organization closer to the customer. The first step in the process is to clearly define what this looks like and how it will be accomplished. This requires that the reason for transformation be clearly defined.

At the heart of this research process are the questions, Who are the customers? and What will they pay for? As we have seen, the new economy has made the customer king. The high number of product and service providers in the marketplace allow the customers to go where they think they will to receive the best value, highest quality, lowest cost, and best service. Only by developing a close familiarity with the customer can their needs be understood and their wants anticipated. Developing this familiarity is the primary outcome of the research phase. Once this reason has been defined, it must be communicated to all employees.

The role of an organization is defined by customer requirements, and that role can only be realized through its employees. Definition and communication of the reason for the transformation provide the employees with an understanding of what the organization needs, what they can do to contribute to the fulfillment of those needs, and what the impact of their contribution will be on them. Only when the employees have a complete understanding of the cause and effect will they be able to participate in a meaningful manner.

The planning and research elements should produce a clearly defined purpose. After planning and research, the next step in reengineering is to develop an understanding of the business processes.

Mapping the Process

A process is a collection of linked activities that takes input and transforms it to create an output. Its characteristics are:

- Inputs provided by suppliers
- A value-added conversion process
- The output provided to a customer

Processes are often complex, with interlinking relationships that feed the main work flow from multiple sources. Experience has shown us that as part of understanding these interlinked relationships it is helpful to develop a visual picture. This technique is called mapping.

The mapping technique provides a focus for data collection that helps diagnose the process. It also ensures that you don't overlook anything. A block diagram of the process is usually the most straightforward approach to mapping. Once a block diagram of the process has been developed, a more detailed visual display can be achieved by developing a flowchart for the activities within each block in the diagram.

Process mapping reveals the bottlenecks that prevent you from fulfilling your customers' expectations as well as you could. These bottlenecks are often caused by complicated processes that can easily be simplified. Pick this low hanging fruit! These process simplifications provide rapid, measurable improvement. Such improvement goes a long way toward gaining employee confidence and executive support for the effort.

In one form or another the concept of process mapping has been used effectively for years. As a management consultant I have spent plenty of time on the shop floor in a variety of industries, for large and small companies. It became apparent to me that as an organization grows, its processes are patched on, much like the addition of a room to a house. The extra room adds value and capacity, but it never really accommodates the flow of traffic as if it had been part of the original design.

Being new in a facility and not being an employee, I could ask the supervisor, manager, or production lead person to explain how the process worked. I could ask "stupid" and leading questions and eventually we would bring to light the obstacles in the process that were preventing the work from getting done. More often than not, these obstacles were the result of some past growth in the business that added capacity or new product capabilities to the facility.

The necessary patches were added to the original process to make it work and the changes were endured. Soon they became habit, then they became "invisible," just something you had to work around. Once our discussions had mapped the process and made the bottlenecks obvious, process simplification was just a matter of developing a plan to eliminate them.

Analysis of Core Competency Processes

After mapping the process, the next stage in reengineering is the analysis stage. During analysis, the team works to define core activities for each process. (A core activity is one that is essential to the process.) Using performance data from a core activity it is possible to identify those core activities that are strong and weak performers.

At this point the reengineering team has a good picture of the organization. They have mapped the process flow, defined the core activities for each process, and used performance data to identify how well each process is functioning. The next step is to determine which of these processes contribute to the attainment of the strategy. This requires an analysis of the core competency processes.

Competencies are the characteristics that predict superior performance and which can be performed exceptionally well. Organizational core competencies are those characteristics that provide a competitive advantage such as human resources utilization, cost control, quality, innovation, cycle time, or distribution. (Employee competencies are the skills, knowledge, and behaviors that can be performed exceptionally well and that predict superior individual performance.)

Once organizational competencies have been defined, the processes associated with these competencies can be identified. These are an organization's core competency processes. They are the key strategic advantages that the organization performs exceptionally well.

Core competency processes are then compared to those things that the customer is willing to pay for. This is a technique that evaluates how well your competencies align with your marketplace. It looks at what you do best and considers what could be done with that potential. If the core competencies fail to align sufficiently with the customer's qualifications, you're in the wrong business (but you probably suspected that already). If there is a match it is most likely not perfect and, based on the degree of misalignment, may present an opportunity for reengineering. Either way, by defining core competency processes an organization has a clear picture of the strengths that it can bring to the marketplace.

Now that you have this great information, what are you going to do with it? The information is invaluable, but to be of any use it must be shared with the employees. In an open organization the key value derived from this analytical effort is the innovative capability that this knowledge can develop in all employees.

Understanding the core competencies and the processes and activities that create them is a unique and valuable type of knowledge. Only this knowledge can provide the basis for creating innovative strategies.

Breakthrough Thinking

The process doesn't have to be all tedious number crunching; it can be fun too. Idea generation is part of the process. Brainstorming techniques, where no idea is too wild or too unorthodox, are often used to generate breakthrough thinking. Breakthrough thinking generates quite a different outcome than the outcomes achieved by process simplification. Process simplification results in the removal of the bottlenecks and stumbling blocks that inhibit the flow of work. Breakthrough thinking can result in the radical redesign of a company's business process. It can reinvent the way a business operates and, in doing so, result in a new competitive advantage. At the leading edge, breakthrough thinking offers an alternative perspective by rethinking the link between strategy and the core competency processes. Companies such as AT&T, Procter & Gamble, and American Express have applied this approach to identify, define, and strengthen their position in the marketplace.

The Applied Physics Laboratory utilized this process when it reengineered its human resources department. The breakthrough thinking resulted in nothing less than a redefinition of its human resources strategy. Initially, the laboratory prided itself in having state-of-the-art human resources practices. However, these leading edge practices weren't always what the employees wanted. The reengineering process clearly defined the customers and their needs and wants, and refocused the human resources organization in that direction.

According to Dan Brown, manager of central human resources: "Our definition of quality was how we were perceived by our peers in the human resources world, not how we were seen by our customers. That was a painful lesson for us."[6]

A Good Question About Customer Expectations

As an interesting exercise in perspective and focus, try to guess what your customers think is most important to them. Answer the question first, then perform the customer research and compare the difference. If what you think your customers value and what they really value differs significantly ask yourself, What process(es) in the organization created my misunderstanding of customer expectations?

Once these processes are identified, as yourself What changes to the organizational processes are necessary to align my perceptions with the customers? Normally, you will find the answer is associated with a need to capture more information, quicker and closer to the source. We discuss the topic of capturing information at the source in more detail in Chapter 6.

Aligning The Human Resource Element

As the result of all this rethinking, realignment, and reengineering, traditional systems will have been reevaluated and redesigned, but to what end? How will these changes be sustained? The answer is, only through the employees, and only when the employees function and behave differently from before. The organization has been aligned with the customer and now it is time to align the employees with the customer.

Partner With the Customer

At some level, all organizations try to understand and meet their customer's expectations. In a traditional organization senior management understands the customer. They also understand the company. They have access to information and they understand the information. They understand the strategic plan, the marketing plan, the organizational design, the work flow processes, and the financial documents that provide information on which to base their decisions. They see the big picture, understand their role in achieving the business strategy and are paid to produce results. However, only senior management is so educated, enabled, empowered, and engaged.

For the most part, in a traditional organization the only thing employees understand is that if the company does poorly, they will lose their jobs. These organizations are filled with energy-draining we vs. they tension based on misunderstanding, role confusion, and fluctuating commitment. Add to that a heightened level of fear caused by downsizing and layoffs and it is hardly an environment in which customer expectations are met.

In the new economy, customers will be accurately identified by the business strategy and attracted to the company by offerings of innovative, feature-rich products and services that fill current needs and anticipate future needs. They will expect to receive the product or service promised them by the marketing group. They will demand the quality implied by the operations processes. And they will expect all of this from each and every representative of the company—even you. "Well, you work here don't you?"

Partner With Yourself

Open organizations have found one way to achieve a sustainable competitive advantage is to move toward a management system that encourages employees to think and act like business partners. However, employees can't possibly share a business partner's perspective until they have access to the same resources and capabilities that business partners do, namely, education, information, authority, and rewards.

As indicated by Figure 2-5, the outcome of providing these resources and capabilities to employees is a company staffed with a skilled, knowledgeable workforce in a flexible, innovative workplace.

An open environment creates mutual understanding, respect, and partnership. In an open environment there is no we-they conflict. There is only us. This high-performance type of company pushes responsibility down to the front line employee. Relationships are based on partnering, trust, and information sharing. Everyone is considered a critical asset and everyone is focused on serving the customer.

Win-Win

The fundamental criterion for successfully establishing any partnership is that the relationship must be viewed as beneficial by all parties involved. This means that to develop a company of partners, both management and labor must have their needs considered and any process of development or change must benefit these needs. This principle is based on the concepts of shared perspective and shared results.

A win-win relationship is based on a foundation in which all decisions and actions are made with consideration for the following two questions: How will my partners perceive this? and Will my partners benefit from this?

Disaster Awaits in Detail

Creating a high-involvement/high-performance company based on an open organization is a process of change that entails a monumental level of detail. The potential to get lost in the details of any major change process, or worse yet, leave out a critical detail, is the greatest single threat to success. Negative outcomes of the process can severely affect morale and employee relations for years to come.

Although there are many proven techniques for involving employees and sharing gains, until now there has been no single overarching checklist of management practices with which to:

1. Categorize details
2. Ensure key perspectives are considered
3. Identify and address the needs of all parties

Chapters 3 and 4 present such a checklist. This checklist provides a guideline for transforming the relationship between management and nonmanagement employees into a partnership that is capable of sustaining and building on change.

Figure 2-5. Human resources: internal and external alignment.

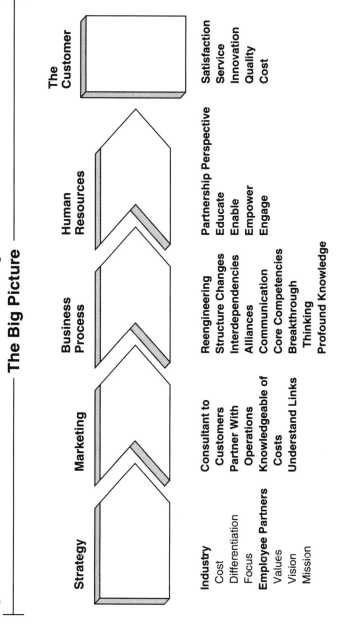

The Big Picture

Strategy

Industry
Cost
Differentiation
Focus
Employee Partners
Values
Vision
Mission

Marketing

Consultant to
Customers
Partner With
Operations
Knowledgeable of
Costs
Understand Links

Business Process

Reengineering
Structure Changes
Interdependencies
Alliances
Communication
Core Competencies
Breakthrough
Thinking
Profound Knowledge

Human Resources

Partnership Perspective
Educate
Enable
Empower
Engage

The Customer

Satisfaction
Service
Innovation
Quality
Cost

Notes

1. *High Performance Work Practices and Firm Performance,* U.S. Department of Labor, Washington, D.C., August 1993.
2. Mike Niedenthal, Time Based Management. Mid-America Manufacturing Technology Center, 1994.
3. Michael E. Porter, *Competitive Advantage: Creating and Sustaining Superior Performance* New York: Free Press, 1987.
4. Thomas J. McCoy, *Compensation and Motivation: Maximizing Employee Performance With Behavior-Based Incentive Plans* New York: AMACOM, 1992.
5. The Big Picture, *Business Week,* November 7, 1994, p. 6.
6. Re-engineering HR. *Human Resources Executive,* June 3, 1994.

3

The E$_4$ Management Practices and Employee Partnership

How are decisions made in your organization? How fast are they made? What would happen if all employees were able to make decisions that affect customer satisfaction and company profitability? What kind of checks and balances would be necessary to allow this without stifling it with bureaucracy? Other than the executives in your company, who has a clear line-of-sight from his job function of Net Income? What would be the results on the business if everyone had this line-of-sight? Are everyone's ideas valued? Does each employee have the authority to act on her ideas? Does senior management have confidence that each employee has the capability to make decisions that are based on data and focused on the business strategy? Are all stakeholders getting what they want from the organization in terms of social rewards, material rewards, and personal satisfaction? These are typical questions that are asked in open organizations. In searching for answers to these questions, senior management and human resources professionals will be required to initiate actions that change the company's culture.

In this chapter we examine a combination of four management practices that senior management and human resources professionals can implement to create an open, partner-oriented, high-performance organization. These management practices make up half of the E$_4$-R$_4$ Partnership Checklist. (The other half is a combination of employee expectations developed in response to the management practices and is discussed in Chapter 4.) We define these practices, analyze their elements, and explore their relationships to each other. We start by examining an issue critical to open organizations—personal satisfaction.

Ownership Or Partnership?

We know what stockholders want from their company. They want to maximize their return on investment (ROI). Some look to maximize in the short term and some look to maximize in the long term. Whatever the time frame, ROI is their focus.

Companies with open organizations have a greater opportunity to maximize ROI because they are staffed with employees who have an enhanced capability to perform effectively and seize opportunity. The Office of the American Workplace recently reported on a detailed study of over six thousand work groups in thirty-four firms. The study found that attributes of an open organization, such as an emphasis on workplace cooperation and the involvement of employees in decision making were positively correlated with future profitability.[1]

Companies that are basing their sustainable competitive advantage on their human resources find themselves developing an open organization. In doing so, they find themselves moving along a relationship continuum with their employees. Figure 3-1 illustrates this point.

At one end of the continuum is the traditional relationship of employer and employee. In this relationship, employees implement the directions given them by management. They have a basic understanding of the company's products and who buys them. They may know who the company's competitors are.

This relationship evolves as the open environment process is implemented. Employees become more like partners. Involvement on all levels is nurtured by using processes that enable and empower all employees. In addition, employees are provided access to education that relates to the general business. They become knowledgeable of the industry, the competition, and the company's market strategy. They are familiar with the internal processes and develop a better understanding about the various sources of revenues, costs, and their relationship to net income.

The result is employees with enhanced levels of understanding, responsibility, and authority. Decisions are no longer made at the top and employees have a greater voice in the day-to-day operations of the business. They also share in the rewards of their effort through gainsharing, profit sharing, or some other form of variable compensation.

In its completed state, employees in an open organization have the same focus and intensity on net income and ROI as owners do. To achieve this, developmental emphasis is placed on education, information sharing, and systems that engage their commitment. Em-

Figure 3-1. The relationship continuum.

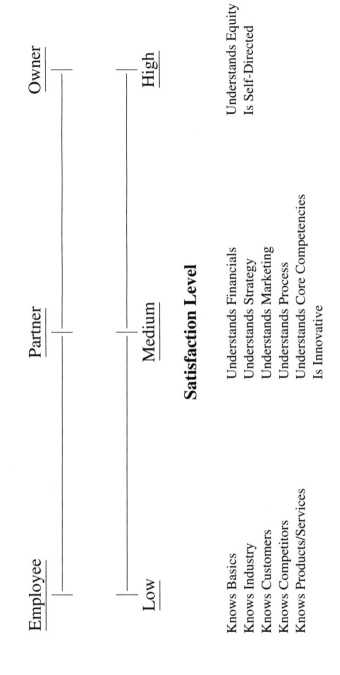

Organizational Maturity

Employee	Partner	Owner

Low	Medium	High

Satisfaction Level

Knows Basics
Knows Industry
Knows Customers
Knows Competitors
Knows Products/Services

Understands Financials
Understands Strategy
Understands Marketing
Understands Process
Understands Core Competencies
Is Innovative

Understands Equity
Is Self-Directed

ployees develop a clear and extended line-of-sight that enables them to understand the financial ramifications of their actions. They fully comprehend their role in the production of profit and the generation of cash.

Their knowledge of the marketplace and their understanding of process capabilities and the organization's core competencies give them the ability to change the way they perceive a situation and enables them to think of fresh or unusual ideas. Employee stock ownership plans (ESOP) or some other form of equity linkage literally makes them owners. Behavioral scientists refer to this state as being fully connected with the organization.

Creating a true ownership mentality on the part of all employees requires education in the concepts of stock, the actual transfer of the stock to the employees, and the realization of the significance of stock ownership by the employees. This degree of organizational maturity requires a significant period of time to achieve. With rare exception, open organizations are too new to have achieved this level of sophistication. Instead, most organizations work on developing a strong level of *partnership* between labor and management, between owner and employee.

Satisfaction and the Empowerment Wall

Do we really know what employees want from their work? Remember the high failure rate associated with efforts to involve them? Empowerment, it seems, is only one part of a more comprehensive process. If we are going to use workplace cooperation and employee involvement to develop a partnership we need to look at work from the employees' perspective. Only then will we be able to identify and incorporate the elements necessary to create a lasting partnership. Only then will we be able to achieve a *sustainable* competitive advantage through people.

Information about how employees perceive the opportunity for involvement and empowerment is provided by companies that have worked hard to incorporate employee involvement as part of their business strategy. Employee involvement techniques have been in use long enough to have developed performance cycles that provide information as to what employees want from their work. One cycle that employee involvement professionals speak about has been dubbed the *empowerment wall*.

The empowerment wall refers to that phase of the employee involvement process in which the upward trend of gains, improvement, and participation reaches a plateau and may even fall off. In a discussion with John Savageau, an associate and experienced professional in the field of employee involvement and TQM, states, "At some point in the process, it appears that employees just don't want to give anymore. Analysis of the phenomenon indicates that employees who hit the wall do so because they don't understand the impact of their contribution on results and/or they don't share in the rewards." This and similar information tells us that what employees want from their work is:

- A shared notion of why they work
- A common understanding of the results of their efforts
- An equitable distribution of the gains

So we see that the process of employee involvement doesn't automatically produce a partnership. The data show that a partnership is established between management and employees only when the relationship produces a sufficient level of satisfaction such that they become committed to participate toward goals compatible with their values.

Any model we use to develop an open, partnering organization must build satisfaction into the job function, into the company culture, the work environment, and into the compensation package.

The Partnership Perspective

Creating a satisfying relationship is a two-way effort. Both management and the employees must do their share. In order to create a mutually satisfying relationship it is necessary to understand the perspectives that each group holds.

Management, acting as representatives of the owners, has a responsibility to strive for a satisfactory ROI. This return must make the business attractive to investors by generating a net profit greater than that available with other investments. In addition, management must manage the company's cash so that it will be available for the payment of expenses. So the foundation of management's perspective is based on running the business and on attaining business objectives that achieve a profit and generate cash.

Employees, acting as independent agents, are selling their time and skills. They have certain expectations of what should be received in return for their commitment and involvement. The foundation for the employees' perspective is based on running their lives and on attaining their personal objectives.

In order for the partnership to be successfully developed, management must understand the expectations of their employees. They must then establish a set of human resources practices that will align and link these expectations with the business objectives and fulfill these expectations as business objectives are achieved.

Employees, for their part, must understand the expectations and perspective of management. They must concern themselves with the business objectives of profit, cash, and customer expectations and understand how the attainment of these objectives will result in fulfillment of their personal expectations. Only then will they become connected to the organization.

Every checklist and model we develop in this book includes the concept of mutual perspective as a background element. Each group has valid perspectives that the other party must be aware of and that must be understood by the other party.

To establish a sustainable partnership it is not enough just to be aware of the other group's perspective, it must be understood as well. Only when the other group's perspective is understood will it be truly accepted (walk a mile in my shoes). Ownership perspectives need to be learned by the employees and employee perspectives need to be learned by the management.

Figure 3-2 illustrates the point that any process of developing a partnership requires consideration of the needs of all groups concerned. In the process of developing an open environment, management has certain practices they perceive will achieve the business objectives when implemented. In participating in an open environment employees have certain expectations that need to be addressed in order to gain their involvement and access their highest potential. These perspectives are represented in Figure 3-2 as the foundation of the E_4-R_4 Partnership Checklist.

Partnership Practices

Management, in the role of leader, should take the initiative to build an enduring partnership. It is obvious that no single act will accomplish this. In a report on a study of human resources systems and productivity in the steel industry, thirty comparable steel finishing lines were analyzed for work practices that had an impact on productivity. The work practices analyzed were job flexibility, communication, labor relations, teamwork, recruitment, incentive pay, knowledge and skills, and employment security.[2]

When examined in isolation the specific work practices were individually correlated with higher productivity. However, it was found that the introduction of any single practice without a change in the overall system had no significant effect on productivity. These data reinforce the need for management to take a multipractice approach to creating a partnership.

Figure 3-2. Partnership perspectives.

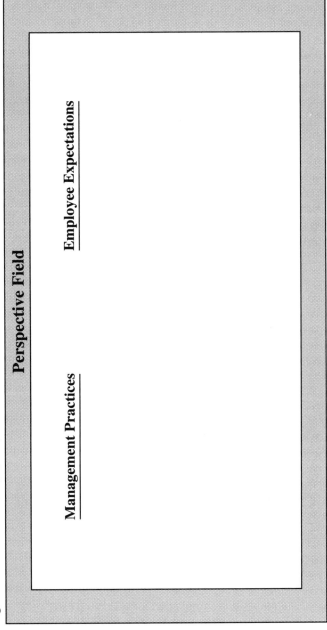

Perspective Field

Management Practices

Employee Expectations

The Four Management Practices

A series of human resources-oriented practices must be established by senior management and the human resources professionals in order to successfully develop a sustainable partnership with all employees. Review of organizations that have focused on achieving a competitive edge through their employees has identified a set of management practices that have a positive correlation to the development of an open partnership. Figure 3-3, the E_4 Management Practices Checklist illustrates these practices and represents the first half of the E_4-R_4 Partnership Checklist.

Every company that has experienced success in the movement toward an open organization has one or more management practice designed to Educate, Enable, Empower, or Engage their employees. Implemented as a holistic package of management practices, these four Es can successfully develop a long-term partnership by connecting all aspects of employee expectations to business objectives.

Implemented together, the four management practices provide all the elements necessary to break through the empowerment wall. For example, the E_1-Educate management practice provides specific fulfillment to the stated employee expectations for a shared notion of why they work and a common understanding of the results of their efforts. The E_4-Engage management practice provides specific fulfillment to the stated employee expectations for an equitable distribution of the gains.

In order to effectively implement this holistic process it is necessary to understand the function of each of the four management practices. It is necessary to understand the elements that comprise each practice, the relationships that exist between them, and how they affect employee perceptions and behavior. In this chapter, we will overview each management practice and analyze them in greater detail individually in Chapters 5, 6, 8, and 9.

The E_1 Management Practice: Educate

The definition of the word *educate* in the *Random House Dictionary of the English Language,* is "to develop the faculties and power of a person by teaching, instruction, or schooling." In the past, education efforts in the workplace consisted mainly of a one-time exposure to company policy and the ongoing development of the skills needed to perform the job function. The old education paradigm centered on a need-to-know basis. It was developed in a work environment in which management made the decisions. Management was differenti-

Figure 3-3. E_4 Management Practices Checklist.

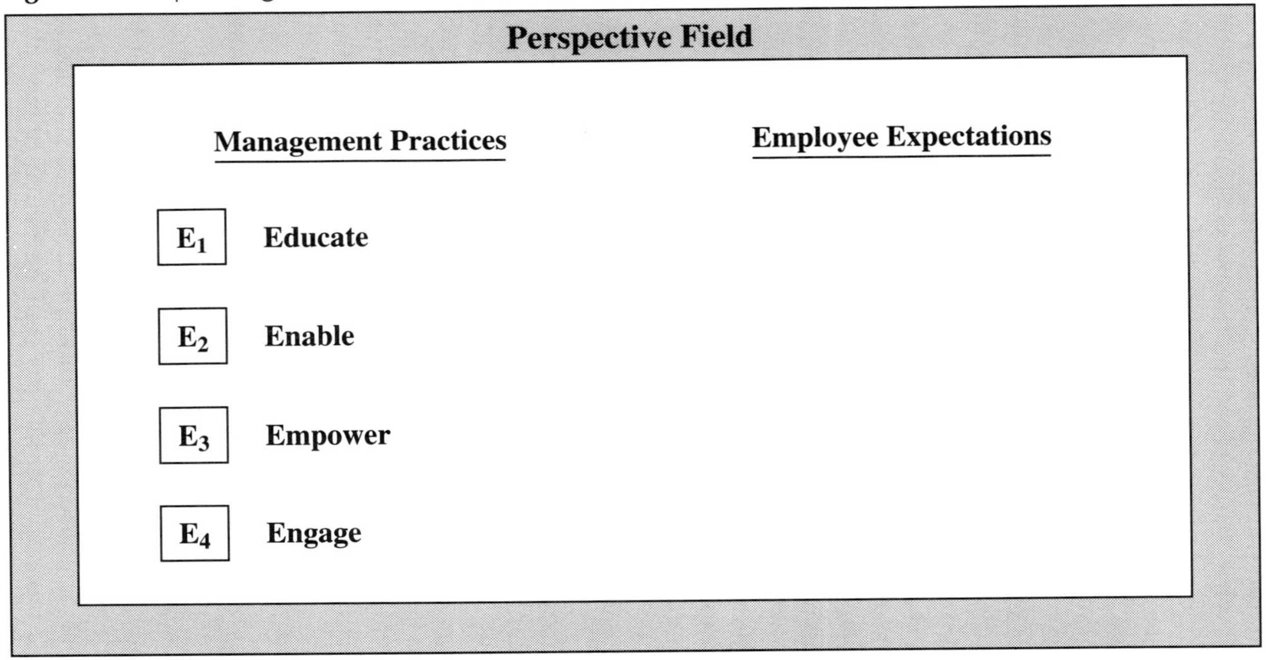

Perspective Field

Management Practices

Employee Expectations

E_1	Educate
E_2	Enable
E_3	Empower
E_4	Engage

ated from the workers because they possessed the knowledge to understand what was best for the business. However, more and more, work is becoming composed of knowledge jobs. These jobs, because of their nature, tend to be more complex. As a result, work is done in a more integrated manner. Workers performing integrated work require a substantial amount of "ancillary" information—ancillary in the sense that it is not information directly related to the job activity. Rather it is information about the impact of their performance on upstream providers, downstream customers, and the performance of the organization as a whole.

The new education paradigm is centered on "the more you know, the more you are needed." It is based on a flatter, more flexible, self-directed organization. In this style, partner employees are expected to make decisions at the level where it will be most effective. Only if they are educated in the cause and effect of their actions can they make rapid, high-quality decisions. In the new education paradigm, employee partners possess the knowledge that enables them to understand what is best for the business.

The Elements of the Education Management Practice

By definition, the practice of educating employees makes sense in establishing a partnership. Who wouldn't want their partner to have well-developed faculties and power? The question is, What type of education is needed?

The Education management practice focuses the employee education on issues of cause and effect. Elements of the Education practice provide every employee with an understanding of the effect their decisions will have on the business objectives. The Education elements of the big picture, the customer, operating process details, and financial results all contribute to an understanding of how the company makes money and competes effectively. Every employee must have this information to function effectively as a partner.

To develop a better understanding of the intent of this practice we examine each of these elements more closely. By understanding the intent, you will be able to implement this practice in a method and style most appropriate for your particular organization.

The Big Picture Education

The big picture element provides an overall understanding of such information as the company's chosen business strategy, the industry, who the competition is, why the company is positioned in the market the way it is, what products and services the company is offering, and what the company's strengths and weaknesses are.

BASF, an international fibers company with offices in Irvine, California, is an example of a company working to provide a bigger picture to its employees. It created a program to educate all managers in the company about the key features of its primary products. BASF realizes that all employees are part of the team that moves the product into the marketplace. As partners, this education would assist each one in working more effectively with the sales team to satisfy the customer.

In thinking about appropriate big picture education for your company, consider elements that will help your employee partners understand the external business environment.

The Customer Education

The customer element provides an understanding of information such as who the customers are, what their expectations are, what their current needs are, what their future needs will be, what the company's capabilities are, how the products and services have been positioned by marketing and advertising, and what the sales strategy is.

Federal Express is a good example of employees understanding the customer and their needs. Who can forget their marketing campaign slogan "When it absolutely, positively has to be there?" The response of every employee in the organization is focused on that definition of customer need.

In thinking about appropriate customer education for your company, consider elements that will help your employee partners understand the customer's expectations, how they have been established, what the company's core competencies are, and how these capabilities are being used and could be used in the future to satisfy customer needs and fulfill their expectations.

Operating Process Education

The operating process element provides an understanding of information such as organizational structure, how orders are processed, how work flows through the organization, what the process capabilities are, how inventory is controlled, and how production is scheduled.

The Hallmark Card Company is a good example of this element. Hallmark recently went through a major process reengineering activity that reduced the concept-to-market cycle time of their greeting cards by almost 50 percent. That was a one-time improvement. The real benefit to the organization is the understanding of how the processes are linked and what contribution each employee makes in every step of the process.

In thinking about appropriate operating process education for your company, consider elements that will help your employee partners understand how raw materials flow through the organization and exit as finished goods that meet customer requirements.

This element is applicable for service companies as well as manufacturing companies. Every company is a grouping of structures and processes designed to provide fulfillment to the customer. Employee partners should understand their role in these structures and groupings. In doing so, they can be more flexible, efficient, and innovative.

Financial Results Education

The financial results element provides an understanding of information such as how the company makes a profit, how the company generates cash, where the company's revenue comes from, what costs and expenses are associated with the business, and what financial ratios are indicators of the company's performance.

Financial education is perhaps the most innovative of all education elements and the most influential in breaking through the empowerment wall. The old thinking was that financial information was to be guarded and understood by only the chosen few. The new paradigm is that financial information is to be shared.

How can a business partnership be successfully developed if one group of partners doesn't understand how the company makes a profit or generates cash? How can employee partners make accurate and timely decisions about cost and productivity issues unless they understand the financial ramifications of the decisions? Financial education helps employee partners understand their role in the attainment of the organization's business objectives and is critical to understanding cause-and-effect relationships.

This type of financial education for all employees has sometimes been referred to as *open-book management* (OBM). This term expresses the core intent of this element of the education practice. However, for companies who are still working to create an open organization and develop a partnership with their employees, the term can be somewhat worrisome.

The mental image of opening the books to the employees is just too much for many managers and executives. And rightly so. As we see from Figure 3-1, that level of maturity and partnership is only reached after considerable development on the part of both management and the employees. And only through the planned implementation of all four management practices.

Companies just entering the process of open environments should understand that the volume of information is secondary to the ability to understand the information. Small amounts of key cause-and-effect information, well understood, is the way to start. However, a mature, open-book environment can be achieved.

Springfield Remanufacturing Corporation (SRC) is one of the classic examples of this approach. SRC is an engine rebuilding company located in Springfield, Missouri. The management group initiated an open organization approach in 1983, shortly after they purchased the company from International Harvester in a leveraged buyout. Over a period of eight years they developed a company environment in which the books are open. All employee owners understand how their performance affects the company and their personal income. Anyone at SRC will tell you that this was not an easy path nor a rapid process. But the benefits to the partners at SRC speak for themselves.

In 1983 the company had a debt-to-equity ratio of 89 to 1 (in millions of dollars). The bank owned the company and could foreclose any month the payment was missed. Cash was flowing out of the company to pay interest debt, not to fund growth. Job security was nonexistent. Ten years later, in 1993, the debt-to-equity ratio was 1.38 to 1.

Springfield Remanufacturing is an ESOP company and the employees have matured to the point of equity owners. They own a healthy company that provides both job and income growth. SRC is obviously on the mature end of the relationship continuum.

In thinking about appropriate financial results education for your company, consider elements that create an understanding of financial cause-and-effect relationships. This education will help your employee partners understand how their actions affect profitability.

The cost structure of a product or service, the expenses associated with overhead and capital expenditure, sales revenues, margins, and the cost of quality are all examples of education that provides partners with the ability to make decisions and take actions focused on bottom line improvement.

Breakthrough Thinking

W. Edwards Deming was perhaps the first to acquaint us with the concept of profound knowledge. The general concept is one of deep insight or understanding.

How can you develop within your employees the capacity for

Figure 3-4. Breakthrough thinking.

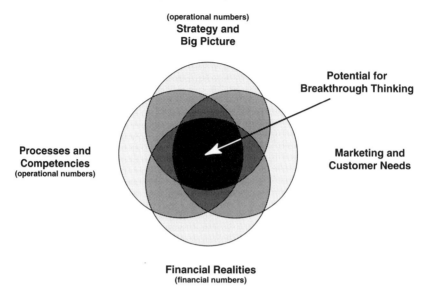

breakthrough thinking? The answer is simple, use the Educate management practice to develop within them a profound knowledge of the organization and the critical elements of the business.

The management practice of education develops a profound understanding of critical business elements, such as business strategies, marketplace issues, business processes, core competencies, financial realities, and customer needs. Breakthrough thinking comes from understanding the critical relationships between and among these functions. The link-pin to seeing these relationships is understanding financial numbers.

The language of business is numbers—financial and accounting numbers. Numbers span the length and breadth of business. Their real power is the ability to translate into a common language the relationships between units of inventory and dollars of finished goods and profit margins and financial ratios.

Most employees are familiar with the operating numbers of their immediate job. Units produced, reports generated, and time on line are all operational indicators. Education in business finance translates those operational indicators into financial results, therefore it is perhaps the most critical element of the Educate management practice.

When profound understanding of the critical processes is translated into the common language of financial results, relationships become evident and the capacity for breakthrough thinking will have been developed. Figure 3-4 illustrates this idea.

The E₂ Management Practice: Enable

Many people confuse the word *enable* with the word *empower*. However, as we will see, although there are close relationships between the two concepts, it is important to keep them separate. Each concept defines a certain set of actions that is critical to developing a partnership. Keeping them separate will ensure these actions are not overlooked.

The definition of the word *enable* in the *Random House Dictionary of the English Language* is "to give means, competence, or ability to." In his workshops, Wayne Dyer, the influential speaker on personal development, uses a cause-and-effect example to demonstrate the concept of the word *enable*. He says: "I hear and I forget, I see and I remember, I do and I understand." In an open environment, employee partners are enabled; they are given the means to "do" it.

The old organizational paradigm was one of command and control. The new organizational paradigm is one of partners who are educated, involved, and participating in the business. In order to function as partners once they have been educated, employees must have access to information and have the means to become involved and participate.

The Elements of the Enable Management Practice

Management's responsibility is to provide the systems that enable employees to affect business results. Key elements include:

- Information sharing
- Information exchange systems
- Employee participation and involvement systems

These three Enable practice elements provide employee partners with the link between education and practical use of knowledge.

We have seen that a critical element in the Education practice is in the area of business finances. A critical element in the Enable practice is freedom.

The Enable management practice promotes freedom of movement. Freedom of physical movement, freedom of position movement for one's career to move throughout the organization, and freedom of information movement. Of all these, information movements is the most influential and has the most day-to-day impact on performance. The decision to share information and make it available is a key element of the Enable practice.

Information Sharing

The old information paradigm was centered on "Information is power." Those who had the information or had access to it maintained control. However, this approach is no longer valid with today's employee. According to a 1993 National Study of the Changing Workforce performed by the Families and Work Institute, open communication was ranked as the most important reason that employees reported for taking their current position.

The new information paradigm is centered on "Information makes us powerful." It's a whole new way of thinking. Power no longer resides in the possession of information. Power now resides in the development of partnerships, and the flow of information throughout the organization enables those partnerships to function. The alchemy of open environments has transformed information from a precious collection of facts, safely hidden in a vault, into life sustaining nourishment coursing throughout the communications channels of an organization.

The strength of the four management practices is the synergistic relationships between them. The strong relationships between these practices creates a sum that is greater than its parts. An example is the relationship between the Education practice and the Enable practice. Education is the source of ideas, but without information, the process for information exchange, and the involvement systems to apply knowledge, education remains purely academic. Educated employees can have very little effect on business results until they have become enabled.

The information element of the Enable practice consists of any information that has value in helping the individual achieve business objectives. The point isn't how much information employee partners have, rather it is how useful the information is that they have. In order to be valuable, information needs to be pertinent to the business at hand.

We are all familiar with the example of documents copied and circulated to a distribution list only to find their way, unread, into a drawer or desktop pile. How much more valuable, and worth distributing, is information that provides the ability to make cost, productivity, and customer satisfaction decisions at a local level, on a daily basis?

In thinking about appropriate information-sharing elements that would enable your employees, consider any information that would focus partner efforts on internal effectiveness, customer satisfaction, and the external competition. Consider what information currently exists that is not widely shared or available. This will normally be financial information. Stand firm on the issue of sharing financial information with the employee partners because it is an essential part of partnership development.

To be effective, partners must understand the business. To achieve a competitive advantage they must understand how the elements of the business relate to revenue, cost, and net income. As Wayne Dyer pointed out, when people "do" it they understand. Employee partners must receive and work with financial information or they will never be able to understand the business.

Information Exchange

The information exchange element of the Enable practice addresses the issues of timeliness and freedom of movement. In order to be valuable, information needs to be timely. A memo notifying the employee partners in the purchasing department of a pricing discount on raw materials has very little value if it is received (or read) after the discount period has expired.

Information exchange systems are both formal and informal systems. Formally, information flows through structured channels designed to control distribution. Whenever I perform communications audits for a client, all too often I see information flowing in channels that have been patched together without the benefit of a comprehensive consideration for the information needs of all partners. As a result, the available information, even when authorized for distribution, often does not get to the employee partners to whom it can be most useful.

Traditional organizational structures tend to create functional silos. These departments develop a "language" applicable to their business discipline and use this language to communicate information in a vertical flow. The result is the isolation of information both within the group and between other silos.

The Enable information elements change the formal distribution of information so that it flows to the partners who can use it. The environment is open, the information is available, accessible, and of value, that is, relative to the achievement of business objectives. The result is the creation of companywide common language around the information most critical to the business.

This language normally takes the form of numbers such as revenue, cost, net income, or key financial ratios. Functional work groups still maintain a "dialect" of their own that relates to their operational measures such as scrap, productivity, downtime, schedule attainment, or product returns.

Information exchange systems are emerging as a major strength in the Enable practice, driven in part by the emerging technologies in computing and telecommunications. These systems have the capacity to provide partners with real-time line-of-sight between their actions and profitability. Line-of-sight is a critical element in developing and maintaining a partnership. It is the outcome of understanding the cause-and-effect relationships. We discuss this concept in much greater detail in Chapters 6 and 7.

In thinking about appropriate E_2-Enable information exchange elements for your company, consider defining each functional group's role in achieving the intent of the organization. The information should allow them to make data-based decisions about real-time problems and opportunities. Ask the question, "What has this group done for the company today?" The answer will most likely be in some form of operational indicator that must then be translated into a financial measurement to be really meaningful. Once you have defined the measurement, the mechanics of information distribution will become evident.

Participation and Involvement

Involvement systems provide the means for employee partners to participate and make a contribution. It gives them the ability to take action and make decisions. The value of involvement systems is widely accepted and successful processes are well documented. Therefore we will not pursue this topic in depth. However, it is important to note that employee involvement practices are critical to the development of an open environment and partnership.

One element of the Enable management practice that integrates directly with employee involvement techniques is goal setting. Studies in behavioral psychology have shown that people who have the opportunity to participate in the goal-setting process show a significantly higher commitment to achieving the goal. Intuitively that makes sense too. Those who are being asked to achieve the goal are often close to the action and have insight as to the realities of achieving the goal. Not only will they identify problem areas, but they will also see shortcuts and easier ways to reach the objective.

Goal setting is an important aspect of the involvement element of the Enable management practice. It enables the employee partners to express themselves. It provides them with a sense of self-worth and adds value to their job function. It provides them with reassurance and encouragement by validating their partnership role.

The E_3 Management Practice: Empower

The definition of the word *empower* in the *Random House Dictionary of the English Language,* is "to give authority to, to authorize by legal or official means." At the very heart of it, empowerment is a single management action that authorizes employees to behave or perform in a certain way.

Earlier we noted that it was important to differentiate between the concepts embodied in the words *enable* and *empower* because each concept defines a distinct set of actions that is critical to developing a partnership. The following story provides insight into the differences.

I was working on an assignment for a client and had purchased a presentation software application as part of the project. Being new to this software application I was experiencing difficulty in executing certain commands. So I contacted the manufacturer's help desk by phone and, after a reasonable wait, was connected to a technician. During our conversation the technician informed me he was going to *empower* me to correct my problem by giving me a list of changes to make to my computer's operating system.

Having spent hours attempting to solve operating system problems in the past, I was less than encouraged by this statement. By right of ownership I was empowered to solve the problem. What I wanted was to be *enabled* to solve the problem.

And so it is with many attempts at employee involvement. The lack of clear distinction of all the necessary process elements results in incomplete implementation and over a 65 percent failure rate. In the E_4 Management Practices Checklist, each practice is a separate set of actions that produce a separate but interlinked set of outcomes all aimed at connecting the employee with the organization.

Empowerment in the sense of the E_4 Management Practices Checklist is the formal proclamation of the transfer of authority and responsibility to the employee partners. Unfortunately, many employees have a relationship with management that is saddled with the historical baggage of fear and mistrust. Any of us who have been involved with empowerment efforts will attest to the fact that a single declaration of empowerment, no matter how sincere, will not be accepted at face value by the employees. To reinforce this new reality, it is necessary to initiate actions that formally verify the transfer of authority and responsibility.

The Elements of the Empower Management Practice

Employees have two concerns when it comes to empowerment:

1. Can I "do" it?
2. Does my boss mean it?

We have seen that the Educate and Enable management practices address the first concern by providing employees with the education and ability to do it. The intent of the Empower practice is to convince employee partners that they actually have the authority to become involved in the business. This is accomplished through a combination of leadership and action.

That's all that the management practice of empowerment is—convincing employees they have the right and responsibility to make decisions and take action. That is why it is so important to separate the concepts of the words *enable* and *empower.* One practice provides the ability to connect with the organization, the other provides the authority to behave in certain ways. The fundamental function of the Empower management practice is to convince the employee partners that the management team really means what they say about empowerment.

Leadership

Leadership has many roles. To empower employees, leaders must become role models because as the leader does so the followers will do. Lasting behavioral change can only be realized through continuing visible management support.

Anyone who has ever worked for someone else will tell you that in an employment situation, the primary job is to do whatever the boss wants done. And this basic reality goes all the way to the top. With this knowledge as a foundation, it becomes critical that senior management indicate their total commitment to empowerment. They need to indicate this commitment through words and actions.

Strategy is great for planning, but tactics get the job done. In a conversation with Cory Rosen, executive director of the National Center for Employee Ownership, he states many top executives fail to take a tactical approach to empowerment. "Of all the companies using Employee Stock Ownership Plans, most of them share information with their employees, some of them help them understand the information, but only a few of them ask their employees to make changes based on that information."

How can senior management demonstrate their commitment?

First, they must clearly define their expectations concerning the practice of empowerment. They must identify the outcomes they want and the behaviors that will achieve those outcomes. This process will help form a mental image that is the "vision" of empowered employees. This mental image becomes the definition of empowerment for the organization. Then management can begin to take actions that represent their expectations.

Writing It Into Law

Part of the process of convincing partners they are empowered is providing them with this mental picture. Only after the concept of empowerment has been defined can it be communicated to the employees in some formal statement of empowerment. This statement should include the company's definition of empowerment, the results expected from the process, and a vision of what the organization will look like when fully empowered. This formal statement is a critical element of the Empower practice. Policies are used as a source of stability in an organization. The attendance policy, the customer satisfaction policy, the pay policy, and all the other policies of a company are a source of guidance and authority in the decision-making process.

In the traditional organization, policies have been used to control the employees. In an open organization, policies are used to empower employees. Establishing a "policy" of empowerment provides strong assurance to all employees that they are, indeed, partners with rights and responsibilities.

Content Actions and Process Actions

The old bromide that actions speak louder than words is never so true as it is here. A policy of empowerment may offer tentative reassurance, but only solid management action will provide the needed support for empowerment to become a reality. Actions such as sharing information, active listening, and participative decision making are *content* actions that connect employees to the organization. However, they are often less tangible than *process* actions, which exist as tangible statements of commitment. The following example illustrates this point.

A company that manufactured farm implements asked me to assist in developing a more open environment. It had announced to all employees that the company was moving toward a "culture of empowerment." As part of the move it instituted a problem-solving team approach centered around functional work groups. Because of the history of labor relations, the employees were initially reluctant to embrace the concept of empowerment. They wanted to grow as individuals and in their jobs, but they continued to defer all decisions to the shift supervisor. Not until management acted to change the work process did employees begin to develop trust. Lasting behavioral changes began when management involved frontline workers in a workplace redesign effort to improve the flow of work. Only then did they begin to accept the fact that they had the rights and responsibilities to solve problems and make decisions.

In thinking of appropriate E_3-Empowerment elements for your company, it will be quite helpful to define the desired relationship between management and the employee partners. The definition of this relationship is the core of any empowerment statement or policy. Once developed, it can be used as a guiding statement in developing actions that will result in educated, enabled, and empowered employee partners.

The Triangle of Educated and Enabled Empowerment

The process of developing employee partners is based on establishing relationships. We should be aware of three basic relationships. The first is interpersonal relationships, people coexisting together for their common good. The second is the relationship of performance to objectives, the behavior and actions of employees relative to the operational and financial objectives of the company (subcategory of this is the relationship of operational indicators to financial results). The third is the relationship of the four management practices to each other.

These four management practices are the means to achieve the interpersonal and performance relationships. Because of the synergy between the practices, the strength and balance of their relationships determines the degree to which a successful partnership will be established. Figure 3-5a, the Triangle of Educated and Enabled Empowerment, illustrates the relationships.

A triangle is one of the strongest and most stable forms in nature. However, even this form can be strengthened or weakened depending on where the emphasis is placed. Figure 3-5a illustrates the relationship among the first three management practices we have discussed. In Figure 3-5a, there has been a balanced emphasis on the practice to educate, enable, and empower the employees. The result is an employee population that knows what to do, knows how to do it, and knows they have the authority to do it.

Figure 3-5. a. Triangle of educated and enabled empowerment. b. Triangle of enabled empowerment.

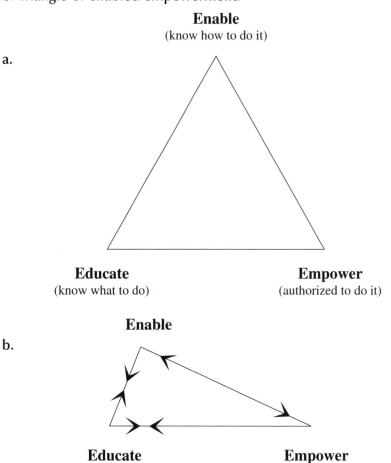

Enable
(know how to do it)

a.

Educate   **Empower**
(know what to do)   (authorized to do it)

Enable

b.

Educate   **Empower**

Figure 3-5b illustrates a common problem encountered in employee involvement efforts. It illustrates those elements of the empowerment wall that employees refer to when they speak of not being connected to the results of their efforts. It illustrates a situation in which one of the management practices, in this case the education element, is under emphasized.

The employees are enabled. They have been given access to plenty of involvement processes such as team building, problem solving, quality circles, or TQM. And this access is represented by the strong and powerful side of the triangle that extends out from Enable to Empower.

The employees are empowered. They have been given the formal authority to become involved. Management encourages decision making at the lowest level and has made each department a profit center, responsible for results. The empowerment statement is policy, and placards supporting this policy can be seen on the walls throughout the organization. Empowerment is represented by the strong and powerful side of the triangle that extends from Empower to Educate.

However, in this example, the practice of education, specifically education in how the company makes a profit and the employee's role in that process, has not been adequately addressed. As a result, employees remain in their functional silos, without a shared notion of why they work nor a common understanding of the results of their efforts.

Figure 3-5b illustrates how a weak relationship is established between the management practices as a result of inadequate education. Employees cannot be fully enabled until they are fully educated. This weak relationship is represented by the short side extending from Educate to Enable.

As long as the three practices are present, a triangle exists and employees will generate performance improvement. However, the degree of partnership and sustained competitive advantage an organization will realize is in direct proportion to the relationship of the three management practices. Figure 3-5b is not as stable, overall, as Figure 3-5a, which illustrates a strong relationship among all three practices.

The E_4 Management Practice: Engage

The definition of the word *engage* in the *Random House Dictionary of the English Language* is "to occupy the attention or effort of a person, to attract and hold fast." By definition, this management practice is in a completely different category from the other three practices.

We want each employee to perform and make decisions with the same degree of attachment and attention as any partner would. The first three practices—educate, empower, and engage—all focus at preparing employees to participate and encouraging their development as partners. Partners, however, not only share information and decision-making authority, but they also gain benefits or suffer loss based on the results of their decisions and actions. This opportunity to acquire benefit or suffer loss based on the results of decisions and actions creates commitment.

The Engage management practice is a dynamic practice. It consists of a variety of reward systems that offer employees the opportunity share in the benefits and risks of the business. Say the word *rewards* in an employment setting and immediately issues of compensation and pay come to mind. Pay is very important, no disputing that. But there is more to rewards than pay.

A recent Gallup poll reported in *Newsweek* found that only 11 percent of Americans think the rich are happier than they are (36 percent thought they were less happy). Only 17 percent said they envied the rich (82 percent didn't).[3] Employees don't seem to be out for riches so much as they seem to be striving for satisfaction. To reach a level of organizational maturity where all employees are satisfied with their role as business partners requires us to look at rewards as a system.

Reward Systems

Reward systems are those groups of elements so combined as to function interdependently and harmoniously to fulfill personal desires, needs, or demands.

The old paradigm of rewarding employees was based on the concept of "hired hands" and was limited to pay and benefits. Work was broken down into its smallest activities and employees were hired to perform activities without thinking about relationships or end results. Compensation was viewed as an expense.

The new paradigm of rewarding employees is based on the value of the whole person to the organization and is expanded to provide satisfaction through the delivery of intrinsic and extrinsic rewards. Figure 3-6 illustrates the point. The pyramid represents the work in behavioral psychology performed by Abraham Maslow, a professor at Brandeis University. In his research he identified that universal human needs are either of an attraction/desire nature or of an avoidance nature. He identified a set of human values that he arranged into a hierarchy of needs. He theorized that these needs could be prioritized. This priority would lead from avoidance of discomfort to the acquisition of psychological states of growth that provide a positive feeling.[4]

Figure 3-6 illustrates how a comprehensive reward system will include elements that offer fulfillment to both the physical (or external) needs and the psychic (or internal) needs. Material rewards are the ones we are most familiar with because they are defined by formalized company policies. Although we often utilize the social rewards, we are less familiar with them as an engagement process because they are less clearly defined as such.

The Elements of the Engage Management Practice

Social rewards are designed to provide fulfillment to the internal needs of social acceptance, self-esteem, and self-fulfillment. In the E$_4$

Figure 3-6. Needs/rewards relationships.

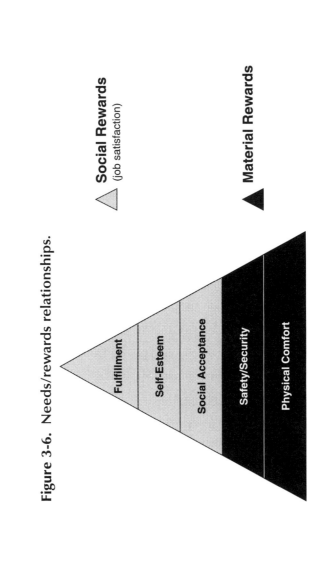

Fulfillment

Self-Esteem

Social Acceptance

Safety/Security

Physical Comfort

Social Rewards
(job satisfaction)

Material Rewards

Management Practices Checklist, the first three management practices that Educate, Enable, or Empower offer the opportunity for fulfillment of these internal needs. The specific tactics such as financial education, skill development, job redesign, team-building, TQM techniques, and performance feedback are all geared toward making each job more engaging and satisfying to the employee.

Material reward systems are designed to engage the employees by providing fulfillment to the external needs of physical comfort and security. The risk/reward relationship is developed through incentive compensation and equity pay plans that are linked to business outcomes. For example, the opportunity to earn an additional 15% of base pay as the result of improved productivity or reduced cost provides each employee partner with the ability to fulfill material needs.

Properly designed reward systems engage employees and get them to connect with the business profit objectives by linking personal fulfillment to the attainment of financial and operational objectives. This linkage between the individual and the business builds positive job attitudes, builds partnerships, and eventually leads to ownership thinking.

Obtaining Commitment to Operating Income

Figure 3-6 illustrates how critical it is to provide this opportunity to share in material rewards. It is literally the link between performance and financial results. As many involvement efforts have discovered, employee satisfaction can be obtained from the workplace without regard to the financial results of the company. Social rewards such as meaningful work, personal growth, and the opportunity to participate on problem-solving teams gain participation in these processes by providing fulfillment for personal internal needs. Yet they do not have a direct link to the bottom line.

On the other hand, material rewards such as equity ownership or incentive compensation tied to financial results provide a direct link to the bottom line. They offer the opportunity to share in either the current or future success of the organization, or both. Material rewards generate a high level of commitment to achieving financial results. They focus attention and efforts on the business issues to which partners should be committed.

Material reward systems are fast becoming an accepted management practice. *Business Week* recently reported that nearly two-thirds of midsize and large companies have some form of incentive pay for nonexecutives and that these types of pay plans have increased by 40% in the past two years. While initially used on the executive and

Figure 3-7. The Management Practice Pyramid of Power.

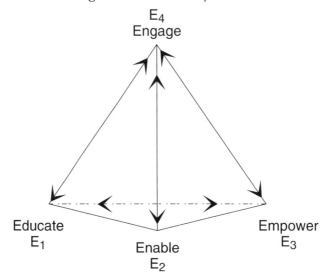

management levels, the trend is to extend this linkage to all levels of the organization.[5]

The Management Practice Pyramid of Power

Figure 3-7, the Management Practice Pyramid of Power, illustrates the relationship between the management practice to Engage and the other three management practices. As the figure indicates, reward systems interlink with each of the other management practices and, in doing so, they add a critical new dimension to the process of educated empowerment and partnership.

Reward systems change the perspective of empowered employees. When material rewards are based on financial outcomes, work groups tend to view themselves as profit centers with profit and loss responsibilities rather than as cost centers, detached from the financial outcome.

When financial education is provided to frontline employees as part of the Education management practice it is often viewed as threatening, uncomfortable, and inapplicable to the daily efforts. When reward systems are linked to financial performance, employee partners view financial education as a measurement tool that will enable them to increase their standard of living.

One of the key strengths of the Engage management practice is the relationship between financial education and incentive reward systems. By linking material rewards to financial outcomes, everyone's attention is focused not so much on how to divide the pie, but on how to make the pie bigger. Financial education on how the company makes a profit, generates cash, and controls cost is a critical tool each employee partner will want to utilize in his or her commitment to increasing the size of the pie.

Aligning Objectives and Getting Satisfaction

Is it important for company goals to be perceived as being relevant to employee aspirations? Professional employee trainer Pam Lontos thinks it is: "People don't reach other people's goals—they only reach their own." So the flexibility necessary to offer satisfaction and thereby obtain commitment is developed by reward systems that link to management practices that educate, enable, and empower. This linkage creates an environment in which people can grow personally, feel fulfilled, contribute to the common good, and share in the material results. The Rolling Stones were wrong when they sang "I can't get no satisfaction." The Engage management practice will provide satisfaction linked to results.

Enabling People to Solve Their Problems

The concept behind the E$_4$ Management Practices Checklist can be summarized in the following statement. "People have the solutions to their problems." These four management practices create an environment that allow people to develop and implement these solutions.

In his book *The Ultimate Advantage: Creating the High Involvement Organization*, Edward E. Lawler III suggests individuals should be involved throughout the organization in the business of the organization. They should receive ongoing information about it, make decisions that influence the organization's success, and be rewarded based on how effectively the organization operates.[6]

A recent market research survey of small and medium manufacturing firms conducted for the National Institute of Standards and Technology (NIST) reports that the top actions planned over the next five years emphasize training, empowerment, and compensation and benefits systems. Use of the E$_4$ Management Practice Checklist will ensure none of these practices are overlooked and the proper emphasis is placed on each to ensure a strong partnership.

Benefits

Used in concert, the four management practices have a positive impact on organizational effectiveness and economic value. They develop a sustainable competitive advantage focused on short- and long-term improvement to operating income. They develop core competencies of flexibility, responsiveness, innovation, and customer focus. They create a culture that attracts, retains, and develops qualified employees.

These practices make each member of the workforce as productive as possible. They provide a process for developing skilled, qualified employees, knowledgeable in the company operations. Once developed, these employees are a powerful strategic asset. They have the ability to generate a large number of ideas or responses to any given situation. They have the ability to expand a single idea by making changes or adding details and they have the ability to think of fresh or unusual ideas. They represent a significant investment and have the capability to significantly improve financial and operating results.

A balanced application of the four management practices creates an intelligent organization in which each employee understands the business goals and his or her role in achieving them. Because all employees are thinking differently and acting differently in this new organization, the results change. A partnership develops that results in real employee involvement and empowerment. Action is no longer focused on symptoms. Instead, the problems are highlighted, their causes identified and solved by individuals or teams of partners.

Communication is direct and immediate. Open sharing of financial information and material rewards based on results generates more pressure to perform. Each team and every partner is focused on making a contribution every day.

Fear Could Stop This

This chapter developed the E_4 Management Practices checklist. The next chapter develops the R_4 Employee Expectations checklist. Together they form the E_4-R_4 Partnership Checklist, a comprehensive tool that can be used by all levels of management to develop and maintain an open, partner-oriented, high-performance workplace.

What could cause such a powerful change initiative to fail? In one word, fear. Fear of change, fear of failure, fear of consequences. We address this issue of fear in Chapter 4 as we examine the employees' perspectives and expectations of an open environment and in Chapter 6 as we discuss the issues surrounding the rights of employee partners.

Notes

1. Daniel Denison, *Corporate Culture and Organizational Effectiveness* (New York: Wiley, 1990).
2. Ichniowski, Casey, Kathryn Shaw, and Giovanna Prennushi, "The Effects of Human Resource Management Practices on Productivity," Columbia University, June 10, 1993, Mimeograph.
3. The More and Less Deserving Rich, *Newsweek*, April 25, 1994, p. 43.
4. Thomas J. McCoy, *Compensation and Motivation: Maximizing Employee Performance With Behavior-Based Incentive Plans* (New York: AMACOM, 1992), p. 115.
5. "Bonus Pay: Buzzword or Bonanza?" *Business Week*, November 14, 1994, p. 62.
6. Edward E. Lawler III, *The Ultimate Advantage: Creating the High Involvement Organization* (San Francisco: Jossey-Bass, 1992).

4

The R$_4$ Employee Expectations

The logic of the four management practices that can be used to effectively manage change is so compelling that senior management and human resources professionals may want to begin immediate implementation of those practices that augment and enhance their organization's current human resources initiatives. However, experience shows that prudent up-front design work is time well spent. In a fast-moving, competitive environment, management tends to seize the newest employee involvement or performance improvement technique and thrust it onto the organization. Normally, the theory associated with each of these techniques is sound. Yet the business landscape is littered with ineffective quality, performance, and participation initiatives.

One of the keys to a successful cultural transformation as outlined by the E$_4$ management practices is the ability of senior management and human resources professionals to understand and manage employee expectations. To be accepted by employees, these management practices must be developed with an awareness and sensitivity as to how they will be perceived by the employees. If the employees' perspective is understood and the specifics of each management practice are developed to support their expectations, then the chances are good that this process will succeed where others have failed.

Understanding Employee Expectations

Managing Employee Expectations

Employees will be most inclined to enter into a partnership with their company if they feel their needs will be met by doing so. However, what exactly are these needs? Are they homogenous throughout the employee population or does each employee represent a unique set of needs that must be addressed?

The answer of course is that each employee has a set of needs based on his or her expectations. Does this present a problem for us? How can we possibly provide fulfillment to this myriad of needs and still run a business? What system could be flexible enough or generic enough to provide the opportunity to fulfill each of these needs? Fortunately building an employee partnership does not require us to address needs on an individual basis.

When employees come to work for an organization they bring with them certain assumptions about how employment will fulfill their personal needs. These assumptions are internal expectations and often have very little to do with the actual terms of employment. Ours is not an attempt to solve all of our employees' personal problems. Rather, our focus is to establish a relationship that defines employee expectations relative to the work environment and business objectives.

A new skill requirement has emerged for managers in open organizations. It is the skill to manage expectations. By managing expectations, management is in effect defining the needs that will be addressed in the workplace. Traditional organizations may make a passing attempt at managing newly hired employee expectations with an "orientation" process. This usually takes the form of a series of group meetings in which employees are informed about company policies and procedures. Most often, this process is focused on transferring information about work rules rather than setting the expectations of new partners. Once through the orientation process, employees are seldom exposed to any additional information about the worker/manager/partner relationship. As a result, most employees continue to maintain an outmoded set of expectations about their relationship with the organization. The following example illustrates this point.

Expectations of the Hired Hand

Recently I spent some time with a colleague who is employed by a Fortune 500 company. The company is in an industry that is global in scope and was one of the first to experience the effects of the new economy. The past several years have been difficult for the company and were filled with constant change. Margins have been reduced, there is fierce competition for market share, and the company's stock price has fallen below that of their competitors.

The company has made the decision to relocate a complete business function to another city. The relocation is just one of many actions the company has taken over the past several years in an effort to maintain a competitive position. The relocation action will result in the displacement of approximately four hundred workers and their families. All of these employees have been provided the options to either retain their positions if they relocate, find another job within the company, or look outside for employment.

Naturally, this action has created significant distress among the employees within this business function. To address the distress, the company facilitated focus groups to help the employees deal with the issues of change.

A vast majority of the employees who attended these meetings voiced anger and disappointment. They expressed a sense of having been betrayed by the company. Several employees stated their position as "I try to do what is good for the company in my job and the company owes it to me to take care of me." Unfortunately, this is the altruistic expectation of the hired hand. It is a set of expectations based on the unspoken employment agreements of the old economy.

The new economy has forced organizations to redefine the terms of this unspoken agreement. However, very few organizations have progressed to the point where they are able to express this new agreement in terms the employees can understand and accept. And until they do, the employees will continue to maintain their old expectations.

Expectations of Employee Partners

An open organization, with the E$_4$ management practices in place, establishes a quite different set of expectations on the part of the employees. These management practices develop a partnership in which employees understand the business imperatives of revenues, expenses, net income, market share, and competition. They understand that their relationship is a business relationship that is ongoing and, at some point in time, may no longer match their personal expectations.

The Employee Expectations

The pragmatic expectations of a partner are based on the realities of the business. Partners understand why decisions are made. Rather than resenting them, partners help to make them work. Their expectations are based on a clear understanding of the four elements that define their relationship. These elements are called the R_4 Employee Expectations and form the employee's half of the E_4-R_4 Partnership Checklist. They are:

1. Roles
2. Rights
3. Responsibilities
4. Risks/Rewards

Figure 4-1, the E_4-R_4 Partnership Checklist, illustrates the four elements that work to define employee partner expectations. Examination of each of the four employee expectations and understanding their relationship to the four management practices will enable us to use the E_4-R_4 Partnership Checklist as a partnership building tool.

The R_1 Employee Expectation: Roles

Employee Roles

First and foremost in the process of managing expectations is to define the role that each partner will assume. The *Random House Dictionary of the English Language* defines *role* as "the proper or customary function, the expected behavior patterns." In a company in which the four management practices are implemented, the roles of both management and employees are quite different from traditional roles. The company develops an open, high-involvement, high-performance culture centered on the potential of the employees.

In this environment, each employee assumes the role of an entrepreneur and partner. The management practice of Education directly supports the employee partner role. The employees' proper and customary function is to use this education to become connected with the organization. They are expected to use their understanding of both the big picture and the detailed cause and effect for the betterment of the endeavor. The other management practices that enable, empower, and engage, also help define the employee partner role by providing information on how and why to act as a partner. As partners, employees are given education, clear direction, and autonomy, and are expected to participate and become involved.

There is active participation and there is passive participation. Active participation occurs when employees have had a voice in goal setting and decision making. Then they are in agreement as to the feasibility of the venture and actively committed to achieving "their" goals. Passive participation occurs when employees have been told

Figure 4-1. E_4-R_4 Partnership Checklist.

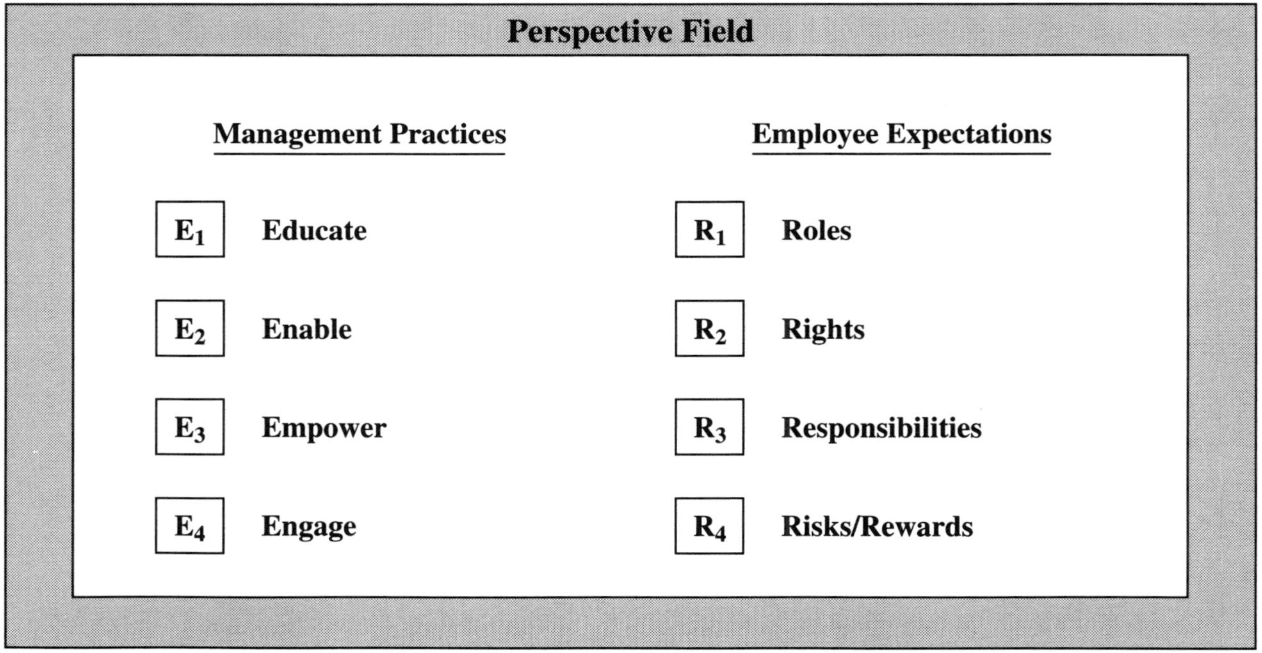

Perspective Field

Management Practices

E_1	Educate
E_2	Enable
E_3	Empower
E_4	Engage

Employee Expectations

R_1	Roles
R_2	Rights
R_3	Responsibilities
R_4	Risks/Rewards

what the goals are and have been directed to participate in the attainment of them. The process used to determine these goals is normally conducted without employee input. Employees go through the motions as they pursue these goals but rarely exercise initiative to overcome obstacles that may develop.

Partners actively participate. By taking the initiative to define the employee's role as that of a partner, the organization establishes the expectation of participation by all employees. One business associate defined the expected behavior patterns of an employee partner role with the following statement: "Employee partners use their business knowledge and best judgment skills to make decisions and take actions that will further the strategic and financial objectives of their company."

Role Definition

Defining the role of a partner requires both a formal and informal process. Formal statements must be made to provide assurance to each employee that the words spoken today will remain in effect tomorrow. A good example of this is the formal process used at Ashton Photo.

Ashton Photo is located in Salem, Oregon. The company is a high-volume producer of photo prints for professional photographers. By all accounts, Ashton is an open, partner-oriented, high-performance company. The employees have been educated in and have weekly access to the financial statements. They understand the numbers and their role in affecting them. The company organization is based around teams and each team receives a weekly profit-and-loss statement that reports their output. Employees are expected to train each other in both technical and social skills.

The company enables and empowers the employees through a team-based management approach in which teams schedule their own workloads. They are empowered to take the action necessary to satisfy the customer and are held directly accountable to the customer for their work.

The employees are engaged through several social and material reward systems. Hourly workers receive a monthly incentive payout based on sales revenues. There is a 401(k), an employee stock ownership plan, and a pay-for-knowledge plan. A culture of trust and openness provides the social rewards necessary for a partnership. Each employee has a key to the building and has the ability to flex their work time to balance their personal life with the production schedule.

Significantly, Ashton Photo manages expectations by clearly defining roles and relationships. The company has developed an employee handbook that is distributed to each employee. This handbook contains the "social contract" that one enters into upon becoming an employee. The handbook is a powerful communication device, complete with graphics, which defines the roles of the employee and employer.

Equality

Informal actions on the part of all employees must encourage openness and sharing. This informal process is the most difficult part of demonstrating partnership. It is achieved by the diligent demonstration of respect and equality for each individual.

Do formal or informal practices in your organization delineate a caste system? Most organizations have practices that, to some degree, set one group of employees apart from another. It is difficult to convince all employees they are partners when parking spaces are reserved for a select group or a dining area or a certain level of furniture or office decor is reserved for a select group.

These practices, although comfortable for the recipients, defeat the concept of equality and mutual respect that is embodied in real partnership. Most organizations recognize this divisive force and many have taken tentative steps to eliminate it. However, change is difficult and the result is often a toe-in-the-water approach such as "casual day" where all employees wear everyday clothes rather than formal business attire.

I have seen both extremes to this approach and they were a reflection of senior management's attitude toward partnership. On one extreme, business suits and ties were mandatory because, in the words of the president, "You can't act professionally unless you dress professionally" (an odd type of form-over-substance approach). At the other extreme, there was no dress code other than a general definition of what would be considered "distracting" to fellow employees. The intent, as expressed by this president, was "Sometimes an artificial level of dress can get in the way of communication." Obviously, this second approach is a much stronger statement of equality.

Unity

A big concern in developing an open culture that supports a partnership is how to develop an overall sense of unity. Unity is important because if sensitive information is to be shared with all employees, everyone must associate closely with the organization. Otherwise there is a chance the information will find its way into the hands of the competition.

This is not as significant a concern as it initially appears. The strategic advantage achieved through information sharing is not in the information itself. Rather it is in the dynamics of an employee population that has access to and understands the information. And unity is almost always a by-product of these employee dynamics. After all, it is difficult to develop a sense of unity unless everyone is speaking the same "language" and focused on the same objectives. The E_4 practices help develop this sense of unity.

In traditional organizations, especially those under pressure to perform, I have often observed that those who "produce" tend to resent those who don't have a direct link to the product delivery. In the manufacturing industry this often appears as a separation between the shop floor and office staff. In service or sales it appears as a separation between the field locations and headquarters. In an open organization this sense of separation and resentment is replaced by a willingness to become part of a bigger team. Underneath the general role of partner, each employee has a specific role defined by the contribution he makes through his job function. This individual contribution is identified during implementation of the Education practice when the link between job function and operational performance indicators is developed.

Because of their understanding of the organization's processes, employee partners understand the contribution each department makes to the business objectives. In larger organizations they may not know the individual roles within each department. However, they will be joined through the common understanding that the process has ensured there are no noncontributors in an open, partner-oriented, business-focused company. Information sharing eventually results in an organization in which each role adds well-defined value.

Service Roles

Having trouble defining the role of your service employee partners? What would happen if you thought of them in more of a sales role? For companies that are sales driven, a sales position holds a certain élan and level of prestige. The service role often has many of the attributes of a sales role. Like sales employees, service employees have direct contact with the customer and their primary function is (or should be) to satisfy customer expectations. What better opportunity to identify additional customer needs and offer goods or services to fill those needs? In a sales-driven organization, redefining the service role as another aspect of the sales role could build unity and enhance the self-esteem of the service providers.

Whatever direction you take, it is important to reevaluate the roles of the employees within your organization and, if needed, redefine them to be more in line with the concept of partnership. This role redefinition does not have to be burdensome. It is a natural outcome of the alignment process discussed in Chapter 2, and the implementation of the four management practices.

No Management Roles

Companies that have implemented the four management practices report a reduction in the ranks of managers. Management goal setting, decision making, and problem-solving responsibilities are being assumed more and more by the educated, enabled, empowered, and engaged employee partners. What does this mean for middle management? Will they be downsized? Rightsized? Outplaced?

Companies that implement the concepts contained in the E_4-R_4 Partnership Checklist tend to partner with all employees. Rather than off-load their current level of managers, they recognize the valuable knowledge and depth of experience these professionals have. They redefine the role of supervision and management. The AT&T Service Center in Atlanta is a good example of redefining supervision's role.

The AT&T Service Center in Atlanta is a telephone remanufacturing and repair facility. After deregulation of the telephone industry, both management and union labor realized they would have to work together more closely to compete in the new economy. As a result, the service center developed a self-directed team structure in which each team is organized around a specific product or group of products. Being self-directed, the teams are educated, enabled, and empowered to plan, schedule, and manage their own work.

When the facility started the developmental process there were forty people in supervisory positions. Currently there are nine remaining and they are no longer supervisors. This reduction was achieved through attrition rather than layoff. The remaining supervisors were moved into newly defined positions such as new business managers, performance managers, and coordinators. These positions were the result of identifying the potential inherent in the competencies held by these employees.

The issue is not whether front line supervision and middle management can contribute. They can. The issue is how to redefine their role to support an open, educated, high-involvement environment. The roles of the people currently in management will change. Their traditional oversight functions are being eliminated and their technical functions are being assimilated by the employees. Management in the new economy will look very different from the management of today.

"New" Management Roles

The primary function of the "new" manager is to provide support. The roles that are most effective in supporting employee partners are the roles of teacher, coach, advisor, and facilitator. These roles help partners to reach their full potential.

A "command and control" management style doesn't work with partners. Partners don't need an overseer. They can schedule and implement work for themselves. Partners don't need an autocrat. They can set goals, solve problems, and make decisions for themselves.

Partners need facilitators to run interference for them. They need expediters to remove the bottlenecks and access the resources so they can perform their functions. Partners need trainers to provide them with guidance, wisdom, and sources of new information and education. They need mentors who stimulate their thinking with new ideas. And they need coaches who provide them with encouragement, who show appreciation for their efforts, who make them feel like a team member.

Many managers will have difficulty with their new role. Part of the human resources professional's responsibility in the Education management practice is to provide training to educate both employees and managers in their new roles. Classroom training needs to be augmented by firsthand doing. As the structure of the organization changes and teams of partners become the norm, managers will need to become team leaders who share their insights with team members while on the job. We discuss the changing role of managers in greater detail in Chapter 6.

Leadership Roles

In an open environment everyone must assume a leadership role. In this role, each partner has an obligation to share personal knowledge and ideas with colleagues. I saw a good example of this type of leadership exhibited by the janitor of a machine shop.

The machine shop manufactures gears, shaped frames and other semifinished goods out of steel and other raw material. It is precision-tolerance work, with products manufactured to extremely close specifications. This employee partner's job was to maintain a clean work environment and ensure the removal of all waste from the facility. This function provided him with a unique perspective of the organization. He was not tied to a single machine all day. Rather he could move about the facility, traveling throughout each department and outside the building. This freedom of movement allowed him to see a big picture of the overall manufacturing effort.

The management at this company was concerned about competition and realized their employees could provide a strategic advantage. As part of the process of developing employee involvement, the entire organization participated in a form of open-book education. All employees were educated about the company's products and customers, the current growth plans, the key operational indicators of each major department, and the key financial profit and expense elements of the company.

As a result of this Education practice, the janitor learned that the company was experiencing a profitability problem. This problem was due mainly to difficulty with quality on a project for a major client. The client represented over 40 percent of the company's product volume and the margin on this project was projected to be a significant portion of operating income for the quarter. Unfortunately, quality problems were affecting profitability, the schedule delivery date, and the relationship with the client.

A team of company engineers had narrowed the source of the problem to a highly complex machining work station. Semifinished work arrived at the work station within design specifications but, after being processed at the station, was found to be out of specification.

The manufacturer of the machining station had sent a technician to recalibrate the machine but the accuracy seemed to last for only a day or two, then the machine would begin to produce out-of-spec product. When the solution could not be found the machine operator, supervisor, production manager and vice-president of sales all began to point fingers at the manufacturer of the work station.

The combination of individual job perspective and the awareness of operating and financial issues created by open-book education develops within an individual a state of understanding I refer to as "local wisdom." Armed with his local wisdom, the janitor observed a material handler bump the machining station with a forklift as he was transporting material from one location in the facility to another.

This was not an uncommon event. The machining station was a large piece of equipment and had been located at the intersection of two material flow paths. The material handlers passed the machine and turned the corner over fifty times each day. Occasionally they would misjudge the angle of the turn and nudge the machining station.

The janitor's local wisdom allowed him to conclude that this event was throwing the machine's calibration off, thus creating the quality problem. Although he had seen this event in the past, he was not able to attach significance to it until he had developed local wisdom, until he had received open-book education and been made aware of the quality problem.

He informed the plant management of his breakthrough thinking. On the basis of his observation and recommendation the plant maintenance partners set a series of metal pipes into the cement floor at the corner of the intersection. The pipes prevented the forklifts from coming into contact with the machining center and the quality problem disappeared.

Respect for Local Wisdom Leadership

Defining roles in an open organization creates two universal leadership expectations: obligation and responsibility. All partners from the executive on down understand their obligation to encourage and respect local wisdom leadership. Sharing thoughts and ideas can be an uncomfortable process for many employees. The traditional workplace has often extinguished this behavior rather than encouraged it.

This clearly defined expectation of respect nurtures self-confidence and the sharing of local wisdom. Each partner is secure in her responsibility to come forward as a leader and share her local wisdom. By defining roles, the four management practices promote and protect employee involvement.

Leader Leadership

Senior management has a new leadership role also. They cannot afford to be removed strategists, remote from the day-to-day action. Management must be the spokesperson, the source of enthusiasm for the company. They must energize the workforce to the cause. They must hold forth the vision of a future state so clearly that all employee partners clearly understand the intent of the organization.

This assumes that senior management is committed to creating an open, partner-oriented environment. By actions and words management must communicate their expectation that each employee will assume the role of partner and act accordingly. This form of leadership assures all employees that, as partners, they are performing in the manner their leaders want and expect.

Is it really necessary to change the senior management style? Can improvements be made without this change? Senior leadership is at the heart of success in creating a sustainable partnership. Without committed and visible leadership the effort will fail.

The reality is that it is not an equal partnership. Senior management has a leadership role that will always set it apart. The essence of this role is captured in a public statement by Oliver White, author and manufacturing process guru. He said, "For a boss you do what you are told. For a leader you do what needs to be done."

Supplier Roles

Suppliers have a key role in an open, partner-oriented organization. Like the employees, the supplier is a partner. Suppliers are relied upon to provide quality goods and services on a timely basis. They provide the input to the organization. Any problem with the input will cause problems within the organization.

The supplier partnership is very similar to the employee partnership. It is built on relationships, trust, and the four management practices. Suppliers must be educated to the needs of the organization. In order to be effective partners, they need to understand the big picture and how they fit into the company's success. They need to be provided with information and systems that enable them to contribute to the organization. They need to be empowered to suggest changes to processes, policies, and procedures, and to make recommendations that benefit the company. And, of course, they need to be engaged through a variety of social and material reward systems that make it worth their while to be a partner.

Several years ago one of my colleagues was working on an assignment for a supplier to the automotive industry. He was in a meeting with the primary manufacturer to whom the client was providing goods and services. During the course of the meeting the topic of supplier relations came up. One of the managers from the primary manufacturer made the statement, only half in jest, "We treat our suppliers like oranges. We suck them dry and then throw them away." Of course, no company, no matter how dominant, can afford such arrogance in today's economy. Today the emphasis is on developing long-term relationships with a few valued suppliers.

Inventory costs have a significant effect on profitability. Large stores of inventory tie up cash that can be used to reduce interest costs and improve net income. Companies that have implemented just-in-time (JIT) inventory practices have partnered with their suppliers to reduce these costs. These companies share with their partner suppliers detailed, accurate, and timely information about production scheduling.

Sharing this information enables suppliers to plan delivery of materials to coincide with production demands. The result is a mutually beneficial partnership. The producer experiences lower inventory costs (and often lower materials costs). The suppliers achieve a steady source of business that enables them to achieve lower operating costs.

Customer Roles

Customers have a role in the organization also. The company that uses the four management practices to define and manage the customer's role will achieve a strategic advantage over the competition. In the old economy, customers were considered an external entity whose role was to "complain" to the company when their expectations were not met. In an open, educated, high-involvement organization, customers are considered partners and, as such, have a key role in the partnership. Their role is that of an advisor.

An open organization views any customer interaction as an opportunity to receive advice from their customer partners as to how well their expectations are being met. Many organizations solicit customer feedback through special programs and occasional focus groups. In an open organization, whenever the customer and employee interact, the partner employee makes the most of the opportunity to define and reinforce their mutual partnership.

Understanding the customer's role and communicating this role to the customer is critical to an organization's success. All too often in my conversations with consumers I hear statements like: "I never thought I would, but I have quit complaining (read advising) to the management about the service. Now I just don't go back." When questioned further, the reason they cease to participate in the process is that they don't feel it will make any difference. They don't feel their advice is being heeded.

In the new economy no company can afford to sustain such lost opportunities. National data show on an average it is five to eight times more expensive to acquire a new customer than it is to keep a current customer.

Employee partners are educated in the value of a well-maintained customer relationship. They understand the cost to their company of a seriously disenchanted customer. Educated employee partners can readily calculate how the loss of a customer affects operating income and, ultimately, their pay and job security.

Educator and Salesperson Roles

Acquisition costs aside, think of the opportunity for improving the product, process, and profitability that is being lost by not capturing the customer partner's advice. To seize this new customer retention opportunity, each employee must assume the roles of educator and salesperson, educating customers on their role as advisor and selling them on the value of that role to the company and, ultimately, to them as consumers.

Done properly, this education will develop customer loyalty. Who of us wouldn't want to do repeat business with a company that treated us like a partner, a company whose employees resolved our disputes, satisfied our expectations, and displayed an interest in a long-term relationship by soliciting information about our future needs?

Universal Roles

In an open, partner-oriented company each employee has a job-specific role. However, each employee also has a set of universal roles that must be assumed. These are the roles of leader, partner, educator, and salesperson/company representative. While these roles are intuitively part of the four management practices, at some point during the implementation process it is necessary to formally discuss them with all employees. This discussion defines management's expectations of the employees' role and becomes the social contract.

This process changes expectations from those of a hired hand to those of a partner. This social contract enables employees to clarify the meaning of these roles for themselves, thus speeding their ability to internalize them.

The R_2 Employee Expectation: Rights

The next step in the process of managing expectations is to define the rights of each partner. If roles are one side of the partnership coin, then rights are the other side. The Random House Dictionary of the English Language defines *rights* as "that which is due anyone by a just claim." It also refers to rights as "moral principles."

Just like the United States Bill of Rights, an open organization that applies the four management practices needs a Bill of Partner Rights. At this point the legal red flags go up and progress grinds to a halt with the thought of the potential for litigation such a document would create.

Good news. Recent legal rulings have indicated that such a document can be interpreted as a set of aspirations rather than a contractual statement. Naturally one would want to partner with the legal department during the development to ensure this intent is clear.

The intent is to provide each individual with a sense of security as to the type of treatment they can expect as a partner. In Chapter 3 we noted that fear was the primary force that could defeat a partnership effort. The R_2 Bill of Rights is a key element that counteracts fear. It outlines the personal liberties and freedoms that can be expected from an organization in return for entering into the partnership.

The employee expectation of Rights is the lens through which each individual partner interprets the Enable management practice. If a company values a multiskilled workforce and initiates practices that enable employees to achieve this end, then each employee partner has the right to seek skill training. If a company values an organizational design based on rapid work flow and initiates practices that enable employees to achieve this end, then each employee partner has the right to, in a coordinated effort, make changes to the organization such that it supports a rapid cycle time. If a company values customer satisfaction and initiates practices that enable employees to achieve this end, then each employee partner has the right to make decisions and act to satisfy the customer.

A classic example of the moral support provided by employee rights is the story told about a well-known overnight delivery service. This company built a strategic advantage around enabling each employee to provide customer satisfaction. As the story goes, an express package was to be delivered to a scientific team at a mountaintop location. Because of a snowstorm, the roads were impassable and it appeared as if the delivery date would be missed. An employee at the branch location decided to charter a helicopter to deliver the package. The result was an on-time delivery. The employee was recognized by her management for making the right decision and satisfying the customer's expectation.

This situation was risky for the employee. The employee was not a management level employee and the expense was far greater than the revenue generated by the transaction. Nonetheless, the employee knew she had the right to make any reasonable decision that would provide customer satisfaction. Her decision was based on the principles and vision of the company. Her ability to make the decision was due to the absence of fear. Her understanding of the company's position that every employee has the right to take a calculated risk removed the fear of negative repercussion and enabled her to fulfill the intent of the company.

The R_3 Expectation: Responsibilities

In an open, partner-oriented, high-performance environment each employee has certain responsibilities that accompany their roles. *Re-*

sponsibilities is defined in the *Random House Dictionary of the English Language* as "answerable or accountable for," and "something within one's power, control, or management." The employee expectation of Responsibilities is the lens through which each individual partner interprets the Empowerment management practice. The logic of this relationship is clear. If employees are empowered to act they will most certainly want to know what their responsibilities are.

All employees have their own expectations as to what their responsibilities are in relation to their roles. In the old economy these responsibilities were narrowly defined and most often related only to the job function. The role of a hired hand was to be responsible only for the activities and output of those hands.

The four management practices in an open environment define partner responsibilities in broader terms. These broad terms set broad expectations on the part of each employee partner. By setting broad expectations, management provides all employees with the ultimate responsibility: to use their local wisdom on a daily basis to make decisions and take actions for the good of the business.

The self-directed team members at the AT&T Service Center in Atlanta are expected to implement change in the work process as they see fit. If changes in the process will affect other teams or have an impact in another area, they are expected to communicate and coordinate the changes with the affected groups.

Partners have the responsibility to understand the intent and the process of the organization. They have the responsibility to understand the products and economics of the business and how the company makes a profit and generates cash. Partners have the responsibility to actively participate and become connected to the organization. They have the responsibility to be concerned about the well-being of their company and to make decisions and act to enhance that well-being.

They have the responsibility to develop their skills and talents, thus becoming more valuable to the organization and to themselves. Personal development is part of the responsibility they have as partners with the company. More and more the human resources community is talking about how employees must take responsibility for their careers.

The four management practices provide a clear and understandable framework that enables each employee to define and internalize these responsibilities for him- or herself. The result is an environment in which employees think proactively rather than reactively. They are constantly focused on personal, professional, and operational improvement because they understand the responsibilities of their role as partner.

The R_4 Employee Expectation: Risks/Rewards

Employees in a traditionally managed company have a much different set of expectations about risk and reward than do employee partners in an open, educated, high-involvement company.

Risk is defined as "the exposure to the chance of injury or loss." In a traditionally managed company most employees are risk averse. They try to minimize their exposure to the chance of injury or loss. Is this aversion to risk a genetic trait? Is there a bell curve for risk-related behavior? Or is it the result of nurturing and the environment? Can the majority of employees, those risk-averse legions of salaried and wage earners, be converted into partners who are excited by the opportunity to take a well-thought-out risk? Or are partnership efforts doomed to failure when the going gets tough and tough decisions need to be made?

Experience and observation indicate that risk aversion is not an inherent trait. For the most part, risk-averse behavior appears to be a default position developed in response to a lack of reward opportunities. Reward is defined as "something received in return for service, merit, or hardship given." For the average employee, reward comes in the form of base pay and benefits. The employment arrangement is based on selling personal time for an established salary or wage. Since this employment arrangement provides for a livelihood, anything that puts this arrangement at risk is viewed as something to be avoided. For this reason, employees tend to dislike, and resist, anything that changes the established way of doing things.

Why Cultural Change Fails

Most change that occurs in the workplace results in a change to performance requirements. Employees have a long history of experience that tells them that compliance to performance requirements is fundamental for continued employment. From the employee's point of view, change is a high-risk, low-reward proposition that should be avoided at all costs.

Their perspective is focused internally. It is focused on maintaining the stability of their position within the organization. In conjunction with this focus on stability of position comes a focus on the equity of their paycheck. As we saw in Figure 3-6, Maslow's hierarchy of needs places security and self-esteem as primary motivational forces. Pay equity in a traditional organization is perceived as being strongly linked to issues of risk, security, and self-esteem.

In more traditional organizations, performance appraisals take place annually. As a result, the process of providing more timely performance feedback goes by default to the paycheck. In these environments the size of a paycheck defines an individual's worth to the organization. Employees who are "worth more" to the organization receive more pay. Perceived pay inequity is an indicator of an unstable position and therefore, is a high-risk position and something to be avoided by the individual. The same logic applies to the paycheck as a measure of self-esteem.

This understanding of risk and rewards helps explain why cultural change processes have such a high failure rate. It is because they fail to recognize and deal with this risk/reward imbalance. They tend to offer the "challenge" of taking on more risk while not clearly defining the social and material rewards that accompany the risk.

Analysis of these failed efforts reveals that, in many cases, employee attention was never successfully redirected from the internal issues of security and self-esteem. The employees remained focused on avoiding loss of security and self-esteem either because they never really understood their ability to gain in these areas (E_1-Education) or, there was no real opportunity available to them (R_4-Risk/ Reward).

Risk as an Opportunity for Reward

In the new economy, change occurs daily. In order to take advantage of the opportunities that change presents, certain process must be used to overcome this risk-averse attitude.

Open, partner-oriented companies understand the risk/reward relationship and develop a more balanced approach to change. In this approach, change is viewed by all as an opportunity rather than a threat. Employee partners look at the company as a business. They are educated in the marketplace economics and competitive pressures and understand the relationship between success in the marketplace and the continued existence of the company.

They understand the risk that investors have made in the stock of the company. They understand the risk that unless the company can make an acceptable level of profit, it will not remain in business. They understand their job security is based on how well the company performs.

However their interest goes beyond that. Their interest is focused on their ability to affect their standard of living and enhance their level of self-esteem. As partners, they have a vested interest in the profitability and viability of the company and they have the knowledge, ability, and responsibility to manage those interests.

Executives in open, partner-oriented companies offer their employees the opportunity to share in the financial outcomes above and beyond their base pay and benefits. They offer a variety of opportunities for short- and long-term material rewards based on how well the company performs. Some offer short-term incentive pay linked to key performance indicators. Others offer long-term deferred profit sharing based on financial performance.

In the most developed stage, these companies offer their employees the opportunity to become owners. They offer equity opportunities such as ESOPs and employee stock purchase plans that work to change partners into true owners.

External Focus on Customers and Competition

Open, partner-oriented companies offer an environment in which an employee can become educated, enabled, empowered, and engaged. In doing so they offer fulfillment to a complete spectrum of employee needs.

As a result, employees focus their perspective outward. They realize they can contribute and affect the outcomes. They focus on the performance of the company and its relationship to customers and the competition. They fully understand the need for change and embrace it as an opportunity to exercise their partnership and share in the rewards.

In these companies, risk takes on a different characteristic. Exposure to the chance of injury or loss is no longer perceived as an individual issue. In this culture, risk is perceived as the hazard that competition will seize market share or a customer will go elsewhere. Risk is the chance that a slow cycle time will bring a new product late to the market and cost market share or new opportunities that leverage the core capabilities will go unrecognized.

Matching Practices to Expectations

Figure 4-1, the E_4-R_4 Partnership Checklist, is an invaluable tool that portrays the elements and perspectives necessary to develop a sustainable employee partnership in an open, educated, high-performance environment. To complete the graphic presentation of these concepts we add Figure 4-2, the Employee Expectation Pyramid of Power. Figure 4-2 is a mirror image of Figure 3-7, the Management Practice Pyramid of Power.

Together these three graphics illustrate the relationship of the eight key elements in the E_4-R_4 Partnership Checklist, as shown in Figure 4-3. They can also aid in the analysis of your design, development, and implementation efforts. Although each company will have

Figure 4-2. The Employee Expectations Pyramid of Power.

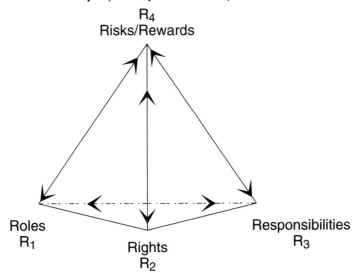

its own cultural priorities and ownership issues, the design process should strive for some degree of symmetry among relationships. Using the checklist and graphic concepts to develop your own pyramids will provide you with a clear picture of conceptual strengths and weaknesses in your overall implementation design.

Figure 4-3. The three key graphics.

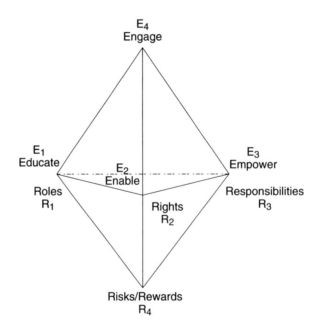

Perspective Field	
Management Practices	**Employee Expectations**
E_1 Educate	R_1 Roles
E_2 Enable	R_2 Rights
E_3 Empower	R_3 Responsibilities
E_4 Engage	R_4 Risks/Rewards

The E_4 - R_4
Partnership Checklist

E_4
Engage

E_1
Educate

E_2
Enable

E_3
Empower

Roles
R_1

Rights
R_2

Responsibilities
R_3

Risks/Rewards
R_4

Joined Pyramids of Power.

5

E_1-Educate:
The Management Practice
R_1-Roles:
The Employee Expectation

"Man's mind, once stretched by a new idea, never regains its original dimensions."

—Oliver Wendell Holmes

In an open, business-focused company the challenge to managers and human resources professionals is to make facts available to all employee partners in a manner that will allow them to make use of the data. This goes beyond just identifying information that management would like to share and then posting it on the bulletin board.

The Education management practice requires that information not only be available but also be relevant, understandable, and applicable. Relevant information is information that bears on or is connected with the business. Dealing with relevant information is a bit like peeling an onion. The removal of each layer reveals yet another layer below it. And the process of getting to the core can be so arduous that the thought of it makes your eyes water.

Fear not. Like any large-scale effort, providing relevant, understandable, and applicable information is achieved through a project management technique that divides the tasks into manageable segments. As we saw in Chapter 2, the vision of the company acts as a reference point in determining relevant information. Any and all information that pertains to the organization's strategic intent can be considered relevant. This could include, but not be limited to industry trends, financial performance data such as sales and profitability, operational performance data such as productivity and quality, and social data such as results from employee surveys.

In this chapter, we focus on the techniques of educating employee partners. We examine an education model that presents four distinct yet interrelated levels of understanding. We will see how these levels of education interact to create a degree of comprehension that transforms employee thinking into partner thinking.

The Education Onion

Information that is presented and explained in an organized, linear manner is normally understandable. For that reason, the Education management practice builds on previous learning as it moves from macro to micro in detail. It starts with general information and proceeds through information that is specific. Figure 5-1, the E_1 Education Onion, illustrates this concept.

The benefit of the Education management practice is a company of employee partners who understand and accept their roles and who possess relevant and understandable information. They then have the potential to apply this information in the form of creative thinking.

Peeling the Onion

The outer layer of this education onion consists of general economic information, such as the industry, the competition's relative performance, customer expectations, pricing, and demand trends. The second layer consists of more company specific information, such as the strategic plan, organizational priorities, budget constraints, new technology plans, the marketing plan, and the production or service processes. The third layer consists of performance-related information on how effective and efficient the organization is on a day-to-day basis. It consists of information such as financial costs, quality, and operating results and about stockholder issues. The fourth layer consists of personal information about rewards, interpersonal relationships, personal leadership, stakeholder issues, and how success for the organization results in success for the partners.

The Four-Stage Progression

The Education Onion model views education as the process of building a body of knowledge. Note that education is a process rather than a program. It requires ongoing communication, cooperation,

Figure 5-1. The E$_i$-Education Onion.

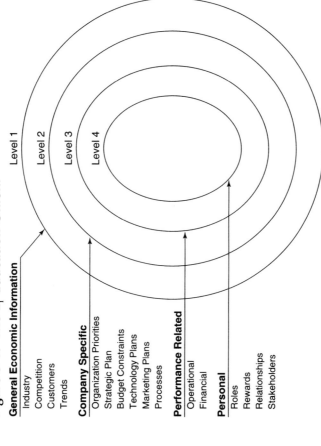

General Economic Information
Industry
Competition
Customers
Trends

Company Specific
Organization Priorities
Strategic Plan
Budget Constraints
Technology Plans
Marketing Plans
Processes

Performance Related
Operational
Financial

Personal
Roles
Rewards
Relationships
Stakeholders

Level 1

Level 2

Level 3

Level 4

trust, and time. It also requires an emotional feeling (interest) for or about the information on the part of the recipient.

This approach to education presents a four-stage progression for developing educated partners. The four stages are information, knowledge, profound knowledge, and local wisdom. Figure 5-2 shows how these stages match with the four layers of the Education Onion.

Knowledge is the result of understanding the meaning of information. Each layer of the Education Onion develops a certain level of knowledge by presenting information and providing education about that information. By progressing from a big picture perspective to an individual perspective, this process leads to the development of profound knowledge.

Profound knowledge is the result of understanding the implications and relationships between a series of information layers. An education process that proceeds from an understanding of the general economics, through company specific information to operational and performance information provides the recipients with an opportunity to see these relationships and to develop profound knowledge.

The philosopher Dr. Emmet Fox has stated that wisdom is a blending of knowledge and concern.[1] This is where the emotional feeling for or interest about the information comes into play. The inner layer provides information of a personal level. It is information that is linked to the fulfillment of personal needs and therefore, is of interest and importance to each employee partner.

This level of concern acts as a connector to the outer layers of business information. It engages the partner in the business knowledge in such a way that it creates local wisdom. As the example in Chapter 4 revealed, it is at the level of local wisdom that information becomes applicable.

Figure 5-2 provides us with a tool to address the challenges of making information relevant, understandable, and applicable. It shows us the types of information that must be provided to create a partnership.

The Leadership Role

Local wisdom is the result we want to achieve through the Education management practice. Yet educating employees can be a daunting task. According to the U.S. Department of Education, over twenty-seven million people in the United States are classified as functionally illiterate. Over three-quarters of American workers are without college degrees.

In order to achieve local wisdom throughout an organization,

Figure 5-2. The four stages of E_I Education.

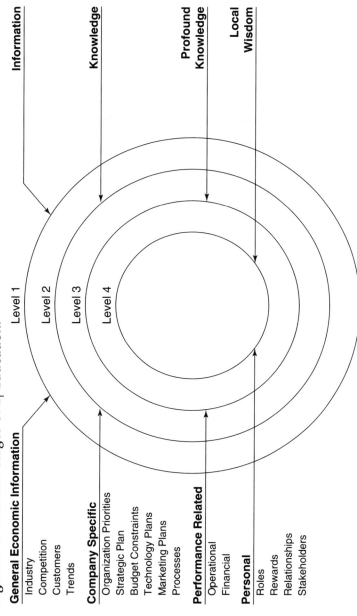

General Economic Information
Industry
Competition
Customers
Trends

Company Specific
Organization Priorities
Strategic Plan
Budget Constraints
Technology Plans
Marketing Plans
Processes

Performance Related
Operational
Financial

Personal
Roles
Rewards
Relationships
Stakeholders

Level 1
Level 2
Level 3
Level 4

Information

Knowledge

Profound
Knowledge

Local
Wisdom

senior management must signal early in the change process that learning is what the company is after. They must commit the necessary resources to bring everyone in the organization up to a base level. Only then can the organization move forward with the education process. And senior management must realize that education is never ending.

Baldor Electric Company is a good example of this type of commitment. Baldor Electric is a publicly owned company in Fort Smith, Arkansas. It manufactures electric motors and drives. It has 3,100 employees, is nonunion and has eleven plant facilities in seven states and Germany. In 1990 it earned the President's E-Star award for Exports, presented by the U.S. Department of Commerce. In 1993 *Fortune* magazine named it as one of the fifty "buy now" stocks.

In the late 1980s Baldor initiated a TQM process that required the active participation of every employee. During the implementation of this process management discovered some of their employees were not literate enough to participate. Thus began the education effort at the company. Management successfully developed a literacy training program aimed at bringing all employees to an eighth-grade literacy level. Baldor believes employees can make improvements only when they have a level of knowledge that enables them to understand how they affect the company's financial results. The extent of this commitment is demonstrated by the construction of a $150,000 training facility. At any one time, there are over 30 training programs in effect. Currently the company trains its employees in both soft skills and technical skills. The soft skills address leadership, team, and interpersonal relationship issues.

To develop a level of profound knowledge, the company distributes financial and operational performance information in each local newsletter. To develop a level of local wisdom, education aimed at making this information relevant and understandable is provided to each employee.

What's the Payoff?

Assuming that educated people are easier to train and to work with, are there any data to support a financial ROI for this education effort? Recently, the National Center on the Educational Quality of the Workforce (EQW), in conjunction with the U.S. Census Bureau, surveyed approximately 3,000 companies in both the manufacturing and nonmanufacturing sectors.[2] The intent was to document the contribution that the level of education makes to an individual company's productivity. Figure 5-3 illustrates the results of the survey.

Figure 5-3. Factors for increased productivity.

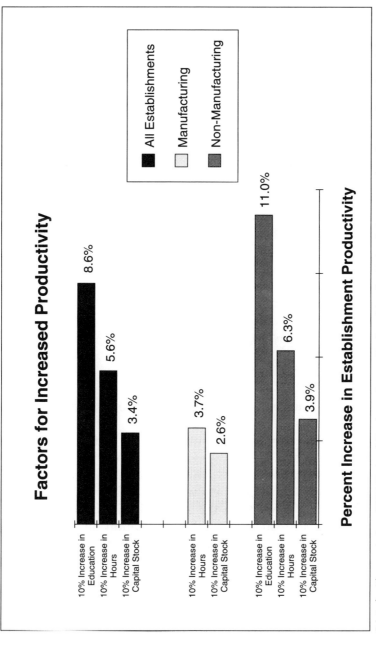

Factors for Increased Productivity

All Establishments
- 10% Increase in Education — 8.6%
- 10% Increase in Hours — 5.6%
- 10% Increase in Capital Stock — 3.4%

Manufacturing
- 10% Increase in Hours — 3.7%
- 10% Increase in Capital Stock — 2.6%

Non-Manufacturing
- 10% Increase in Education — 11.0%
- 10% Increase in Hours — 6.3%
- 10% Increase in Capital Stock — 3.9%

- All Establishments
- Manufacturing
- Non-Manufacturing

Percent Increase in Establishment Productivity

Printed with permission. EQW National Employer Survey. Designed by the National Center on the Educational Quality of the Workplace. Administered by the Bureau of Census. Funded by the Office of Educational Research and Improvement. U.S. Department of Education.

The survey considered annual sales, principal products and services, investments in equipment and new facilities, costs of materials used in productions, and the average wages and level of education of their workers. The survey found that a 10 percent increase in the average education of all workers within a company (slightly over one additional year of schooling) is associated with an 8.6 percent increase in output for all industries. In the nonmanufacturing sector the effect was an 11 percent increase in output. To ensure validity of the data, the survey controlled for materials used, employee hours, age of equipment, industry, size, employee turnover, and the key indicators of human capital.

To place this productivity increase in perspective, the same survey document reports that a 10 percent increase in the book value of capital stock is associated with a 3.4 percent increase in output. Obviously the cost of education is well worth the investment.

The Purpose of Education

There are three general goals in the process of education:

1. Acquire knowledge
2. Build skills
3. Change attitudes

The challenge is to focus these educational goals so they support the strategic intent of the organization.

Each organization has its own vision of where it is going and what it wants to become. The specific information embodied in each level of the Education Onion is unique to each organization. It reflects the degree and type of knowledge, skill, or attitude needed to achieve that vision. Whatever the vision, the Education Onion model illustrates how to focus the goals of education on the intent of the business. Figure 5-4 shows how economic awareness, company specifics, performance information, and personal information all focus attention in the same direction—toward the organization's strategic intent.

If your company's vision calls for superior execution, the various levels of education should provide your employee partners with the knowledge, skills, and attitude to focus on issues such as process improvement, responsiveness to change, flexibility, and problem solving. If your vision calls for organizational unity, the levels of education should provide the knowledge, skills, and attitude to focus on issues such as group participation, a partnership attitude on all levels, and a sense of mission. If your company's vision calls for manage-

Figure 5-4. The focus.

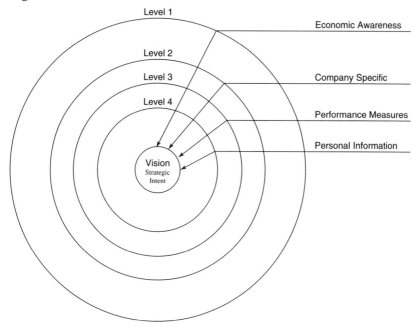

ment skills on all levels, the levels of education should provide the knowledge, skills, and attitude to focus on issues such as leadership, data-based decision making, interpersonal skills, and consideration for others.

The Education management practice creates this focus on strategic intent through its process. This process should be aimed at providing all employee partners with the knowledge they can use to assess opportunities and requirements, analyze options, identify improvement opportunities, and develop and implement innovative solutions.

Emmet Fox said, "Look where you are going because you will inevitably go where you are looking."[3] It is a natural law that, over time, you go where you are focusing your attention. The Education Onion model is designed to tap into the energy of that law. Use this model to help focus the attention and energies of your partner employees.

Level One: General Economic Awareness

As illustrated in Figure 5-1 the first level of education deals with general economic information. This information is so important because it provides a big-picture perspective to all of the partners. It provides them with an understanding of why things are the way they are and the general economic environment that defines the basis for their business's operations.

In an open, business-focused organization, each employee assumes the role of partner, and each partner assumes multiple subroles. Among these subroles are those of problem solver, decision maker, self-manager, and entrepreneur. The first level of education provides background information that each employee can use to be successful in these roles.

A Level-One Example

I recently worked on an education assignment with a company that wanted to expand the perspective of their employees beyond the day-to-day level that most employees had. The company's core competencies were research and distribution. They had several key patents that were going to expire within the next few years. The expiring patents would permit competitors into their marketplace and force them to reduce their margins. This squeeze on profits, coupled with an aggressive growth target established by the CEO, created a need to more fully engage the employees in the financial and business issues of the company.

Management started the educational process by developing a first-level economic awareness workshop. This workshop was a series of day-long sessions in which subject matter experts assisted the attendees in learning about the industry that the company was competing in. They were educated about the barriers to entry and the governmental regulations by which all players were constrained and protected.

The employees participated in a team exercise in which they defined the core competencies that enabled the company to compete successfully. Then they identified and discussed areas where there were opportunities for improvement. The senior management had chosen to maintain a certain position in the industry and this process enabled the employees to understand this position. It also provided them with insight as to why certain strategic decisions had been made.

During the next session, the attendees focused on the competition. They applied the same strength and weakness analysis process to the competition as they had to their company. The outcome of this analysis was a matrix that portrayed the competitive relationships that existed between the key companies in the industry. This matrix helped explain why each firm held the position it did in the industry.

The third session addressed the customers and their needs. Past, present, and potential customers were identified. Another matrix was developed to define the current and future needs of each customer. This matrix was compared to current products. A list was developed of R&D

projects needed to fill the gap between company products and customer needs.

At this point, the participants were becoming energized. They had been given information and education and had participated in a creative, problem-solving process that got them thinking out-of-the-box.

At the fourth session, a member of the executive staff presented the strategic plan for the organization. Because of their creative-thinking exercises, the participants could understand and appreciate how the plan addressed the competitive issues. The heart of the competitive plan's short-term focus was the impact to the company of the expiring patents. On a high level, the staff discussed four key scenarios that projected ten years into the future. These scenarios were:

- Where the company will be based on current levels of performance
- Where it will be with the addition of new business initiatives
- Where it will be when new products exit the R&D pipeline and are introduced into the market
- Where it will be with the addition of performance improvement, cost reduction, and employee partner initiatives.

The marketing staff added to this with an overview of the economic, consumer, and marketplace trends. A forecast based on key events in each category was discussed and its impact on the industry was analyzed. Working together, representatives from marketing and finance overlaid on the industry trend a series of trend lines that indicated the company's profitability and market position based on each scenario.

At the end of the four-day workshop, the participants had a new-found confidence in their senior management. They received information and a level of education that enabled them to understand how the company was going to achieve its aggressive growth plan even with their key products losing patent protection. As a result, they recognized and respected their partners' goals and priorities and were committed to helping achieve them.

Level Two: Company Specific Education and Overcoming Resistance to Change

As illustrated in Figure 5-1, the second level of education is the level that addresses company-specific information. The education and understanding developed at the second level defines an organization's ability to cope with change. Change, in the business context we are discussing, can be defined as "the awareness of, and adaptation to the customer's interests."

In order to *cope with* change, each partner must become a member of a team. As a team member each individual cooperates and shares his or her body of knowledge with others. The role of team members is to use their knowledge to anticipate problems and to work together to improve quality and avoid interruptions to output.

In order to *take advantage of* change, employee partners must develop an adaptable attitude. This attitude will enable them to adjust their focus, action, and commitment to the customer's interests as these interests change. An adaptable attitude enables employee partners to avoid the debilitating frustration and paralysis that so often accompanies change.

The second level of education provides the information and knowledge that form the basis of an adaptable attitude. This education is primarily focused internally. In the broadest sense, it is an understanding of how the company's strengths and core competencies can be used to fulfill the needs of the customer.

There is a strong indication that frustration and resistance to change occur when there is no apparent appropriate response to the change. Providing partner employees with second level knowledge enables them to identify and initiate the appropriate response and thus eliminates frustration and resistance to change.

What and How to Respond to Change

Second level knowledge is the understanding of What and How. It is the understanding of *what* capabilities the company possesses and can bring to bear on customer issues and *how* this can be accomplished.

The What aspect is more or less a static element of information. Here the employees understand the actual resources, skills, and knowledge that exist within the organization. Physical manufacturing facilities, special equipment, and unique materials are examples of resources that can be brought to bear on customer needs. Technical expertise, multiskilled workforce, self-directed work teams, and educated partners are examples of the skills and knowledge available to fulfill customer needs.

The How aspect is a dynamic element of knowledge. It is an understanding of how the resources, skills, knowledge, and processes can be organized and coordinated to fulfill customer expectations. The strategic plan is an example of a dynamic element of education. It acts as a guiding document that outlines how resources will be organized and coordinated to take advantage of opportunities presented by the industry.

Guided by the strategic plan, a marketing plan can be developed that defines how the company will approach the marketplace. In theory, the marketing plan defines how the organization will overcome marketplace and economic obstacles. Placed in this context it is easy to understand the value of educating all partner employees in the details of the strategic and marketing plans. Doing so provides them with a picture of how the company's resources will address the issues of market share and revenue generation.

Organizational priorities, technology plans, budget constraints, and business processes define how things are done to support the marketing and strategic plans. Sharing this information with employees creates an understanding of how things are done internally: It provides a picture of how the company's resources will address the issues of productivity, cost, quality, cycle time, and other issues that affect profitability, cash flow, and customer satisfaction.

The benefits of being educated in the What and How of an organization are that employee partners have the potential for creative thinking that can uncover problems and foresee how to proactively adapt to change.

Changing by Big Leaps and Small Steps

By the time partners have received level two education, they have the potential to make improvements in big leaps and small steps. Big leap changes are normally associated with breakthroughs in technology, new product, or process reengineering. They are the result of significant, one-time changes in what a company brings to bear on the market. Small-step changes are the basis for continuous improvement. They are the refinements and improvements that each partner makes to his/her daily effort. They are the result of partners making changes to how resources are organized and coordinated.

The four management practices are focused on supporting the small-step change capabilities of partners. Many advocates feel that these day-to-day improvements provide a greater yield than big leap changes. Because they are daily and ongoing, they represent a sustainable strategic advantage and require less capital investment to achieve. Whether it is big leap or small-step improvements, they both occur only as the result of partners being educated in the company specifics.

How: The Dynamic Element of Knowledge

Among the first things I ask for when I start an assignment is the client's organization chart. An organization chart is one of the primary elements of level two information because it is essentially a map of how resources are organized and coordinated. However, receipt of this document is simply a receipt of information. In order to gain the knowledge it represents, I have to understand the reality of the organization. I have to understand the relationships and links that exist between and among the resources. I have to turn information into knowledge.

Figures 5-5 and 5-6 illustrate this point. Figure 5-5 illustrates a typical organizational chart. It consists of boxes that symbolize departments and connecting lines that indicate links and reporting relationships. It is a command-and-control artifact that, by itself, imparts very little knowledge. The "org" chart represents how things are done in the company. It represents work flows, information flows, and hierarchy. The challenge is to unlock the tremendous potential for knowledge it represents.

Unfortunately, although full of potential, the traditional organization chart is not an accurate representation. Reality is more like the organization depicted in Figure 5-6. Take a moment to examine Figure 5-6. For the sake of learning, assume for a moment you are an employee in this company. Picture yourself as working in department H. You were hired into department H several years ago and, except for a short period when you participated in an ad hoc team, you have always worked in department H. Having been with the company for these many years you are somewhat familiar with its structure. You know that department G provides you with input and that you contribute to the output that is passed on to departments I and K.

As a long-standing employee, attempt to answer the following questions: What does your company produce? Who are the customers? What are their expectations? What is your department's function? How does your department affect the performance of the other departments in the process path? How do the relationships between departments result in satisfying customer expectations? How could departmental linkages in the process cause poor quality, late shipments, high costs, low productivity? Now ask yourself if this illustration is all that much different from your reality.

Most people, when shown this illustration and asked these questions have difficulty answering them. Like every employee who has been insulated in a functional silo, it is almost impossible to describe how the company's resources, skills, knowledge, and processes are organized and coordinated to bring about fulfillment of customer expectations. So what does this company produce and how does it do it?

Here's How It Works

The company portrayed in Figure 5-6 produces fresh-squeezed orange juice. The process was designed by cartoonist Rube Goldberg

Figure 5-5. The "org" chart.

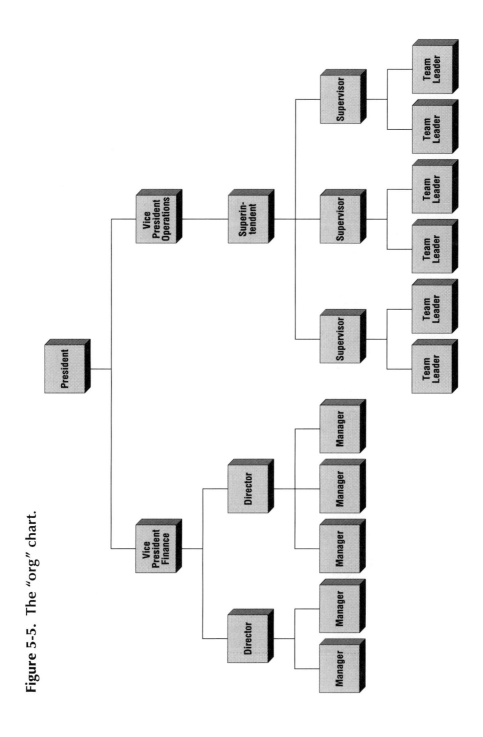

Figure 5-6. The real organization.

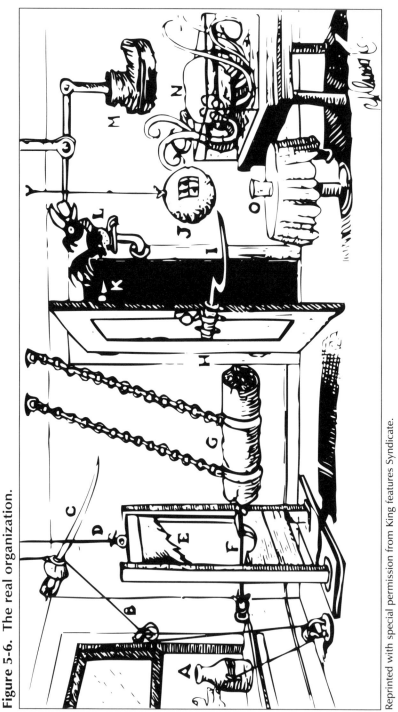

who was well known for his drawings that made simple tasks laughingly complex. Here is how the resources have been organized and coordinated to produce fresh orange juice on demand.

The milk bottle (A) has been placed on the window sill for collection by the milkman. When the milkman takes the bottle he pulls on string (B), which causes sword (C) to swing forward and cut restraining rope (D). Guillotine (E), no longer held in tension by rope (D), falls and cuts restraining rope (F), which allows log (G) to swing forward and slam into door (H), closing it.

Door (H) (your department) performs a dual function. As it swings shut, sickle (I) slices the bottom off the orange (J). Tack (K) pokes the Prune Hawk (L). The Prune Hawk holds a prune in his mouth and, when agitated, releases the prune that allows the diver's boot (M) to descend and stomp on the sleeping octopus (N).

As part of preproduction preparation, the face of a diver has been painted on an orange (J) which has been suspended above glass (O). The sleeping octopus, aroused by the diver's boot, sees what appears to be the diver and, reaching out with his tentacles, angrily squeezes the orange. The orange releases its juice out the sliced bottom and into the glass.

An Analysis

Now that you have been educated in the orange juice company's specifics you have the knowledge to think creatively about how best to use these resources to fulfill customer needs. Is it easier to answer the questions posed earlier? How would you improve quality?

Perhaps the addition of a strainer department placed just below the orange would prevent seeds and pulp from entering the glass. If you understood your customer and knew that seedy juice was an issue, you could take action that would improve the acceptance of your product and gain market share.

The point of this exercise is to realize the value to each employee of understanding the specifics of the resources available to the organization, how they are organized and coordinated, and why they interact the way they do. It was easy to identify the resources: a bottle, a sword, a log, a boot. But this was only information. Knowledge occurred only when the relationships between the resources were understood sufficiently so as to see how they interacted to create an outcome.

Level Three: Performance Information

As illustrated in Figure 5-1, the third level of education consists of performance-related information—how effective and efficient the organization is on a day-to-day basis. This information consists primarily of key performance indicators (KPIs). These indicators can be nonfinancial or financial.

The effectiveness of these relationships determines the efficiency of the process that, in turn, determines the level of productivity, cost, cycle time, and other critical success factors of a company. Understanding why things interact the way they do to produce an outcome provides the opportunity to think creatively about how changes can be made that will improve results.

Operational KPIs

In any operation or process, resources are consumed by activities and transformed into a value-added output. (This, of course, is assuming that all processes add value.) The value-added output of the process can be viewed as a nonfinancial or operational KPI.

A good example is the Rube Goldberg exercise we just completed. The key performance indicator of sword department (C) is how well it performs its function of severing the restraining rope (D). If the sword is dull or misaligned, it will not perform its function efficiently and the entire downstream process will suffer. To accomplish its mission, the dull sword department (D) will require additional resources in the form of ongoing tugging activity on the part of the milkman.

Although several performance indicators may exist internal to the process, the KPI is that essential indicator that tells how successful the process or operation is in achieving its mission. In its best form, it indicates the ability of the process to synchronize supply with demand in the most cost-effective manner. The essence of a KPI is its ability to provide information about the usefulness of the activities within a process.

KPIs as Indicators of Cost

All processes have activities, and all activities have a cost associated with them. The cost of an activity may not be identified or readily apparent, but it exists nonetheless. The amount of activity required by a process is in relation to how efficiently the process is operating. When a process is not performing as efficiently as it could it will consume additional resources and activities and contain excessive costs.

By understanding the KPIs of a process and comparing them to some standard or norm, employee partners can identify when a process may contain inefficiencies, extra activities, and excessive costs.

Herein lies one of the real values of level three education. It provides employee partners with tactical data they can use on a daily basis to make continuous improvements.

The ABCs of Effectiveness

KPIs provide information as to the efficiency of a process or operation. Two techniques related to this concept can help employee partners pinpoint the causes of inefficiencies and excessive cost. The first is a concept called activity-based cost management (ABC) and the second is a concept called time-based cost management (TBC).

ABC management is an established management science. We will not attempt to provide an extensive education on the mechanics of it, however, it is a valuable tool that employee partners should be aware of. ABC management techniques can help them reduce the cost and improve the effectiveness of their processes.

ABC management is a technique for identifying the cost of doing business by identifying the activities that make up a process, deciding which activities add value and which do not, and assigning a cost to them. It is most effective when it is applied by employee partners in their own area of expertise because it addresses the issues and events they are knowledgeable of and have responsibility over.

Essentially, the partner or a team of partners develop a block diagram that represents the processes they are responsible for. Then, using their knowledge of the process and by soliciting input from the customer or recipient of the output, they define the intended output of the process (the KPIs).

Once the KPIs have been defined, each activity or step in the process is described and the exact content is verified. At this point in the technique, the partners can use the KPI as the standard to evaluate the worth of each activity by asking the questions, Is this activity necessary? Does it add value to the output? Does it enhance the KPI? This exercise identifies those activities that add value to the process and those activities that are waste activities. The outcome is a clear understanding of the process capabilities and the identification of wasteful activities that can be eliminated.

The following is a good example of the application of this type of education. The company is a medium-size machine shop that builds specialty products to meet customer specifications. Materials arrive at the receiving dock and are moved by forklift to a staging area where they are held until needed. This same staging area is used to store semi-finished goods, material that is in between operations, and finished goods awaiting shipment.

Customers had begun to complain about incomplete shipments and missed schedules. Management was concerned about customer satisfaction and had asked the employees to assist in improving the process. The employees in the internal transportation function initiated their improvement process by defining their KPIs. They defined their KPIs as the ability to deliver the proper type and amount of material where it was needed, when it was needed, at the lowest possible cost.

Applying the ABC technique to the transportation process they saw that internal transportation costs were high because the average travel distance per part was 1.5 miles and the average part was handled over 12 times. Timeliness was suffering because the disarray in the staging area often made it difficult to keep track of work-in-progress. Not getting the right materials to the right work centers at the right time resulted in machine downtime, lower throughput ratios, missed schedules, and partial shipments.

By including the operating centers in the analysis process they found they were performing many material-movement activities that had no value to their customers. One example was the constant shifting of loads of material around the staging area to free up access to other stored material.

Identifying these waste activities enabled the partners to design the transportation function to more effectively service their customers. One of the changes recommended was to cut doorways in walls where it made sense to shorten the transportation distance. Material-in-process was staged closer to the work areas where it would be needed. This resulted in less travel time and more organized material storage.

The improvement in the KPIs of the transportation process resulted in improved throughput and more on-schedule shipments. The level three performance information for this process is now tracked on a daily basis and displayed on a wall for all to see. When the indicators begin to trend negatively, an ad hoc team will form to investigate the cause on an activity level.

Morale, Slash-and-Cut, and ABC

ABC management is well established and, in its purest form, is a highly detailed process. Because of the level of detail required, not many organizations have embraced it as a formal management process. However, that is changing, in part perhaps, because of the ability this technique has to counteract the negative effects of the recent rush to downsize, cut spending, and reorganize.

The greatest negative effect of these actions on morale is the perception on the part of the employees that the decisions and actions are arbitrary. Employees, informed only in the most general terms as to the reasons for the decisions (no level one or level two education), have no understanding of the underlying issues or how they can affect them. They are simply told that the company must cut spending.

Obviously, senior management thinks there is good reason for such a strategy. However, the tactics they implement often lack the necessary focus to successfully address the issues. Tactics often take the form of unilateral budget cuts or an across-the-board freeze in promotions and merit increases. Or worse yet, a predetermined percentage reduction in headcount.

Several colleagues who, as employees, experienced this type of management action observed that, although the workforce was reduced, the amount of work was not reduced. The result was more work for those who remained. Morale plummets in this type of situation because the employees closest to the action see the results as unfocused and often negative. Spending is cut, yes, but costs are not reduced and quality and service often suffer due to increased workloads.

On the other hand, companies who apply ABC management techniques as part of their Education management practice, not only cut spending but actually eliminate waste. In many organizations, allocated costs are 50 percent to 60 percent of the cost of the product. These allocated costs are often poorly defined and much of their value is questionable. The ABC technique defines the activities that make up these allocated costs and identifies the value, if any, which they contribute.

Educated employees understand the need for and contribute to the cost-reduction process. When a position needs to be eliminated they support the action because they understand how the action will create a positive outcome for the organization. Moreover, many companies that implement the four management practices make a point of addressing such eliminations through attrition and reassignment.

The Cost of Time Travel

Would the ability to travel forward in time, to get ahead of your competition, be of value to your organization? Cutting cycle time, reducing product lead time, and shortening delivery time are all forms of time travel relative to the competition. Assume it takes you and your competition both thirty days to deliver an order. If, through some process you could reduce your cycle time, the time between receipt of order and product shipment or service delivery, by 50 percent you would have transported your company fifteen days ahead of the competition—time travel.

This form of time travel, the second improvement technique related to key performance indicators, is available to your organization today. It is a derivation of activity-based cost management and is called time-based cost management. Time becomes the key performance indicator for any process. Critical questions about a process all relate to time: How much time does the process require? How can this time be reduced?

ABC management defines the processes and activities and identifies all non-value-added elements. Once this technique has been implemented, TBC management can be used to focus on the time that each process and activity consume. Time is the next dimension of competition. It is a critical element of responsiveness.

The ability to get to the marketplace first with a product or service provides an incredible competitive advantage. High-tech companies like Apple, IBM, Compaq, Dell, and others base their business strategy on this ability. Service companies use time as a competitive advantage to delight their customers and thus retain them. As we have seen, nothing happens in an organization until someone sells something. Then it is up to the operations or service people to deliver on the sale because revenue isn't generated until the product is delivered. The faster the product or service can be delivered, the more revenue a company can generate.

A Higher Level of Understanding

What is the outcome of educating your partner employees in operational performance measures and techniques such as ABC and TBC management? Well, if they take them to heart and use them as tools in their everyday business, it will change the way they think about their role and their group's role.

Activities are what employees do and activities have cost associated with them. Participation in the process of identifying value-added or time-based activities links employee thinking to cost. This linkage to cost leads to an understanding of the impact their actions have on profitability.

A change of perspective takes place as profound knowledge grows. Rather than seeing themselves as a cost center, each group of employees sees themselves as a profit and loss center responsible for their own financial outcomes. Employees responsible for a process understand the activities involved and the costs associated with them. When improvements are made, such as shortening the time an activity requires or eliminating an activity, the employees understand the dollar value of that increment of improvement.

In order to understand how these incremental improvements improve the company's before-tax earnings it is necessary to provide all employee partners with the understanding of how their company accounts for its financial transactions, how it makes a profit, and how it generates the cash needed to pay the bills (and the payroll).

How Do We Make Money Around Here Anyway?

Custom Editorial Productions (CEP) is a Cincinnati, Ohio, based company that provides editorial and electronic book production services to publishing companies, businesses, and organizations. The president, Mary Lou Motl has a profound knowledge of how to be successful in business. "It's all a matter of focus," she said during a personal interview, "you need to know what you do that makes money, then go do it."

Genius in its simplicity? Easier said than done? Perhaps, but in this instance, Ms. Motl is talking about each employee knowing what she does that makes money. And for CEP the results of this type of thinking are well worth the effort. For the past thirteen years, CEP has achieved an annual growth rate of over 20 percent! It has achieved the status of preferred supplier with three major accounts and, during a time when most companies are downsizing, CEP is adding to its staff.

As part of the employment process, all employees receive first-and second-level E_1 Education. They understand the customers, and services, and the processes used to deliver these services. Ms. Motl shares the company's growth and marketing strategies with all employees. On the basis of this knowledge, everyone understands how budget constraints help define technological growth plans. In a close knit group, working under deadline pressures, this level of understanding goes a long way toward maintaining high morale.

Perhaps more importantly, management has taken the time to educate the employees in the company's operational and financial key performance indicators. As a result, each employee understands the cost and margin elements of every project. When a project estimate is being developed, representatives from each department have the opportunity to evaluate the project requirements and develop their commitment to operational key performance indicators such as productivity, schedule, materials, and labor costs.

Operational indicators are tracked as the project moves from process to process. If a variance occurs, immediate analysis of the situation is conducted by the employees and management closest to the project. Because the operators are involved in the problem-solving process, adjustments can be made within the process to keep the project within acceptable KPI thresholds, and therefore within acceptable operating profit margins.

These operational KPIs are linked to the company's costing system and the financial KPIs. As a result, they become indicators of the project's profitability. Employees understand how their operational effectiveness translates into the organization's competitive advantage. If they can meet or exceed their operational KPIs they know the company will be profitable and will be able to bid competitively in the marketplace for business.

Financial KPIs

Understanding relationships and linkages provides employee partners with the opportunity to think creatively about what changes can be made to improve results. Operational performance measures such as schedule, labor hours, or materials, provide a detailed, micro perspective of the situation. Financial performance measures such as revenue, cost of goods, and operating expenses, provide a different, more abstract perspective of the efficiency and effectiveness of an organization.

Risk Management

Companies are beginning to share financial performance information with their employees. Some are even educating them in financial fundamentals so they will understand the significance of this information. The senior management in companies that ask me to help them educate their employees in financial fundamentals all have the same concern about sharing this type of information.

Since the concern centers on risk, I usually take them through a risk management process. Together we identify and list all the benefits associated with educating their employees in the financial performance measures of their business. We then clearly define how these benefits will be measured and list all the actions that can be taken to maximize them. Then we identify and list all the risks associated with educating their employees in the financial performance measures. We clearly define how these risks will be measured, and list all the actions that can be taken to minimize them.

Once we have thoroughly explored the risks and benefits associated with financial measurement sharing and education, management compares the two and decides if it makes good business sense to do this.

A decision to share financial information is not usually the starting point of cultural change. Companies considering this have normally proceeded through the first two levels of the education onion and are building on success. The risk management process is performed primarily as a final step to relieve anxiety and establish a clear vision of the outcome.

Financial Understanding: Top Down, Bottom Up

It isn't necessary, or even advisable, to turn everyone in your organization into accountants. What is important is to provide them with enough information and education so they can understand the business objectives and how they can affect them with their day-to-day activities.

We have seen how employees can relate their local operational performance measures to specific costs of resources or activities. An educated machine operator will be knowledgeable of the labor, materials, power, and other direct labor costs associated with his or her process. This is a bottom-up understanding of performance measurement. The cost accounting system, a process that allocates costs to a finished product, links an employee's bottom-up understanding to their top-down understanding of profitability.

The top-down understanding of financial measurement is an understanding of how their company makes a profit and generates cash. Three financial performance measurement categories are important to almost every business: profit, ratio analysis, and cash. These key performance indicators can be used by employees to evaluate how well their company is performing and how well the competition is performing.

Profit: The P Word

Unless a company makes a profit, that is, takes in more revenue than it pays out for costs and expenses, it will not be able to stay in business. First and foremost, employee partners need to understand this fundamental concept as the heart of the company's effort. In order to contribute to this effort, they need to be educated in how their company makes a profit. This means they should understand how sales generate revenues and how the company's costs and expenses reduce them.

Part of what determines profitability is the difference between the selling price and the costs directly related to producing the product or delivering the service. Is it wise to provide employees with information on product margins? It is if they are your partners. Understanding the level of profit that each product or service produces enables them to focus on what is important.

An Application of This Understanding

Trigger Plastics is a good example of sharing margin information with the employees. Trigger is a medium-size manufacturing company producing over thirty different plastic-based consumer products. The opportunity arose when sales of certain products increased and the company began to develop a backlog. This trend had all the indications of a longer term increase in market share and demand.

Initially, management considered adding another shift of workers until additional machines could be purchased and brought on-line. Expanding capacity to meet demand was going to be an expensive proposition. Employees in Scheduling performed an analysis of product profitability. This analysis revealed that ten products made up 80 percent of their gross profit margin and that the increased sales were for these products. Further analysis revealed that by eliminating over 50 percent of their low-margin products they could increase the capacity of the plant to produce the higher-margin products.

On the basis of the marketing forecasts and the observations and recommendation of the Scheduling employees, it was decided to eliminate the low-margin, low-volume products. This decision eliminated the need to add shifts or purchase additional equipment.

An additional benefit was the increase of cash made available to the company through the reduction of slow-moving inventory. This increase in cash was used to pay down some of the company's short-term, high-interest debt. By reducing interest payments the company automatically improved its profitability.

Ratio Analysis

Ratios are relationships that identify the source of a company's profitability, efficiency, solvency, and liquidity. Each company chooses its KPI ratios based on the type of business it is in and its strategy. Ratios can be quite valuable to your employee partners if they understand the underlying elements that make up the relationships. For example, return on assets (ROA) is a profitability ratio and is determined by dividing income (earnings before interest and taxes) by assets. The ROA ratio indicates how efficiently assets are being used to generate income. In capital intensive industries, this can be a general indicator of how well the employee partners are managing these assets.

As a general indicator, ROA is a good tool for employee partners. Asset intensive processes that are out of statistical and quality control will have a low ROA. In this situation, the employees would focus their attention on issues such as cost control, process control, scheduling and planning, inventory management, or receivables management because these are the underlying operational elements that make up ROA.

There are other return type ratios, such as return on investment and return on equity (ROE). However, these are higher-level ratios and contain elements beyond the average employee's control and are more removed from the day-to-day operations. The closer the relationship is to the actual performance, the more problem-solving information it conveys. For that reason, whenever I provide employees with financial education, I include the cost and expense ratios that are relative to their job responsibilities. Remember, not every employee has to be an accountant, but employees should understand how their contribution affects the business results.

Cost or Expense?

Most employees don't understand the difference between cost and expense. This is a fundamental yet important accounting concept. Costs are those charges that can be directly related to the production of goods or the delivery of services. Expenses are all other charges that support the business effort but are not directly related to the production of goods or the delivery of services.

The most common example of cost is cost-of-goods-sold (COGS). COGS is defined as the material, labor, and overhead directly associated with the product or service (service costs are COS: cost of service). Raw material and the labor used to process it into finished goods are examples of cost.

The gross profit of a product or service is the price it is sold for (revenue) minus the direct cost incurred in producing it (COGS or COS). The formula is

$$\text{Gross Profit} = \text{Revenue} - \text{COGS}.$$

It is important for your partner employees to understand this concept because it helps them break the intimidating world of financial reporting into manageable segments. Most of what your frontline employees (i.e., production or service delivery) can affect on a daily basis is in either COGS or COS. Therefore, this information will be of most interest and most value to them initially.

Making the Connection

Remember having established the need for employees to "connect" with the business? A good example of a ratio that makes the connection between operational performance measures and financial performance measures is a concept called *variance.*

Most organizations have operational standards identified for a product or service. These standards are expressed in measures of material, labor, and overhead. Assume we are producing fidgets (this is a competitive upgrade to the time-honored widget and is consumed in great quantities at every business meeting). The production of ten fidgets uses ten units of material.

Today the production process was out of specification and twelve units of material were required to produce ten fidgets. There was a negative variance against standard. Because there is a cost associated with the material, the COGS for this batch of fidgets was higher than standard and, therefore, the gross profit was lower than planned.

A good example of this can be found at the AT&T Service Center in Atlanta, Georgia. The center provides all financial information to their employee partners (called "associates"). Each month the self-directed work teams receive a package of both operational and cost data. This information is reported by section and product so each team can identify their impact on the overall business. Operational performance, over which the employees have direct daily control, is linked to financial performance measures through the use of a variance ratio. By looking at the ratio, the employees can tell whether their efforts are profitable. The teams then discuss how to adjust their local activities and performance to improve the business results.

This linkage that we have been discussing is a concept called line-of-sight, and is discussed in greater detail in Chapters 6 and 7.

Day-to-Day Expense

A good example of day-to-day expense is the selling, marketing, or general administrative charges associated with running the company overall. A salesperson's salary and company car are examples of expense. The television advertisement and the order processing are examples of expense. The payroll for clerical support and the utilities for the headquarters building are examples of expense. Most of what your support employees (i.e., nonproduction or nonservice delivery) can affect on a daily basis is in the area of selling and general administration expenses. These day-to-day costs and expense items can be found on the income statement.

Other Expenses

Other expenses can be affected by both the operations employees and support employees. The following are examples of financial education that enables employees to understand the business.

Inventories cost money to hold in stock. This money could be used to pay off debt or earn interest. By reducing unneeded inventories, a company frees up this cash for productive use. Many companies are reducing inventory expenses by moving to a JIT process in which their suppliers deliver material only when it is needed. Production is based on customer demand and finished goods are shipped rather than stored.

The inventory turnover ratio measures the number of times inventory is turned over during the year. This ratio can be an indicator of the efficiency of the operation as well as the effectiveness of the planning and scheduling process and the materials management function. The formula is

$$\text{Inventory Turnover} = \text{COGS} \div \text{Average Inventory}$$

COGS is found on the income statement and inventory is found on the balance sheet.

Do your employees ask for the latest technology that, theoretically, will increase productivity, reduce costs, or expand the product line? Do they wonder what senior management is thinking about when these requests are not approved? Do they understand there are expenses associated with capital investment beyond just the cost of the equipment? Do they know that if the company cannot fund the investment with cash it will have to borrow the money?

Borrowing incurs an interest expense that is subtracted directly from profit. The higher the interest expense, the lower the net profit. The formula is

$$\text{Interest Coverage} = \text{EBIT (earnings before interest and taxes)} \div \\ \text{Interest Expense}$$

EBIT is found on the income statement and interest expense is found on the balance sheet.

Employees should understand how much cash is being used to pay interest expense. Employees working to lower costs and improve cash flow will enable a company to reduce the amount of income paid to others in the form of interest.

Cash

If the customer is king, then cash is the emperor. Cash enables a company to pay costs and expenses. Without cash, the company goes bankrupt. The answer to How do we make money around here? has two elements: profit and cash.

Profit, as we have seen, is the positive difference between the selling price and all the costs and expenses. The positive difference can be large, one hundred million dollars, or small, one hundred dollars. But as long as the difference is positive the company can stay in business and grow. A company makes money by selling at a profit.

Cash is the actual currency that a company holds. This currency, in some form, is used to pay costs and expenses. The fundamental difference between profit and cash is that, although profit may be the source of cash, it cannot be used to pay the bills. Only cash can do that.

As an example, company XYZ sells fidgets at a profit. They deliver the product and invoice the customer. The invoice represents an account that is receivable. Until the account is received, the company has no cash from that profitable transaction. In fact, XYZ had to use some of its cash to pay for the COGS to produce the fidgets and does not have that cash available to pay for other costs or expenses. Until the company receives payment for the sale it is operating at a loss.

Cash is (or should be) constantly flowing into and out of a company. At the most basic level, cash flows in from invoices that are paid and flows out to pay bills. If the customers are slow to pay and there is more cash flowing out of the company than is being received, a company can go bankrupt even if it sells at a profit. If the cash flowing into a company is greater than the cash flowing out, the company can stay in business and grow.

Almost everything in the operation of a company consumes cash. Employees who understand the relationships associated with cash flow will be able to make daily decisions that have a positive impact on the retention of cash.

How important is cash? In February 1995, it was announced that Hayes Microcomputer, the major producer of computer modems (a product in great demand), filed for Chapter 11 bankruptcy protection. The CEO, Dennis Hayes attributed the filing to "a short-term cash shortage."[4] Cash proves itself to be emperor.

Financial Documents

The basic financial documents, the income statement and the balance sheet, hold relevant and interesting information for all employee partners. Once they understand the value of the information and how to extract it they will no longer be intimidated by them. The documents become tools that they use to identify areas for improvement and to measure their success.

However, first each employee must get past the mystique of these documents. Although there are several approaches, I use a board game focused on key financial learning experiences. It is a half-day, team learning event that imitates the day-to-day operation of a business.

By using the income statement and balance sheet as scorecards, the participants develop a sound understanding of the fundamentals of these documents. Once the breakthrough is made, employees build on their understanding with specific ratios related to their function or process.

But I Thought You Said . . .

A caution here. Unfortunately, in the language of finance the words *income, profit,* and *earnings* are used synonymously. This can be very confusing and intimidating to your employee partners during the educational process. Every effort should be made to clarify this communication by choosing a single term and using it universally. This may be a traumatic concession on the part of the financial community in your company but it will be well worth the effort.

Level Four: Personal Information

As illustrated in Figure 5-1 the fourth level of education is the level that addresses personally-oriented information such as redefined roles and relationships. The education and understanding developed at the fourth level cements the connection between the employee partner and the organization. This level provides information and education on the personal costs and benefits associated with being a partner.

These costs are mostly of a social nature whereas the benefits are both social and material. By providing this education, each employee can make his own cost-benefit trade-off analysis and decide whether to participate. Participation in a company with an open, partner-oriented management philosophy appears to be desirable, with the social and material benefits far outweighing the personal costs.

However, almost every company that has implemented this type of management practice has encountered some individuals who cannot or will not make the necessary personal changes. In order for all employees to have the greatest opportunity for success, it is important to provide them with a level four education. Education at this level explains the social and material contracts between the company and the employee partners. It defines the contributions that are required of a partner and it defines the rewards that can be expected in return.

The details of roles and rewards will vary by company, but there is a thread of consistency that runs through this management practice and will be universal to every company. That thread is the understanding that personal relationships are one of the foundations of a sustained competitive advantage.

In a partner-oriented company, each employee is considered to be a stakeholder. This stakeholder position defines the relationship that each employee has with others and with the organization. As a stakeholder, each employee has a vested interest in the outcome of the business. This interest is often manifested in the material reward system that enables her to share in the growth and profitability of the company. As a stakeholder, each employee has an obligation to focus on realizing the intent of the organization.

The social aspect of stakeholders entitles them to certain rights and responsibilities in which they need to be educated. Personal relationships are critical if all employees are stakeholders. Training in the area of interpersonal skills, leadership techniques, group dynamics, problem solving and decision making become valuable tools that enhance personal relationships. Companies that successfully implement this type of management practice include both technical and "soft" skills training in their education process.

A Matter of Fairness and Trust

The data from several employee surveys indicate that most employees tend to think that their company is more profitable than it really is. It might be interesting to survey your employee population to identify their thoughts on this matter. Not to worry, you say, this is only a perception. However, perception is reality to the individual. Therefore, it is an issue that absolutely must be addressed if a company wants to develop a partnership with its employees.

This misperception of profitability doesn't fit with the other messages employees receive in their daily work environment. It is in conflict with the messages of cost cutting, downsizing, and low salary increases they are receiving. Employees hear in the news that their company has made record profits and yet the daily messages they receive ask them to give more. This conflict naturally generates in the employees a sense of being exploited.

In some instances real exploitation does take place. However, for the most part, employee expectations are based on past experience as a hired hand and a lack of knowledge about business finance. This misperception creates a major obstacle to the development of a partnership. Would you partner with someone you thought was exploiting you?

The solution to the perception of exploitation is information sharing and education. Perception is based on known and available information. If we want to change a perception, we can do so by providing education and information. Through the management practice of Education, perceptions are clarified and expectations are based in reality.

Notes

1. Emmet Fox, *Around the Year With Emmet Fox* (New York: Harper & Row, 1979), p. 196.
2. National Center for the Educational Quality of the Workforce, *EQW National Employer Survey (EQW-NES)*, Wharton School, University of Pennsylvania, Philadelphia, 1994.
3. Fox, p. 328.
4. "Bad Time at Hayes," *PC World*, February 1995, p. 51.

6

E_2-Enable:
The Management
Practice R_2-Rights:
The Employee
Expectation

The second element of the E_4-R_4 Partnership Checklist addresses the responsibility all levels of management and human resources professionals have to develop processes and systems that enable each employee to become involved in the business, to become a partner, and to participate as a partner. When management provides these systems they can reasonably expect these partners to develop to a point where they are able to manage themselves. In an open organization where systems enable employees to participate in an educated and informed manner, management can reasonably expect the entire employee population to learn and to grow. On the other hand, employees being asked to assume the role of partner are naturally interested in the rights that accompany such a position. Presenting these rights in conjunction with the management practices establishes the proper expectations on the part of all employees and provides them with confidence and a sense of security.

This chapter identifies and examines the key human resources initiatives that enable employees to realize their full potential in an open organization and shows how these initiatives address and fulfill employee expectations concerning their rights in an open organization.

Employee Expectations and Fear

Freedom from Fear

Fear is perhaps the most destructive aspect of any change process. Apart from lack of support from senior management or the human resources community, fear can derail the process quicker than anything else. Several types of fear can exist in the workplace: Fear of change, fear of failure, fear of loss of power, and fear of the unknown are a few of the more predominant fears. One of the primary expectations that employees have in assuming their role as partner is their right to be free from these fears.

Fear can often be alleviated with reassurances, education, and action. If management has taken concrete actions that verify their honesty and integrity, employees will tend to believe their reassurances. If reassurances are presented in conjunction with education, fear and uncertainty can be replaced with known expectations. Often employees are afraid to participate in a change process because of fear of the reaction of their supervisor. They are afraid their new behavior will not be supported. This fear exists because employees in the organization have not been educated in what the company considers to be "good" behavior.

Zig Zigler, the great motivational speaker has said in public oration that participation must be grounded in a person's passion for the cause. He said that, to achieve this, values need to be established first. These values will then develop an attitude that will lead to commitment and participation.

When the values of an organization are clearly defined and communicated throughout the organization, this fear is removed and replaced with a desire to participate.

Eliminating Fear Eliminates More Than Fear

The philosopher Dr. Emmet Fox says there are only two types of feelings: love and fear. All others, he says, are just manifestations of these two feelings. He uses the allegory of chemistry, where a substance, black lead for example, is exactly the same substance chemically as a diamond. Both of these are allotropic forms of carbon. "In the same way, anger, hatred, jealousy, criticism, egotism are but allotropic forms of fear."[1] Do any of these emotions exist in your organization? Could they be removed by removing fear?

He then goes on to say that, among other emotions, joy, interest, and the feeling of success and accomplishment are allotropic forms of love. Do any of these emotions exist in your organization? What would your organization look like if fear were replaced by these emotions?

Dr. Fox offers a technique for ridding an organization of fear. He states that the only way to eliminate fearful thinking is to supply the opposite type of thinking. "The right thought automatically expunges the wrong thought."[2] In other words, if you want employees to think and act as if they are partners, they have to think about and get interested in the concepts that define partnership.

Partners understand the business, yet I find most employees fearful and intimidated by the prospect of learning about business finance because the mechanics of the basic reporting documents, the income statement and the balance sheet, are unknown to them. Once they have been educated in these fundamentals and understand how their performance can have an impact on profit and cash, this fear is removed and is replaced by an understanding of how to use these tools to become involved in the business.

Fear can be replaced with the positive emotions associated with a process that educates, enables, empowers, and engages all employees. Employees who receive education and information and have opportunities to participate and contribute will be enabled to think about success and accomplishments. As a result, they cannot feel they are in jeopardy.

Trust and Leadership

Integral to the elimination of fear is the development of trust. How is trust developed in an organization? First and foremost, trust is established through the integrity of leadership. Leaders establish trust by their example. When senior managers adhere to moral and ethical principles in their actions and decisions, it creates an expectation in the employees that they will be treated in the same honest manner. Trust is the essential ingredient that enables an organization to develop a partnership with its employees, and trust is a two-way street.

Paul Clay is chief executive officer for the Mid-America Manufacturing Technology Center (MAMTC). MAMTC is a nonprofit organization committed to increasing the competitive edge of small and medium-size manufacturing companies. I have had the opportunity to work with him on several occasions and have found he is very committed to the employee involvement process. During a personal interview, he said:

> When you think about it, what really makes you different from your competition? Is it your processes? Is it your equipment? Probably not. The difference—your primary

competitive edge—lies with your employees. Management must believe in the inherent desire of employees to do a good job. There must be mutual trust and commitment to foster and support risk taking. The process of achieving this trust begins with an exchange of knowledge and continues with communications and training to gain an understanding of common goals.

The Education management practice enables an organization to develop an environment of trust. Employees educated in this manner no longer work in a world of rumor and assumption, where suspicion can breed mistrust. They work in a world of facts and their relationships are based on facts.

Enable vs. Unable

Functional silos are the antithesis of the concepts exemplified in the four management practices. They develop in a company where a rigid organizational structure discourages cross-sectional communication and information sharing. What results from this closed environment is a type of ignorance that makes employees unable to participate or become involved in the business.

This point is illustrated by a colleague who was employed in the marketing department of a Fortune 500 company organized along traditional lines. He worked in this functional silo acquiring technical skills and becoming adept in the role of a marketing generalist. The focus of the employees in the marketing department was on products, sales, market share, and the competition. Communication throughout the department was centered on topics such as revenue volume and income growth. Everyone was aware of the business plan and the performance of the company toward that plan.

After three years he "participated" in one of the company's many reorganizations and found himself in the human resources department. He observed that the employees in this department had the technical skills necessary to perform their function but had very little understanding of the company's products and services. They were only vaguely aware of the major competitors, and had no idea of market share, product profitability, company revenues, or income.

In addition, he found this information was difficult to get and generally unavailable to human resources employees. The finance department, who provided Marketing with information, was reluctant to share this information with anyone who "didn't have a use for it." Because of a lack of systems and processes that would enable the human resources employees to obtain and understand business performance information, they were unable to relate their efforts to the financial performance of the organization. As a result, their focus was on technical issues within the human resources community rather than the company's competitive issues of profit and growth. They were unable to become partners in the organization.

Key Enabling Mechanisms and Employee Expectations

Partner/Manager Relationship: Enabling Managers

What is the role of a manager in this new environment? Many organizations make the fatal mistake of overlooking this question in their rush to gain the involvement and commitment of their frontline employees. The result is a leaderless organization of novice partners. The role of the front line and middle manager is critical in an open, partner-oriented, high-performance organization. It is imperative that any effort to implement change using the four management practices must provide the management level partners with the support systems that enable them to be successful in their new roles.

According to the National Commission on Employment Policy, experts predict that 30 to 40 percent of the seven million middle-management positions will be eliminated during the next ten years.[3] If this prediction is accurate, employees will have no choice but to manage themselves. How will they be able to do this? It appears as if the function of those managers who remain will be to enable them to do so. Obviously, this requires an entirely different set of skills from the traditional role of supervisor or manager. In order for managers to enable employees, they themselves must be enabled. What will this new set of management skills look like, and how will it enable them to be successful?

Employee partners have the right to be heard. In order to fulfill this right, managers will need to develop their ability to hear. They will need to physically cultivate the skill to stop and listen to what the employee partners are saying. All too often important information is communicated "on the fly" in the hallway as people are moving from one location to another or while they are busy performing other tasks. This weak communication process is partially the result of a desire to avoid direct interpersonal interaction and partly the

result of a busy work environment. However, taking the time to physically listen to people provides them with assurance that their right
to be heard is valid and intact. This assurance encourages participation on the part of everyone.

Employee partners have the right to be respected and valued as
individuals. In order to honor this right, managers will need to develop their ability to empathize. They will need to identify with the
feelings, thoughts, and attitudes of employee partners. This skill is
becoming increasingly important in an environment of growing cultural diversity.

Research indicates that people are increasingly protective of
their cultural identity when they are members of an organization that
may impose different cultural norms or offer rewards for behaving
differently.[4] Identifying with the feelings, thoughts, and attitudes of
individuals makes them feel part of the team and assures them of
their right to be included as a partner in the team.

Part of the process of empathizing with employees is taking the
time to analyze the concerns, questions, and ideas the employee is
dealing with. Managers need to distinguish real interests from assumed positions and find ways to accommodate the most important
interests. They need to avoid contests of will and loss of face. Only
by spending time in dialogue together, reasoning out the issues, can
disparate individuals reach mutual understanding and agreement. In
short, managers will have to change their role from parent to facilitator, from tyrant to coach, from director to trainer. The crux of their
responsibilities in managing people will be the ability to develop relationships that eliminate suspicion and facilitate teamwork and
partnership.

Coaches Enable the Process to Succeed

Pat Riley, having coached basketball players for the Los Angeles Lak-
ers, the New York Knicks and the Miami Heat, has said that a team
will be successful only when the members "know they can rely on
you." On a television interview in mid 1995 he said that players go
to a coach to become better—better individual contributors and better team members. What they expect from their coach is someone
who will consistently show energy and intensity, communicate a
message, and be a teacher.

Many companies are currently developing this style of management and leadership, and they find it a difficult task. I interviewed
Tom Hornsby in July 1995 to get his observations about this style of
management. Tom is an organizational development consultant for
the Tennessee Eastman Division of Eastman Chemical Company.

The Tennessee Eastman Division uses a socio-technical approach to its continuous improvement process as a method of enabling its employees. The technical element addresses the work itself. The socio element addresses the people interaction. Hornsby told me that "When people ask why they are taking the social training elements we tell them 'because when people interact effectively it increases the likelihood of improved team results.' Basically, it is a good business decision."

Eastman has been evolving the culture and performance of the company through focus on a Total Quality Work System. Initially, as they moved toward a shared leadership environment the first line supervision was told "You need to coach the teams." Hornsby tells us, "Initially there was little training for first-line supervision and other members of management. They needed to figure out what to do on their own. It was a very confusing time for everyone."

Some of the primary questions being asked by frontline management were What am I supposed to be doing? What is coaching?, and What tools do I need to do it? The company realized that to enable managers to coach they needed to define coaching and create a system that would develop coaching skills.

In response, Hornsby's organization helped develop a three-and-one-half month capability development system for frontline management. The training includes approximately thirty courses, seven books, and thirty videos. Some of the different types of training are in the areas of coaching roles and definitions, principle-centered leadership, valuing differences, quality management, empowerment, and managing change. They also receive coaching tools such as intervention and feedback, problem solving, team facilitation, presentation skills, leadership styles and strategies, performance management, process redesign, decision making, motivation, and counseling.

The training resulted in a comprehensive process that enabled the frontline managers to better understand and perform their new roles and to coach their teams. However, it became apparent that developing the coaching skills of first-line management was not enough. Feedback from the process indicated a need for the second level managers and above to increase their coaching knowledge and skills. The coaches of the coaches needed to be developed. It became apparent that improved coaching *on all levels* was critical to the success of Eastman's approach to continuous improvement.

Referring to the need for direct leadership of the change process, We found that we needed someone to help pull this all together. Hornsby said, So we created a coaching development system that would enable coaches to lead the change process. It is the operator/mechanic's responsibility to manufacture the product: coaches are defined as "capability build-ers" who enable others to succeed. A visible and competent coaching presence is needed to help people perform in their new roles as team members until it becomes habit.

In most organizations, supervisors and managers normally are the ones who know how to arrive at solutions. It appears as if, in an organi-zation that values openness, information sharing, high involvement and high performance, the new role of management is to enable employees to arrive at solutions by asking questions, facilitating discussion, and encouraging problem solving.

Rewards Enable Change to Grow

Implementation of the four management practices requires an orga-nization to change. Developing trust, leadership, and coaching en-ables the employees in an organization to change. Once change occurs, rewards enable this change to be sustained by increasing the level of trust. For example, assume you were asked to change your performance. You were provided the education that would enable you to do so. You were encouraged and supported by your immedi-ate management and assurances were communicated by senior management that this change was considered "good" by the organi-zation. In the past your leaders, by their actions, proved themselves to be people of integrity and so, with trust, education, and coaching, you change your performance.

Would you maintain that change if you were punished for it? Would you maintain that change if you were recognized and re-warded for it? Obviously, reward completes the circle of change and keeps the ball rolling. Figure 6-1, the Circle of Change, illustrates this point.

Education and information sharing create trust. Trust leads to change, change results in some form of reward, and reward rein-forces trust. The Circle of Change illustrates that, with the proper elements—education, information sharing, group technologies, trust, and rewards—change can be maintained as an ongoing proc-ess. Companies who espouse the philosophy of continuous improve-ment would do well to examine their change process for these elements.

Mutually Reinforcing Practices Enable the Growth of Intelligence

A recent survey conducted by the U.S. Department of Labor on the effectiveness of "high-performance work practices" concluded that

Figure 6-1. The Circle of Change.

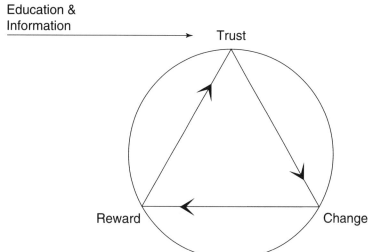

high-performance work organizations provide workers with the information, skills, incentives, and responsibility to make decisions that affect innovation, quality improvement, and rapid response to change.[5]

One of the observations of the survey was that management practices that mutually reinforce each other will create *multiple ways* workers can develop skills, align individual goals with organizational goals, and share information crucial to solving problems. In essence, the resulting organization is a whole that has an intelligence greater than the sum of the parts.

The Education practice and Enable practice combine to create such an environment. They enable all employees to move beyond the realm of emotion and to develop their intellectual capabilities. These two practices mutually reinforce each other to enable a Socratic dialogue that is "the asking and answering of intelligent questions."

Intelligent employees ask the question "Based on what I know, does this make sense?" Research shows that these employees are more effective and successful. Education and understanding provide them with a better perspective of the situation and they are able to act innovatively based on that perspective.

The Great Enabler: Line-Of-Sight

In an open organization the key value derived from an E_1 type of Education is the perspective and capability for innovative thinking this knowledge develops in each employee. Understanding the company's core competencies, the KPIs of their department and team, and the processes that create these indicators provides a type of knowledge that is the basis for experimentation and the creation of innovative strategies, as well as day-to-day improvements. This ability to think and act on multiple mental levels is the result of a perspective developed by an extended line-of-sight.

Line-of-sight refers to the ability to understand how actions contribute to the outcome. It is the ability to see the connection between personal performance and results. Line-of-sight is really a misnomer. It is not so much a line as it is a loop, a performance feedback loop. When an individual understands how actions contribute to the outcome he is able to affect the outcome by adjusting his actions. This understanding is a key element in the process that enables employees to participate and exercise their rights as partners.

Line-of-sight is created through a combination of information sharing and education. How long the line-of-sight extends is a function of the type and amount of information that is shared and how well this information is understood, as illustrated in Figure 6-2.

The question posed to the employees in the polyethylene plant in Chapter 2 was a version of the question What is your job? and was intended to determine the length of line-of-sight that the employees had. A response that indicates a short line-of-sight might be "My job is to lubricate the compressors on a scheduled basis." In this case, the employee sees his performance as having an effect that is no farther than the direct result of his actions. A response that indicates a long line-of-sight might be "My job is to contribute to operating revenue by performing actions that reduce unscheduled downtime, thus increasing machine utilization, throughput, and improving quality." In this case the employee sees the performance as having an effect that is directly related to the profitability of the company.

Efficiency and Effectiveness in Line-Of-Sight

In order to develop a line-of-sight it is necessary to understand the information that is available. Education develops this understanding and the greater the degree of understanding, the longer the line-of-sight will be. Figure 6-3 builds on the original line-of-sight model and illustrates how the information available at each segment in the line-of-sight model relates to a required level of the Education practice.

The model shows that level 3 education (profound knowledge) is related to financial and operational performance information.

Figure 6-2. The Line-Of-Sight model.

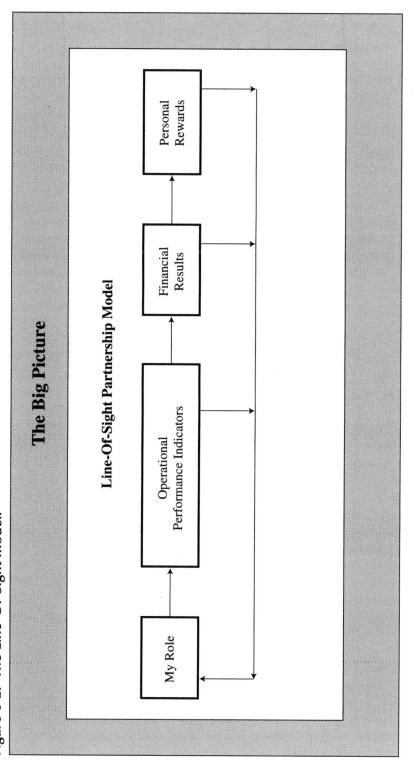

The Big Picture

Line-Of-Sight Partnership Model

My Role

Operational
Performance Indicators

Financial
Results

Personal
Rewards

Figure 6-3. Education, information, and line-of-sight.

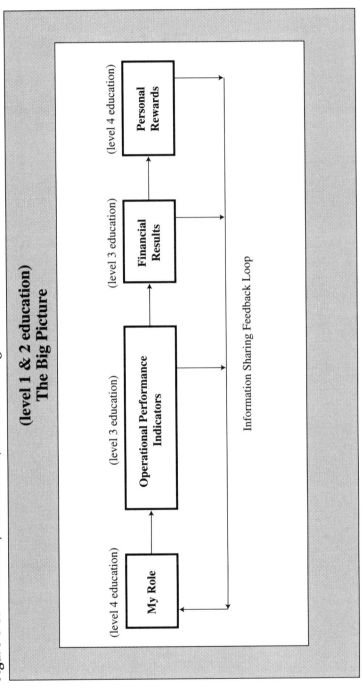

(level 1 & 2 education)
The Big Picture

(level 3 education)
Operational Performance
Indicators

(level 3 education)
Financial
Results

(level 4 education)
Personal
Rewards

(level 4 education)
My Role

Information Sharing Feedback Loop

Level 4 education (local wisdom) is based on an understanding of roles and feedback about how performance has affected operational indicators, financial indicators, and rewards. These levels of education are essential to develop a long line-of-sight. They are essential because they enable an employee partner to understand the efficiencies and the effectiveness of the organization.

Building on our previous discussion, we will elaborate on the concepts of efficiency and effectiveness. Efficiency is an overall indicator of the level of effort required by a system to produce an outcome.[6] Operational results are a type of efficiency indicator. They tell us how much each process or system consumes during implementation. A measurement concept called first run yield (FRY) is a good example of how line-of-sight provides information about a system's efficiency.

First run yield reflects the consumption in a process by comparing input to output. A perfect first run yield would be 100 percent, with zero losses attributed to the system or process. As an illustration, let's assume the system is a manufacturing system that includes the processes of manufacturing, packaging, and distribution. Raw materials enter the system and finished product exits the system.

Losses will occur in and between each process throughout the system. The manufacturing and packaging process may have cost losses in the form of quality defects. There may be productivity losses in the form of unscheduled machine downtime and underutilization. And there may be labor cost losses in the form of excessive material handling. The distribution process may have cost losses in the form of spoilage and misshipment.

A long line-of-sight, created by the management practices of Information Sharing (E_2) and Education (E_1), enables employees to understand how the processes interlink to create a system and how the KPI of each operation indicates the level of efficiency that exists in the system. If these indicators are not within acceptable levels it is a sign that the processes within the system should be analyzed to identify weaknesses and waste that can be improved or eliminated.

Line-of-sight enables employees to identify problems and make improvements to processes. This is critical to the development of a system that consumes the least amount of effort and resources and is the most efficient.

Effectiveness is a measure of functionality. It indicates how well the implementation produces the desired results.[7] Financial results are a type of effectiveness indicator. They tell how well a company's systems achieve the business objectives of generating revenue, producing profit, and maintaining cash on hand. The objective of the orange juice squeezing machine in Chapter 5 was to produce a glass of orange juice on demand. The system was effective because it achieved the objective of capturing all of the juice from an orange upon demand. However, it left plenty of room for improvement in the area of efficiency.

In a company, if the financial indicators are not within acceptable levels it is a sign that the system needs to be either improved or changed in order to achieve the desired results. Financial indicators really tell us how well the company recognizes and applies its core competencies and strengths.

Understanding of the operational and financial performance indicators is necessary for employee partners to fully participate. Operational indicators that are tracked in real-time by employee partners enable them to proactively manage an inefficient process to maximize the intended results. Financial indicators, normally reported "after the fact," enable employees to react to an inefficient system that is not achieving the intended results. These actions and reactions can be coordinated through a company's common language.

Line-Of-Sight and Universal Language

Employees who have a long line-of-sight and who understand the performance relationships it represents possess a common knowledge. When information is shared with all on a daily basis, this knowledge becomes the common language of the organization and communication is greatly enhanced.

For example, employees in a distribution process with a short line-of-sight will only receive and understand operational information about their distribution process. The employees in this process have their own language, which they use to improve the efficiency and effectiveness of that process. Employees in a distribution process with a long line-of-sight will receive and understand operational and financial information about their process and the other processes in the system. The employees in this process possess a common language, which they can use to communicate with other members of the organization.

This common language, used in the information sharing feedback loop, enables employees to work together as partners to improve the efficiency and effectiveness of each process and the performance of the entire system. Figure 6-4 illustrates this point of common, cross-functional communication.

We will use the hypothetical Star Tech company to illustrate this concept. The Star Tech company is a manufacturing operation utilizing precious metals and expensive raw materials to produce exotic space-age electronic products.

Figure 6-4. The universal language.

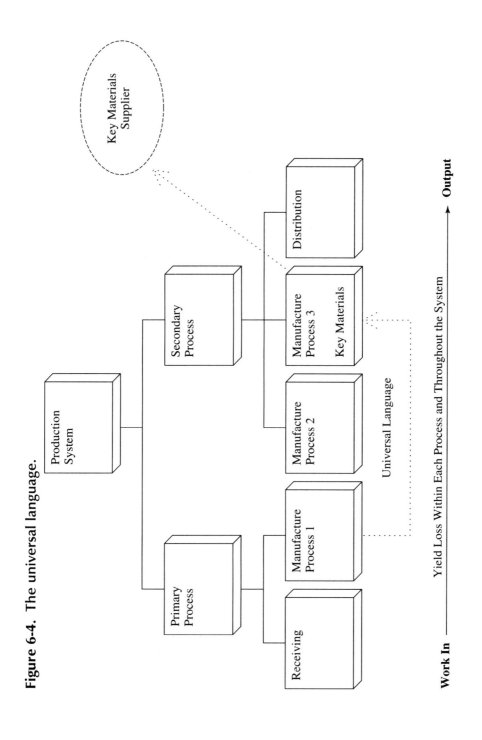

Work enters the organization when Receiving matches raw materials with orders written by the sales force. Work flow proceeds through processes 1, 2, and 3. The finished product exits the production system through Distribution. Process 3 requires the expensive and rare materials that are purchased from a key supplier.

Planning and scheduling are difficult for Star Tech. The company experiences periodic increases in workload based on seasonality, new products introduced, changes in pricing, and increases in volume caused by sales incentive programs conducted throughout the year. Each year process 3 develops an annual schedule of key material needs based on the business plan and sales forecast. It provides this schedule to the key materials supplier and updates it monthly based on projections developed by the production system group.

During one of the anticipated seasonal increases in work input, process 1 experienced a capacity problem with one of their machines. The employees identified the cause of the problem and determined that corrective action would require one month to resolve. However, until the problem could be corrected, work flow would be constrained. Instead of increasing with the seasonal demand, the flow of work to process 2 would be maintained at the normal level.

This change in planned work flow would not adversely affect process 2. Process 2 was labor intensive and they had planned to cope with the seasonal increase through the use of overtime and temporary help. Instead of overtime, they would continue to maintain normal hours and staffing for the month that work flow would be constrained. Process 3 made similar labor plans. However, they had also scheduled an inventory increase of expensive and rare material to coincide with the planned increase in work flow.

Because the employees in process 1 had a long line-of-sight and spoke a common language based on business finance, they understood the unnecessary inventory expense process 3 would incur during the additional month of normal level work flow. To prevent this unnecessary expense, process 3 was advised of the pending capacity constraint and resulting reduction of planned work flow.

Rather than take possession of the inventory and tie up tens of thousands of dollars of cash in inventory for at least a month, process 3 rescheduled delivery of the inventory from the key materials supplier.

The employees' long line-of-sight resulted in improved economic value in the form of improved cash flow for the company. This was the result of processes 2 and 3 not hiring temporary staff and postponing the delivery of expensive materials into inventory. This improved cash position enabled the company to reduce interest expense associated with the cost of capital. In addition, they avoided the cost associated with security measures needed to protect the inventory.

What is unique in this example is the flow of communication. The communication did not go up to management, across functional territory, and down to the employee for implementation. Rather, the information was communicated directly to those who needed it and who could take action. Communication time and potential for error were reduced significantly.

Minimizing Negative Effects With Forward and Backward Thinking

In an open organization, a rule of thumb used to address problems is: When a problem arises, find the cause, don't treat the symptom. But dealing with a problem is more than finding and fixing the cause. We have seen that in interdependent organizations, a problem in one process will have a ripple effect in several other processes. Figure 6-5 provides a different perspective of the action that took place at Star Tech. It shows how a long line-of-sight enabled employees to think in both a backward (cause) and a forward (effect) direction when a problem arose.

Multidirectional thinking is the ability to use operational indicators to identify the cause of a problem and then apply local wisdom to initiate a solution. It is also the ability to look 180 degrees in the other direction, beyond the effect the problem will have on the immediate process, and anticipate the effect the problem will have on interdependent processes throughout the system.

The cross-functional measures used to identify these ripple effects will usually be financial indicators. A problem may show up in an operational indicator in the local process, in Star Tech's case this was reduced throughput. However, it will also show up in cost, profit, and cash indicators throughout the system. In Star Tech's case this was cash that would have been spent on temporary staffing and unneeded inventory.

A long line-of-sight and a common financial language enables partners to communicate efficiently and effectively about performance. This communication enables them to minimize the negative effects of problems that inevitably occur in all processes and systems.

What Information Should Flow and Who Should Control It?

Data is the information that employee partners use to develop their line-of-sight. During the process of developing an open organization, logical questions concerning data should be asked. These questions are What kind of data is needed? and Who should be collecting and reporting it? The answers are relatively clear and simple.

Figure 6-5. Multidirectional thinking.

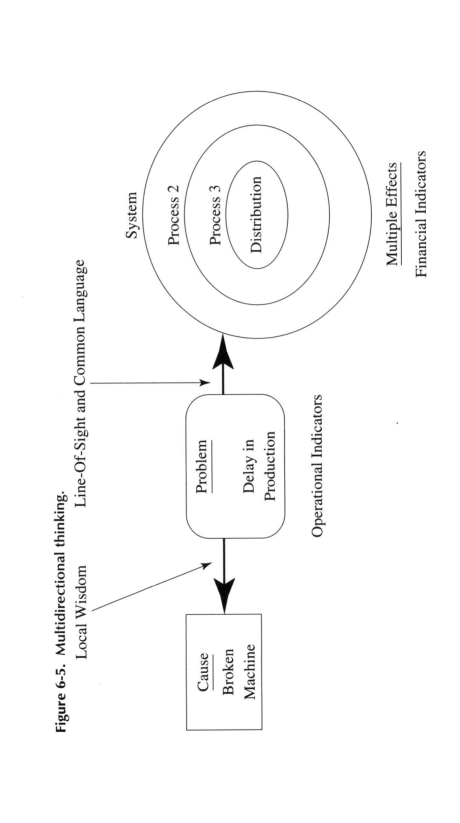

Concerning the type of data: If you cannot or choose not to act on the data you are collecting and reporting, then stop collecting it. Conversely, if you are collecting the data, then do something with it.

Concerning who should be collecting and reporting the data: Michael Theimer, a business analyst with Texas Instruments in Dallas has a keen opinion on this. Texas Instruments is very committed to developing an open environment of high involvement and high performance. According to Theimer, "We are moving data ownership to the source."[8] In other words, the best situation is where management and human resources professionals have enabled employee partners to develop their own real-time performance information. Because they are closest to the information, they are in the best position to define the data, track the data, and report it to themselves and to their associates.

Communication and Information: Dealing With Reality

As you contemplate the changes necessary to partner with your employees in an environment of open communications, ask yourself the following questions: What kinds of problems are being caused by inadequate and inappropriate communications? Is action focused? Are there situations in which communication is weak, perhaps in the support functions? Are communications verbal or written, formal or informal? What changes in communication would improve the partnership? Does management really know what is going on throughout the organization?

The drawback to most performance information is its age. By the time it is collected and distributed at the traditional monthly budget meeting, it is 45 to 60 days old. If management is using this type of information to make decisions and understand events, the answer to the question Does management really know what is going on throughout the organization? is a resounding NO!

Reality, in the fast-paced world of competition, is how well the organization is conforming to the business plan right now. Real-time performance information is immediate feedback of actual performance compared to planned performance right now. The only people who know what is going on are the people who track actual performance against planned performance as it occurs, or as soon as possible after it occurs.

Performance plans are documents that define the estimated cost associated with a projected level of performance. The initial source of these plans is the sales organization, where revenue forecasts are developed. These revenue forecasts are then matched against the expense and costs associated with meeting this revenue forecast. The result is "the plan" of what products need to be produced or what services need to be delivered, when, and at what cost. These plans define a certain profit margin based on forecast of revenues and the associated costs. However, the problem with plans is that they are only estimates of what may be, they are not reality. Actual performance and the associated costs are reality.

Variance From Plan

The key point here is the concept of variance—variance between plan and actual performance. Assuming the forecast is accurate and reasonable, if the variance between planned performance and actual performance is too great, the whole endeavor can become unprofitable. Therefore, to achieve and maintain a competitive advantage, it is critical to continuously compare actual real-time performance to planned performance.

We will use the Arctic Hot Dog Company to illustrate this point. The Arctic Hot Dog company produces wool knit sweaters to keep family pets warm during the winter. One of the key knitting processes experienced a problem which caused the actual productivity to vary from plan by negative 15 percent. In other words, it took 15 percent longer to knit and purl each sweater than the plan estimated.

Pet apparel is a dog-eat-dog industry, with fierce competition from Pacific Rim companies. In addition, demand was declining due to global warming. The Arctic Hot Dog company was aware of this and had based its business plan on very thin profit margins and high volumes. A 15 percent variance would cost the company money rather than produce a profit.

How long can the company afford to be ignorant of the effect of this variance? Five days? Forty-five days? If the company relied on traditional reporting from the accounting system, the business would have gone to the dogs before they had the information on which to take action.

Why? Because financial performance reporting, as provided by the accounting department is a statement of history. It is information that enables only a *reactive* approach to the business. Operational performance indicators are statements of reality as it currently exists—information that enables a *proactive* approach to the business. A proactive ability to anticipate future problems or effects, combined with an understanding of the financial implications, enables employee partners to identify problems, make decisions, and take action on a local level in a confident, rapid, accurate manner.

Communicating Quickly Is the Key

Most companies entering into a partnership with their employees will redesign their communication process. They realize how real-time performance information enables all employees to identify and reduce variances quickly or to make adjustments to other processes within the system to compensate for the variance. They develop systems and establish procedures that enable employee partners to communicate quickly.

The AT&T Service Center in Atlanta shares a large amount of information with the self-directed work teams through weekly meetings. During these meetings managers and production coordinators meet to discuss the performance plan, known to them as their customer commitments. This meeting acts as a forum for performance issues on the work team level to be communicated upward. These issues and events, which may have a negative impact on the plan, are evaluated and adjustment plans are developed jointly as needed. These adjustment plans are then communicated to all employees.

From any point in any process in an open, educated, partner-oriented organization, employees using a common language composed of financial and operational KPIs, have the ability to communicate freely with their leaders, their process suppliers, and with their process customers.

In this environment, communication "downward" from the leadership is primarily focused on information about performance plans based on sales activity and available support. Communication "upward" from frontline employees is primarily focused on reporting actual-to-plan performance, identifying variance, and discussion of support needs. Communication from a process to upstream suppliers should inform them about current and future performance needs, and communications from a process to downstream customers should inform them about performance outcomes and potential problems that may affect them.

Tracking Performance and Forecasting the Future

The sales department is not the only group of employees in the company that is required to forecast their performance. Figure 6-6 is a basic industrial engineering technique that demonstrates how employee partners can forecast future performance, track actual performance, and report variance from plan.

This form, as simple as it may seem, plays a significant role in the communication process. It requires the employee to perform two

Figure 6-6. Variance tracking form.

Department: _____

Team: _____

Partner: _____

Date: _____

Project: _____

Performance	Week 1	Week 2	Week 3	Week 4	Month Total
Plan	150	150	150	150	600
Forecast	150	**162**	**163**		
Cumulative Forecast Variance		−13	0		
Actual	125				
Cumulative Actual Variance	−25				

activities. Prior to the work period they forecast their performance and at the end of the work period they capture real-time performance data and compare it against the plan.

For example, let's assume that the plan for the month is to produce 150 fidgets (or process 150 insurance claims) each week. At the beginning of the week, the employee expects to meet the plan and establishes the forecast at 150.

During the week, the work flow is unexpectedly interrupted. Upstream delivery of materials is delayed, a "hot" job interrupts the schedule, or the machine/computer breaks down. At the end of week 1, the employee has only produced/processed 125 units. The variance, 25 units, is calculated and entered into the form.

Here the real value of this simple reporting device comes into play. The employee forecasts the next week's performance with the intent to get back on plan. She sees the plan for week 2 and the shortfall variance of week 1, and thinks how to make up the difference.

In the example illustrated by Figure 6-6, the employee decided it would be possible to make up the 25 unit difference over a period of two weeks. She indicated this by forecasting a performance level of 162 units for Week 2 and 163 units for week 3.

Sometimes the individual employee is able to resolve the variance. If not, she has an obligation, as a partner, to make others aware of the situation and solicit their support.

This mechanical performance reporting form serves several functions:

- It enables employees to visualize their contribution to the success of the organization.
- It initiates proactive problem solving by enabling employees to identify variance from plan and to think about future actions that can be taken to reduce the variance before it gets too far out of control.
- It acts as a hard copy information tool to communicate to others the degree to which the process is in compliance with the plan. This information enables others to make adjustments in their process to compensate for shortcomings in other areas of the system.
- It can create a direct line-of-sight link from performance to rewards.
- It can be used on a personal basis also, such as tracking a golf score, stock performance, or exercise routine.

We will return to the variance tracking form in Chapter 10, when we examine the relationship between performance and rewards.

Line-Of-Sight and Learning

An extended line-of-sight enables learning to take place throughout the organization on an individual and group basis. Understanding and studying data from the results of good and bad performance as it feeds into the system from sources such as the variance tracking form, enables everyone to learn from past experience. Understanding the stakeholder relationship and the fact that everyone shares in the destiny of the organization breaks down functional silos and enables people to learn from each other.

Enabling Mechanisms

However, all this learning is merely potential. Specific enabling mechanisms are needed to take full advantage of the potential this learning represents. These mechanisms are individual and group technologies that enable all partners to transfer their knowledge into action. In an open organization, employee partners view these technologies as everyone's right to become involved and participate.

The Right to Participate

Of all the rights that partner employees value, perhaps the most valued is the right to participate in the day-to-day process of managing the business. This process generally consists of formal and informal goal setting, problem solving, and decision making. Participating in problem solving and decision making on a local basis is becoming a common practice in today's business. A review of twenty-nine studies on employee participation in decision making and productivity was recently conducted by the Brookings Institution. The studies included eight case histories, twelve field experiments, and nine econometric tests.[9] The studies concluded that participation was greater when:

- It involved substantive decision-making rights rather than purely consultative arrangements such as quality circles.
- It is characterized by a high degree of employee commitment and employee-management trust.

The authors of the study concluded that substantive participation in decision making on the shop floor, or local level, was the most important type of participation and had the greatest long-term effect on productivity.

This information is supported by the findings of an extensive research project of the American Compensation Association and conducted by the Consortium for Alternative Reward Strategies (CARS). This ongoing research examined the link between rewards and organizational performance in 663 companies.[10] In the area of employee involvement, the CARS research found that organizations with more employee involvement programs reported better teamwork results in both manufacturing and service industries.

Group Technologies Are Enabling Mechanisms

The mechanisms that enable employees to participate, solve problems, and make decisions span the scope from individual suggestion systems to self-directed and self-managed work teams. Although the research data indicate that group technologies are more effective than individual efforts, the CARS data indicate that the move in this direction is slow. Figure 6-7 reports on the percent of the 663 companies with performance-reward plans that also use participation mechanisms.

These companies, with compensation plans linked to operational and financial performance, are putting their money where their mouth is when it comes to employee involvement. Yet the data indicate that, in general, the level of involvement in group activities is low. Typically 25 to 40 percent of the employees are active, and they spend less than 35 minutes to one hour a week in formal activities.

The data may indicate the difficulty of generating and maintaining large-scale, ongoing human interaction. (Anyone who has tried to organize and coordinate even a small group will attest to the difficulty.) It may be an indicator of the degree of management commitment to and support of the process. (Although it has been my experience that when senior management has made the commitment to engage the reward system in the process, the commitment is there.) It may be an indicator that the management practice of Education is missing and not everyone understands his role or how he can make a difference. Or it may indicate that not everyone needs to or can participate on a scheduled basis in group activities. It may indicate that most participation is informal, with interaction taking place in the workplace on an individual, as-needed basis.

When you come right down to it, unless you are part of a team hauling granite blocks to the pyramid, most work is of an individual nature. Whether it is working on a computer, servicing a customer, making a sales call, or producing a part on a milling machine, the nature of work boils down to how well each individual is equipped to perform and contribute.

Figure 6-7. Participation — plans and rates. (Data from Organizational Performance and Rewards Survey, 1994 CARS Research. Reprinted with permission from the American Compensation Association.)

Type of Employee Involvement Programs	Percent Using Program	Median % of Employees Participating	Median # of Hrs. Spent per Participating Employee per Yr.
Individual Suggestion Plans	42	20	5
Ad Hoc Problem-Solving Groups	44	20	22
Team Group Suggestion Programs	28	25	10
Self-Directed Work Teams	19	40	56
Employee-Management Teams	19	15	40
Quality Circles	26	16	50
Percent of All Plans Using Any Type Of Employee Involvement Program	66		

Figure 6-8. National employer practices — work organization.

EQW National Employer Survey of Over 3,100 Manufacturing & Service Companies.	
Mean Percentage of Non-Managerial/Non-Supervisory Workers Discussing Work Related Problems in Regularly Scheduled Meetings.	54
Percentage of Establishments Using Total Quality Management Processes	37
Percentage of Establishments Participating in Benchmarking Programs	25

To enhance and support this individual ability to perform and contribute, what appears to be needed on a day-to-day basis is an effective mechanism that enables collective planning, problem solving, and universal information exchange.

Meetings Are a Key Enabling Mechanism

The National Center on the Educational Quality of the Workforce (EQW) designed a survey around such issues. In late 1994 the U.S. Bureau of Census administered the survey to over 3,100 companies in the manufacturing and nonmanufacturing sectors in approximately equal distribution.[11] Each sector covered ten or more industries. The companies included establishments numbering from twenty to over one thousand employees. Figure 6-8 illustrates the results.

The survey data indicate that the most widely used participation technique for nonmanagerial and nonsupervisory workers is regularly scheduled meetings that enabled them to discuss work-related information.

Notes

1. Emmet Fox, *Around the Year with Emmet Fox* (New York: Harper & Row, 1979).
2. Ibid, p. 182.
3. David Pearce Snyder, Future Pay, *ACA News*, October/November 1994, p. 17.
4. John Naisbitt, *Global Paradox* (New York: William Morrow, 1994).
5. Office of the American Workplace, *High Performance Work Practices and Firm Performance*, U.S. Department of Labor, Washington, DC, August 1993.
6. Ichak Adizes, *Corporate Lifecycles*, (Englewood Cliffs, N.J., Prentice Hall, 1988), p. 141.
7. Ibid.

8. Human Resource Executive, *The Enabler—HRIS,* June 1994, p. 26.

9. Office of the American Workplace, *High Performance Work Practices and Firm Performance,* U.S. Department of Labor, Washington, DC, August 1993.

10. Jerry L. McAdams, CCP and Elizabeth J. Hawk, CCP, *Organizational Performance & Rewards: 663 Experiences In Making The Link* (Scottsdale, Ariz.: American Compensation Association, 1994).

11. National Center for the Educational Quality of the Workforce, *EQW National Employer Survey (EQW-NES),* Wharton School, University of Pennsylvania, Philadelphia, 1994.

7

Developing Line-Of-Sight Capabilities Through Information Sharing

Facts, when combined with ideas, constitute the greatest force in the world."

—Carl E. Ackerman

The accessibility and flow of information are at the heart of an open organization. With the proper data, the education to transform that data into information, and a timely process for receiving the data, each employee can develop a clear understanding of how their actions affect the profitability and growth of their company.

But education and information sharing are not enough to develop a clear line-of-sight for all employees. Although many employees have the intuitive capabilities to create this line-of-sight, many will not. Managers and human resources professionals must take the initiative to create a specific set of learning experiences that enable all employees to develop a clear line-of-sight.

In this chapter, we examine the systems and processes that enable employees to develop and utilize their line-of-sight. We analyze in detail a specific technique called the Line-Of-Sight Linkage Tree™, which is used to create a graphic line-of-sight model for each employee.

As most human resource professionals know, the difficulty with human resources initiatives such as TQM, self-directed work teams, and incentive compensation is that they do not affect the organization in a comprehensive manner. Each initiative is limited to producing results in its specific area of focus.

The Line-Of-Sight Linkage Tree is an invaluable tool that can graphically identify the areas in an organization that are affected by each initiative. This capability is quite useful in coordinating and ensuring complete and accurate coverage or for targeting a specific issue.

Meetings and Line-Of-Sight

There are many forms of information sharing—voice mail, e-mail, bulletin boards, memos, video tapes—but, as we observed in the previous chapter, none appear to be as effective as face-to-face meetings. Here not only is information exchanged, but conversation and discussion also take place. Meetings provide a substantial format for involvement, participation, development, and social growth. A meeting is an assembly of people who come together for a specific purpose. Unfortunately, many business meetings are not really meetings because they often lack this defined specific purpose.

Meetings, as they are defined in an open, educated, partner-oriented, business-focused environment are essential communications processes that transfer information critical to the attainment of the organization's goals. How often they are conducted and at what level (work group, department, plant, etc.) depends on the type of information being exchanged and the needs of the participants. Employee partners who have received an E_1 type of Education understand the meaning and value of information and exchange it regularly as needed.

Several different categories of information are exchanged in an open environment. The industry and type of business tends to define the specific information. However, all information exchange events enhance the line-of-sight and sense of partnership throughout the organization. They enable the partners to participate by sharing "future" information about plans and past information about performance. For example, in manufacturing, the content of these "information exchanges" focuses on five basic elements. They are:

1. Sales forecast
2. Customer orders
3. Operations plan
4. Production schedule
5. Team and individual performance

Forecasting and Planning Meetings

At the beginning of each time period (week, month, quarter, etc.) the sales department develops a forecast of estimated future sales.

This is the initial step in a process that is often called *shop floor management*.

Accuracy is a critical aspect of a sales forecast because most other plans are derived from it. To enhance the accuracy of the forecast, it is often developed with participation and input from Purchasing, Customer Service, Accounts Receivable, Operations, and other groups. Experience has shown that the more participation there is from groups that have customer contact, the more accurate the sales forecast will be.

During the sales forecast development meeting the accuracy of the information supporting the forecast is discussed. The importance of this discussion process should not be overlooked. Whether it is in a manufacturing operation or a service environment, the purpose of this meeting is to gain consensus and agreement on the information that supports the sales forecast plan.

After discussion about the underlying assumptions on which the forecast was developed, modifications may be made. The result is a forecast that is agreed upon by both sales and operations. As the saying goes: "There is no right forecast or wrong forecast, only an agreed upon forecast."

This forecast is then used to develop a plan that best matches the organization's resources and capabilities (capacity) with the sales projections (load). The plan determines how the organization will use its capacity to fulfill the sales forecast. This matchup becomes the operations plan and defines the flow of work through the facility. It also defines the type, amount, and flow of materials needed to support the plan and build the product.

Production Scheduling Meetings

The production schedule is then developed based on the operations plan. Employee partners from groups such as Operations, Shipping, Receiving, Inventory, Materials Management, and Order Processing should participate in this meeting. This schedule details when and how each order is to be produced. It is the daily working schedule for the operations and associated support employees.

Organizations with a strong E_4-R_4 culture enable everyone to participate in the process. Enabling every employee partner to participate in development of the plan assures an accurate matchup of load (sales forecast) to capacity (ability to deliver).

Take the test in Figure 7-1 to determine how well this forecasting, planning, and scheduling process works in your organization. Check the box that most represents your planning process. The results of the test are self-explanatory.

Figure 7-1. The involvement test.

Planning Process: Involvement Evaluation Form

(Check one.)

☐ **Full Involvement**

All employees can participate in the planning and scheduling process.

Outcome is an accurate, high quality, realistic plan and schedule.

☐ **Partial Involvement**

Only those employees who are directly related to production and production support participate.

The outcome is relatively accurate and realistic if everything goes right.

☐ **Management Involvement**

Only management and "the experts" are involved in the process.

The plan may or may not work.

☐ **No Involvement**

The planning department develops a detailed schedule tightly linked to the forecast.

The planning printer is hooked to the shredder.

Performance Orientation Meetings

If an employee partner, team leader, or coach/facilitator is not present when the production schedule is developed (and not all will be), they are provided with this information and are responsible for communicating these performance requirements to their employee partners.

Normally a coach or facilitator reviews this information with the team in an informal meeting prior to the start of each shift. At this point, individual contributors have a clear understanding of the plan and schedule. They can use this information to set their levels of performance and understand with whom they need to interact to accomplish their element of the plan and schedule.

Performance Feedback Meetings

Unfortunately, plans are only plans and often go awry. In our manufacturing example, unless the organization is building product to place into inventory (and you better not be doing that), plans based on forecasts will change when the first hard order enters the company. Orders disrupt the plan because, in reality, they rarely conform to the forecast.

Disruptions will also come from within. The process may break down, manufacturing or material problems may cause lost time and throw the schedule off. If all employee partners have an operational line-of-sight and understand the financial implications, they will be able to define how these disruptions affect the critical path, identify counteractions, and implement corrective action.

In an open environment this critical path management process normally begins on an individual level. The schedule allows an employee to identify when the process is out of compliance. Local wisdom and operational line-of-sight enables the employee to take the best action. Information is exchanged on an individual, as-needed basis as each employee partner does what it takes to achieve the objectives.

If the solution cannot be achieved individually, the problem is escalated. In open, high-involvement organizations, employees are partners and are enabled to meet and discuss their performance issues. Any employee partner can convene a meeting of the partners necessary to effectively resolve the issue. These meetings are often on an as-needed basis, but can also be established on a schedule to support the team building and partnership process.

At Republic Steel, crew meetings are held daily for approximately 15–20 minutes. Each crew conducts their own meeting to solve problems or generate ideas. Or employees may meet individually, to pass information about needs and issues to the individuals who have the ability and resources to take corrective action.

Whether these meetings are formal or informal, group or individual, the purpose is the same: to identify the constraining resource or process and to develop a solution. Anyone can attend these meetings, and that generates a high level of trust.

Department meetings are held weekly and last for no more than 2 hours. Each crew sends a representative to the department meeting. The issues addressed are often problems the crews were unable to resolve or ideas they had generated. The department head takes the results of this meeting to the plant meeting.

The plant meeting is held weekly and lasts for no more than 4 hours. Issues of plantwide interest, such as capital acquisition, as well as unresolved issues from the crew and department levels are addressed.

The corporate meeting is held each month and lasts approximately a half day. The purpose is to address continuous improvement efforts, capital improvements, and strategic issues.

Perhaps the two most important elements in this process are that:

1. Problems are identified and resolved on a local level. They are sent to the next level only if the crew is unable to develop or implement a solution.
2. The minutes from all meetings are made available to all employees.

Operational Line-Of-Sight

The forecasting, planning, and scheduling processes develop the information tools that contribute to a long operational line-of-sight, one of the fundamental elements of information exchange in an open, high-performance, business-focused environment.

In general, this line-of-sight enables each employee to understand, by customer order, which processes are involved, their relationships, and the time required for each process in relation to the whole. Essentially it is project management on a micro level. This level of detail may not be possible in a service environment, but the concept remains valid and should be applied with vigor. Figure 7-2 illustrates the operational line-of-sight.

Figure 7-2. Operational line-of-sight.

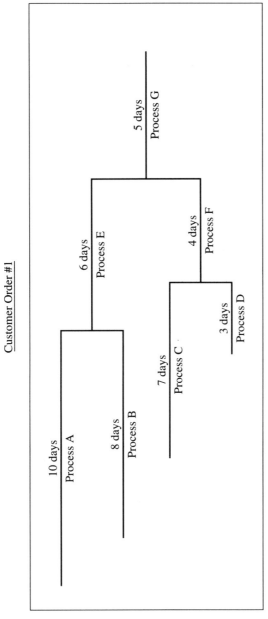

Customer Order #1

10 days
Process A

8 days
Process B

6 days
Process E

5 days
Process G

7 days
Process C

4 days
Process F

3 days
Process D

21 Days Lead Time From Customer Order to Product Completion

Timely Information Is Money

Performance issues such as material availability or shortages, production problems, capacity constraints, handling and storage problems, quality, and productivity issues affect the production schedule and operations plan. The hard data associated with these issues is normally collected by systems that, by their nature, are slow to report. In a traditional organization, this lag in performance reporting means a lag in resolving the problem and results in lost productivity or increased costs.

In our manufacturing example, when a disruption to the schedule occurs, either from a "hot" order or due to process breakdown, the affected employee partners meet to define the problem and formulate options that would compensate for the disruption.

For example in Figure 7-2, if a disruption to process B extended the lead time from 8 days to 10 days, it would have downstream impact on all the other processes. Left uncorrected the disruption would cause the output from process B (in this case semifinished materials), to be 2 days late feeding into process E, which would extend the time necessary to complete process G by 2 days.

The corrective action may be to reallocate 2 days of capacity of processes C, D, E, F, and G to another order, or feed their output into inventory, thus increasing material and interest costs. Either way, customer order #1 will be shipped late.

A different response is to find some way to shorten the lead times in process B. Addressing other elements in the process, such as material wait time, activity lead time, machine setup time, or productivity could compensate for the disruption. The result would be to maintain the schedule and ship the customer order on time.

This same scenario applies to a service organization in which process B could be market analysis data that feed a strategic planning project, or promotional print material that drives a time-sensitive marketing campaign, or it could be data output from the Information Services group that feeds the weekly payroll!

Whatever the decision, consensus is achieved through discussion by educated partners who possess an operational line-of-sight. Group and individual action plans are developed and initiated, and the results of the meeting are immediately forwarded to management and made available to all other partners.

If additional support is needed, this need is communicated to management as part of the results of the meeting. The target outcome of the meeting is a plan of action to correct the effects of the disruption. If this is not feasible, the next outcome is a definition of the cause and effects, with a recommendation of necessary action, the scope of which is beyond the control of the immediate individuals or group.

Utilizing this process, management may, for the first time, be receiving real-time performance information. Such information provides a sustainable competitive edge. Inefficiencies and excess costs are eliminated. Resource capacity can be tuned to maximum utilization, thus lowering costs, improving flexibility, and increasing productivity.

From a financial standpoint, the end result of operational line-of-sight is an increased ROA. With an increased ROA, an organization can compete on price, increase market share, and more effectively weather business downturns. In addition, an improvement in ROA makes a company more attractive to investors and tends to increase the value of the stock price. On an employee partner level, increased ROA provides strong rewards in work and pay growth opportunities.

Developing a Comprehensive Line-Of-Sight

The Value of a Comprehensive Line-Of-Sight

When we talk about line-of-sight we are speaking about the ability to visualize the cause-and-effect relationships between business processes and activities. This ability to visualize relationships between key business elements is a long-sought-after capability in the process of managing employee performance. With it, employee partners can reduce cost, eliminate waste, or add value to every activity. With it they can increase revenues through flexibility and rapid response time. In the new marketplace of specialty demand, a line-of-sight capability supports innovation and results in a greater variety of product and service offerings.

The Design Challenge

The challenge of creating an effective line-of-sight has been to develop a model that is comprehensive, yet flexible enough to be utilized in almost any industry, in any environment. During research for this book it became obvious that an effective approach would require the combination of several key business perspectives.

First we must establish that the underlying premise of a line-of-sight capability is to increase the economic status of the organization—its profitability. Since we are speaking in economic terms it makes sense to include the concepts of supply and demand in the model. Based on these assumptions, a comprehensive line-of-sight model should represent the knowledge and understanding each employee partner has about the following three key business concepts:

1. Profit
2. Capabilities (supply)
3. Demand

Profit

If profit is an underlying theme in a line-of-sight model then employees will need to have knowledge and understanding of financial measures that provide information on the financial success of the organization. ROA, ROE, revenues, costs, and margins are examples of financial indicators that provide information on an organization's financial success.

The knowledge and understanding associated with the concept of profit can be obtained through education in basic business finance and a sharing of the company's financial information. Until this understanding is combined with the perspective provided by other key business concepts, it provides very little line-of-sight capability.

Capabilities (Supply)

An organization's supply is its capacity to respond to the demands of the marketplace. Supply capabilities are often expressed using operational indicators, such as customer service levels, production capacity, productivity, cycle time, and other operational measures. Quality indicators such as scrap, rework, returns, warranty costs, and customer satisfaction can also be considered supply indicators.

The knowledge and understanding associated with the concept of supply can be obtained by using block diagrams and flowcharts to map the process. Flowcharting the process can allocate overhead costs to the activities where they belong rather than lumping them into a single category where unnecessary costs can hide. Process mapping can simplify a process by creating a micro line-of-sight that highlights waste and non-value-added activities. Accurate cost allocation and waste reduction capabilities are fundamental elements in the line-of-sight linkage between profit and supply.

Demand

Demand, for an organization, is defined in terms of customer orders or sales forecasts. It is the level of goods or services that the marketplace desires to purchase from that organization.

The knowledge and understanding associated with the concept of demand can be obtained through frequent and candid communications between the customer, Sales, Operations, and other support functions. Accurate and timely information about projected demand requirements is a fundamental element in the line-of-sight linkage between profit, supply, and demand. For example, if employees have a line-of-sight to both the sales forecast (demand) and the production capacity (or available service capabilities in a service industry) they will be able to increase ROA by synchronizing the organization's supply capacity (assets) to customer demand.

The Line-Of-Sight Linkage Tree™

Figures 7-3a, b, and c, The Line-Of-Sight Linkage Tree, illustrate how, with the proper education and information, employees can visualize the cause-and-effect relationships between the key business concepts of profit, capabilities, and demand.

The Line-Of-Sight Linkage Tree is structured around the basics of an income statement, with its emphasis on the earning power of an organization. However, it is not intended to be an accurate representation of a financial document. It is a combination of a financial instrument and an operational map.

Information is slotted into this map where it can provide perspective and define relationships. The end result is a document that allows employees to visualize cause-and-effect relationships that are directly or indirectly associated with their job. This individual line-of-sight capability also provides them with a clear definition and understanding of their unique value to the organization.

Figure 7-3a is an overview of the tree. Figures 7-3b and 7-3c are detailed expansions of Figure 7-3a. The Line-Of-Sight Linkage Tree is presented in this manner because of the space limitations of this book. A working Line-Of-Sight Linkage Tree would be a single document that presents a unified line-of-sight from individual activity to operating income. This document would include all branches that have direct or indirect links to the function being examined.

Viewing the model from left to right, the perspective flows from macro to micro. The information progresses from general financial measures to specific operational measures. It starts on the far left side with operating income, and winds up on the far right side with specific indicators of activity and/or individual performance. In between there is a process of transition where operational performance indicators are translated into more conceptual financial performance indicators and vice versa.   *(text continues on page 180)*

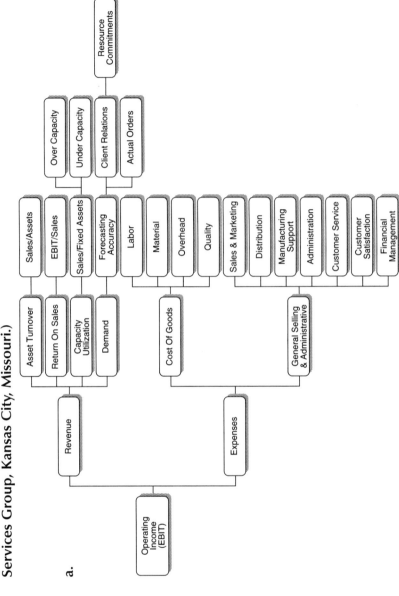

Figure 7-3. The Line-Of-Sight Linkage Tree. (Used with permission from Performance Services Group, Kansas City, Missouri.)

a.

b.

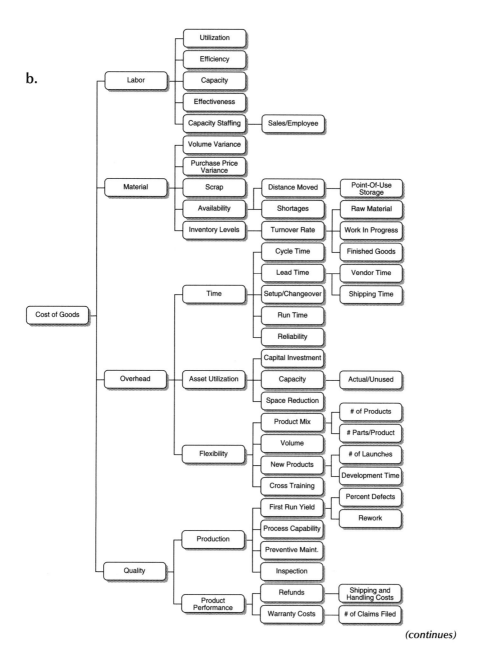

(continues)

Figure 7-3. (*Continued*)

C.

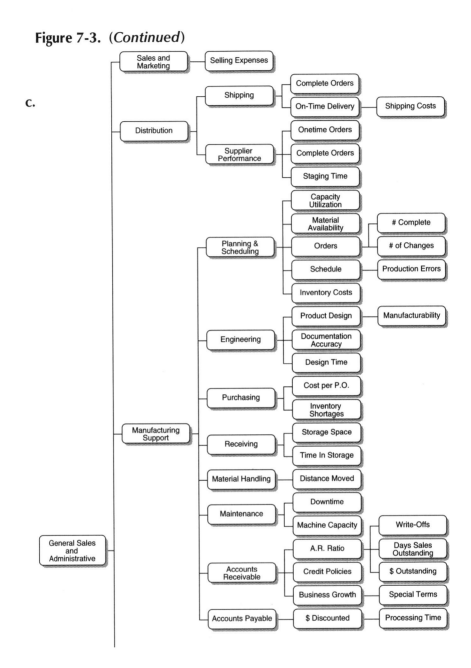

C.

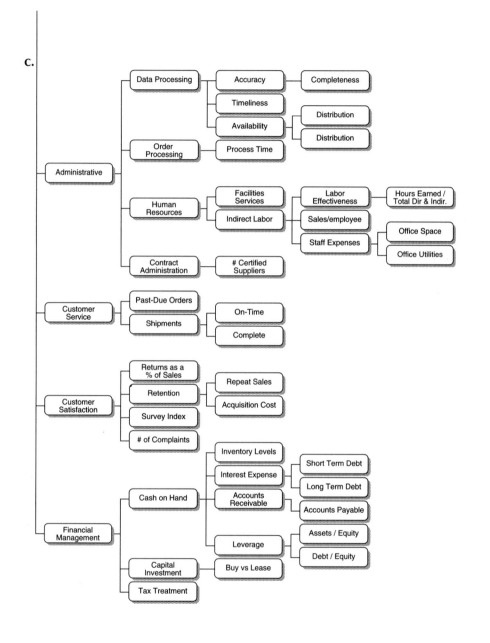

Using the Linkage Tree for Cause-and-Effect Problem Solving

For example, with the appropriate education and information, employees in Material Handling, Purchasing, Planning, Engineering, or Shipping are able to see the cause-and-effect linkage between profit margin and the inventory levels associated with raw material, work-in-progress material, and finished goods material. They understand that inventory costs money and that finished goods inventory is more expensive than raw material inventory because of the value that has been added to it.

They also understand that the money tied up in excessive inventory could be invested in other things, such as interest-bearing notes or other assets. If the inventory is not properly balanced, that is, if there is too much inventory in the system, the money is being used inappropriately. This inappropriate use of money increases the cost of the product or service and negatively affects profit or earnings before interest and taxes (EBIT).

Understanding the cause-and-effect relationships between the concepts of profit, supply, and demand, the employee(s) can identify specific activities that are related to the situation. They may take action to reduce the level of raw material on hand by changing the supplier order system. They may reduce the amount of work-in-process material by increasing the speed at which work flows through the process (perhaps by reducing lead time or setup time). Or they may reduce the level of finished goods by improving the customer delivery system.

Conversely, if there is too little inventory on hand, the organization will be unable to completely satisfy the demand of the marketplace and sales revenues will be lower than they could have been. Understanding the cause-and-effect relationships, employees will recognize that ROA is being reduced and profit margins will be lower as the result of underutilization of the supply capacity of the organization.

Depending on the cause, they may take action to increase their raw material levels or establish better material delivery procedures with their suppliers. They may work to improve the material handling process internally by staging materials closer to the work station thus reducing travel distance. They may improve the material planning process or establish a "pull" system where operators manage their own inventory.

Building and Using the Tree

For the employee partner, developing a personal line-of-sight capability is neither easy nor rapid. It is an ongoing process of education based on information, participation, experience, and discussion. The Line-Of-Sight Linkage Tree displays measurement information for each critical process or activity in both financial and operational formats. As an educational tool it can help employees visualize cause-and-effect relationships and how they add to or detract from economic value.

For the company, developing a Line-Of-Sight Linkage Tree that encompasses the entire organization may not be practical. What may be of greater use is the development of this visibility tool on a department or team level. By meeting periodically to develop a tree that reflects their key performance indicators, the department or team members will share learning and build a common understanding of their roles, responsibilities, and relationships.

For example, one of the key performance indicators of the team may be cash flow. A Line-Of-Sight Linkage Tree that includes cash flow information may include the accounts receivable function. The right-hand side of this tree would include indicators of collection effectiveness: competitor trends, credit policies, uncollectables, special terms, and days-sales-outstanding. Supporting these indicators would be the information that provides meaning to them. This information is part of the E_1 management practice of Education and the more information that is available, the more effective the employees will be at improving the situation.

As an illustration of this point, a company in the food industry with $60 million in revenues and a collection effectiveness in the upper quartile will have an annual positive cash difference of $5 million over a similar company with a collection effectiveness in the lower quartile.

This huge cash advantage provides a significant competitive edge to the company. The company can gain market share by pricing its products more aggressively. It can capture customer awareness by advertising and promoting its products more often. It can use the cash to pay down debt and therefore operate less expensively.

This team's cash flow tree would be customized by them to include pricing, marketing, financing, and other functions that can be affected by the availability of cash. As this information is developed it can be shared with the group's customers and suppliers. Feedback and conversations with these other groups will expand the detail of the tree and the activities that affect the key performance indicators. Using this process, over a period of time the employees in each team can grow a highly detailed and accurate Line-Of-Sight Linkage Tree from the ground up. These team and departmental branches can then be combined to create the company's tree.

Ownership is the ultimate outcome of this development process. Each employee has the opportunity to take responsibility for completing his "branch" of the tree. As a result, each employee creates his own understanding of how he fits into the organization. He understands how he relates to others in the organization, how he can make a contribution, and how he can add value.*

Parker Pen: A Good Example of Line-Of-Sight

Parker Pen USA Limited has been producing fine writing instruments for over one hundred years. It is a union environment whose employees belong to the United Rubber Workers union and the International Association of Machinists (IAM).

At one point during the course of its existence, the Parker Pen Company became a subsidiary of a diversified organization. As the marketplace changed, competition increased and profit decreased for the pen division. Eventually it was separated from the parent company in a leveraged buyout (LBO).

The new owners developed a turn-around strategy designed to create sustained competitive growth. Peter Bentley, now president of Parker Pen, was head of the North American Operations at the time. As part of the turn-around strategy he led a process to change the organization's culture. The focus was on defining the company's customers and satisfying their needs.

A TQM process was initiated as part of the change process. As leader of the process, Bentley assured there was a long-term commitment to the effort from senior management. An educational process was developed that included 12 hours of training on the individual's role in quality, 40 hours of total quality process (TQP) training, and education in statistical process control.

At first the focus was on relating quality to the production process. Where once 15 percent of the workforce were quality inspectors, each employee was taught personal responsibility for quality. Now, less than one percent of the workforce is utilized for inspection, and their focus is on incoming materials.

After experiencing success in the production areas, the quality initiative was moved into the office environment at the Arrow Park facility in Janesville, Wisconsin. A major thrust was the redesign of the planning system. The result was the creation of a comprehensive line-of-sight for all employees in the facility. Management at Parker Pen knew that developing a long line-of-sight would create a significant increase in personal responsibility.

An analysis was performed to determine how capable and effective

*If you would like additional free information on this process, please contact the author c/o AMACOM Books.

the processes were in Operations, Administration, Sales, Planning, Information Services, and Human Resources. For example, the management information services were evaluated to see if the information being provided was needed, accurate, and timely.

The status of the employees was also examined. Management wanted to know if they had the proper skill training, knew and accepted what was expected of them from a performance standpoint, and understood how their activities related to everyone else. The conclusion of the analysis was that the employees didn't understand and were not focused on the business issues.

The survey indicated that first-line management didn't understand the necessity for a business plan or how they related to it. They didn't understand concepts such as ROA or ROE that would make people want to invest in a company. They didn't understand the different ways of financing a company or why financing was important. They didn't understand how budgets were made or why they changed.

The company initiated a process to educate its employees about the business. The first step was to give them sufficient education to understand the information that management wanted to share with them. In addition to the education in quality concepts, managers received over 40 hours of big picture education about the industry, the company's place in the industry, and basic business finance as it related to measuring the company's performance. Each supervisor also spent over 40 hours developing personal facilitation and people management skills. Once this had been accomplished, the frontline employees received an abbreviated version of the same business education.

The company's chief financial officer participated in quarterly supervisor meetings in which employees were educated in the company's products, product life cycles, the cost of goods for each product, and their profitability. They discussed existing and potential markets, new products in development, and existing and potential distribution channels.

The education was designed to support quality in the overall system—quality in operations and in administration. The purpose was to build a foundation so employees could relate to the company's numbers. Management knew that this understanding would enable everyone to make valid commitments and deliver on them. The understanding emphasizes a clean handoff. Each employee made sure that what was handed off by one was picked up and acted upon by another.

The big picture education helped develop an understanding of what was going on, why decisions were made, and what actions were necessary. This education helped balance the TQM process. Employees began to understand that quality at Parker Pen is not just about pens. It is also about the relationships between employees, between Operations,

Engineering, Management Information Systems, Marketing, and Human Resources. The big picture education helped better define who the customer is and what they want.

Satisfying the Customers' Needs

At the time, Parker Pen was an LBO. Because of the structure of an LBO, Parker Pen's primary "customers" included the investors who financed the LBO. They wanted to see the business grow with limited additional investment. In other words, they wanted an increase in ROA. ROA is a profitability indicator. It indicates how efficiently a company's assets are being used. The formula is EBIT divided by average total assets (ATA).

$$ROA = EBIT \div ATA$$

Analysis of the formula indicates that ROA can be improved either by reducing total assets (such as selling off equipment or shutting down facilities) or by increasing EBIT (such as increasing sales or reducing costs).

From an internal standpoint, the company chose to focus on improving operations and reducing costs. Three of the many key areas they addressed were forecasting, planning, and inventory materials management.

Line-Of-Sight and Open Communications

The sales forecasting process was revised. Sales forecasting was conducted jointly with Operations, Sales and Marketing. Each month this group would meet to discuss the forecast. They would examine the plan on a product-by-product basis. Statistical tools, historical data, and market intelligence were used to improve the accuracy of the forecast.

The planning system was revised to provide clear, accurate, and timely visibility in terms of capacity and the ability to respond to changes in product volume and product mix. Once the forecast was developed, representatives from Operations and Sales would discuss how much of the forecast was feasible to achieve based on current capabilities.

When demand exceeded capacity, the options were to postpone the production (and not satisfy the customer's delivery date), lose the demand (such as Christmas retail orders that are not needed after the holidays), or reallocate resources from other areas to meet demand (the flexibility that accompanies a clear line-of-sight of operational capabilities).

This group process gave the organization the ability to synchronize supply to demand. As a result, the company was generally able to satisfy the demand using overtime or routing the customer order to another product line. On the rare occasion when they were unable to fill the order by the customer's due date they were able to advise them of this well in advance and recommend alternatives. This ability supports the quality emphasis by providing a high degree of credibility and strong customer relationships.

Accessible Information Provides Line-Of-Sight

One of the many improvements made was to increase inventory turns. Inventory turns are a tightly focused measure of how well assets are being utilized. They indicate how well the planning process matches supply with demand, how well inventory levels are being matched to demand, and the speed at which inventory is cycled throughout the process.

In general, higher inventory turns indicate a more productive use of capital assets. Higher inventory turns also mean that less material is held unproductively in the process. Because inventory requires money to purchase, higher inventory turns also indicate a more productive use of financial assets.

To address the issue of inventory and lead time, the employees were involved in the design and development of a *kanban* style material management system. Originally developed in Japanese automobile factories, *kanban* is a method of inventory management that keeps inventories low by scheduling materials to arrive a short time before they are needed.

The team developed a low-tech, real-time, shop floor discipline in which items are produced only to fill an order or to replace the inventory that was used to fill an order. It consists of an inventory control and scheduling system in which materials are pulled through the distribution chain based on demand from the production line. The use of status boards in the work area gives visibility to order backlogs, inventory levels, and work flow.

The status boards let employees know at all times where they are in relation to the plan. The nature of the system makes this information available to everyone in the location. It is the responsibility of the people who use it to maintain it and keep it accurate.

Prior to implementing these changes there was no visibility of the consequences of a change in the plan. If an unusual order entered the system, it would take 2 days to decide how to deal with it. There wasn't the visibility of all the information so management made educated guesses. Lack of visibility of all the information had management in a reactive, fire-fighting mode. The order would be produced, but it would cause something else to be missed two weeks later.

With the new system, performance against forecast is measured on a daily rather than weekly basis. Inventory consumption is tracked by market channel. Inventory can be shared between market channels, allowing for a lower overall level of inventory.

Parker management looked at the money invested in the organization with an eye toward improving the ability of the process to respond. The process can now respond within a few hours to what once would take several days or weeks.

Line-Of-Sight and Quality

The changes to the system developed a line-of-sight visibility that forces quality issues to the front. An order card is attached to each inventory container. When the assembler pulls the container for use they place the card in the Needed column of the status board. The status boards were designed to provide a visual impression of the business activity. Lots of cards in a specific Needed column show an issue. The system forces one to ask, Why, in relation to all the other cards, do you need twice as many cards of this material? The beauty of this system is that information is available to anyone who walks through the department.

Line-Of-Sight and Flexibility

The result of these changes was an increase in flexibility. Production lead times were reduced, which increased production flexibility and reduced the amount of finished goods in stock by reducing the time it took to get the product into the marketplace. The company's ability to respond to the marketplace has been greatly enhanced by educating all employees, establishing responsive systems and developing good communications with the sales group.

Line-Of-Sight and Staffing

The enhanced line-of-sight has also allowed for better staffing plans. Operations now gets the best forecast possible from the sales group. Performance is tracked against the forecast on a daily basis. If there is a variance, operations employees talk to the sales group to determine if it is just a spike or if it is a trend. This visibility to the numbers enables employees to understand where and how they can make the best contribution.

Parker management knows there are other benefits also. By educating everyone in the big picture and the finances of the company, every-one understands the need to stay lean during good times, and the company has more credibility with the employees when facing hard times.

During this cultural change process, one of the plant's products was allocated to another facility for production. This necessitated a downsizing at the Arrow Park Facility. Management tells us there was better acceptance of this downsizing as a result of the education that had taken place. The employees understood the business necessities involved. They understood the facility's ROA was reduced because the product left the facility but the overhead remained. According to management at Parker Pen, "It is easier to run an organization in a healthy way when people understand the business issues behind the decisions."

Following its 1993 acquisition of Parker Pen, the Gillette Company is now the worldwide leader in writing instruments with its Paper Mate, Parker, and Waterman brands.

A Diagnostic Tool for Human Resource Initiatives

Once an organization or team has developed a Line-Of-Sight Linkage Tree that reflects its activities and key performance indicators it will possess a powerful diagnostic tool. This tree can be used to identify the areas in an organization that will be affected by other change management initiatives. By identifying these areas on the linkage tree, it is possible to see which functions and activities will be affected by the project and which will not.

For example, if a company is planning to implement a TQM initiative, it can define the functions, activities, and financial aspects that will be affected by the initiative. This information is then overlaid onto the linkage tree and it becomes immediately apparent which functions and elements of the organization are being addressed by the TQM initiative and which are not.

This technique can be used to compare the effectiveness of any or all of the available change management and performance improvement initiatives: process reengineering, TQM, ABC management, self-directed work teams, and even the open-book/partnership process outlined in this book.

By identifying the effects of these initiatives on the Linkage Tree, it is possible to see where double coverage exists and where no coverage exists. In effect, this diagnostic process enables an organization to determine the right mix of change management initiatives and the degree to which they need to be customized to provide the proper amount of coverage to the entire organization. Taking a more focused approach, this diagnostic tool enables an organization to identify the appropriate improvement initiative and customize it to have an impact on specific target areas within the organization.

8

E_3-Empowerment: The Management Practice

R_3-Responsibilities: The Employee Expectation

Ideally a company is staffed with self-starting employees who are dedicated to fostering continuous improvement through creative thinking and proactive problem solving. The reality is that most employees apply a successful personal survival technique, developed in response to a command and control management style. This technique is to automatically excuse oneself from any personal responsibility for results, or the lack thereof. The process is to rationalize away a lack of involvement and participation by placing the blame somewhere else. Familiar excuses are:

- Scheduling and planning didn't consider all the factors.
- The client changed his or her mind.
- My coworker didn't pick up the ball where I left off.
- The product doesn't have all the features it should have.
- The policies and procedures prevent me from taking action.
- The pricing structure is wrong.
- They don't understand the level of detail involved in delivering what they want when they want it.
- The competition has more resources. They are too agile and responsive.
- It's not my responsibility. I don't get paid for that.
- What is the use? They will only change direction again in six months.

This mentality is the product of a management style that is fast becoming extinct. A new, more open management technique encourages a new and collaborative employee response. The concept is called employee empowerment and anyone who has not been living on a desert island has heard of it and most likely had some exposure to it. But do you know what it is and how it works?

In this chapter, we create a definition for empowerment that enables us to examine what it is and how it works. During our examination, we will see how the dual nature of empowerment has a stimulating effect on several elements in the E_4-R_4 Partnership Checklist.

We use that knowledge to develop a tool that we can use to define the outcomes we expect from empowerment and identify actions that can be taken by employees to achieve these outcomes.

The Dual Aspects of Empowerment

Almost every senior manager and human resources professional desires to develop a sustainable competitive edge through a workforce of employees who, individually and as a group, are actively engaged in the business. To have employees who are actively engaged they must be allowed to solve problems, make decisions, and act. This requires a transfer of control and power. Thus the term *empowerment.*

Empowerment is perhaps the most talked about technique of managing employees, but it may very well be one of the most misunderstood techniques. This one word, while powerful, is only a symbol of the concepts involved in the transfer and use of power and control.

The dictionary tells us that the verb "to empower" means "to give official authority or legal power." But how does this single verb translate into an environment in which self-starting employees are dedicated to fostering continuous improvement through creative thinking and proactive problem solving? Not to mention decision making and action taking.

Most companies, in their effort to empower their employees, take one of two obvious paths. They either proclaim their employees are empowered, then send them back to the workplace and wait for the improvements to materialize. Or they initiate empowerment processes, whereby groups of employees are brought together to solve problems and make improvements.

As Eastman Chemical and other companies have discovered, either approach can produce results that range from confusion, to disappointment, to anarchy. The reason has to do with the two aspects of empowerment: the conceptual aspects and the concrete aspects.

Conceptual Aspects

The concept of empowerment deals with the social contract that transfers power and decentralizes control. The power to make decisions, authorize changes, and to take action, and the control over information, are moved from a contained management level to the individual employee level where, presumably, they can be used most effectively.

Any executive who is considering such a dramatic shift in relationships will want to examine how these changes will affect the organization's short-term and long-term bottom line. During a discussion and analysis about the value of empowering employees, those who have the power and control inevitably realize that their paradigm of success must change. Until they see success defined in terms other than power and control, they will be unable to accept the real concept of empowerment.

Often there is a reluctance or inability to define success in terms other than power and control. Occasionally there is a concern about the ability of the employees to effectively fulfill their responsibilities in this new management model. Many times there is a fear about the impact such a change will have on the order, flow, and short-term performance results of the organization.

This reluctance, concern, and fear often result in a limited acceptance of the concept of empowerment. Unfortunately, limited acceptance of the concept of empowerment is like standing with one foot on the dock and one foot on the departing boat—the outcome can be unpleasant. If limited acceptance exists, it becomes painfully obvious during the act of empowerment.

The Concrete Act

The act of empowerment is the actual act in which power and control are transferred. It is where I give, and you receive and accept, the responsibilities and benefits of control and power. In its purest form, it is a social event, providing legitimacy to the transfer of power through its ceremony. How else can you actualize a concept?

This, perhaps, is what makes empowering employees so difficult. If the organization is serious about empowerment, the act of empowerment, like the coronation of a king, can only take place once. After that, "empowerment" deals with the employees exercising their newly acquired power and control.

During the process of considering the wisdom of transferring power, those who currently have the power will focus on the potential negative consequences of such a move. This is good. It is their responsibility to evaluate all the repercussions of any strategic move and evaluate the costs against the benefits.

Unfortunately, all too often the potential of negative effects on the bottom line, of mass confusion or worse yet, anarchy, will so affect their perspective that they will provide what appears to be the power, but in reality will not release the control. They will provide the mechanisms that enable employees to participate, solve problems, and make decisions, while retaining control over their ability to take action.

An example of this is the company that establishes quality improvement teams to identify the root cause of problems and recommend solutions. The management organization directs the teams as to the types of problems and then has the ultimate say as to whether the recommendations are implemented. Employee involvement yes, but obviously not employee empowerment.

The New Social Contract

The transfer of power and control is the new social contract between employer and employee. The old social contract provided assurances of security and care-taking in return for loyalty and proper execution of orders. This new social contract provides the opportunity for self-fulfillment in return for active "self-management." It is an entirely different paradigm.

That this new social contract is worth pursuing has been well documented in the business press. In this new social contract, benefits are realized for the organization, the management, and the employees. The company realizes better operating results through improved internal communications, stronger relationships and cooperation, and customer-oriented thinking on the part of all employees. Management is free to pursue more expansive, strategic, growth-oriented activities, and the employees have a direct say in the primary role of their work.

Defining Empowerment

The key tactics and their subtle linkages necessary to achieve these benefits has been less well documented. Empowerment means different things to different people, depending on the context and culture.

Empowerment is contingent upon employee participation, employee accountability, access to information, an innovative atmosphere, and compassionate leadership.

Shirley Richard is the executive vice-president of customer service and marketing at Arizona Public Services, a utility company in Phoenix, Arizona. The utility has made a strong move toward empowering all employees and Ms. Richard says that empowerment is contingent upon communicating the company's mission, listening to employees, opening the flow of communications, convincing employees their ideas are needed, and giving employees a format for action.[1]

In keeping with the dual aspects of empowerment, the conceptual and the concrete, it is possible to develop a working definition of empowerment: Empowerment is the ability to make decisions, take action, and assume responsibility for the outcomes (concrete aspects), based on the authority and desire to do so (conceptual aspects).

Using this definition, it is easy to see how the E_4-R_4 Partnership Checklist supports the development of empowerment. The Education management practice develops the skills, understanding, and knowledge from which to make intelligent decisions. The Enable management practice is a tangible manifestation of the transfer of authority to take action.

The New Paradigm of Power and Control

The Enable management practice provides a new paradigm of power and control to consider. Do those who enable others have a new and unique form of power and control? Do those who enable others have control over how empowerment is applied? It is an interesting question and not entirely philosophical in nature. Empowered employees must be directed and must have defined boundaries in order to channel their energies and efforts. How these energies and efforts are channeled will have a significant impact on the success of the empowerment effort.

Recognizing Empowerment

Would you know empowerment if you saw it in the marketplace? One key attribute of empowerment is situational leadership. Situational leadership is the ability to assume a leadership role and make information-based decisions when the circumstances require them. These information-based decisions are normally outside the activities involved in the day-to-day work effort.

I observed a good example of this exercise of empowerment at a local pizza kitchen in Kansas City. The pizza kitchen provides only carry-out services. Customers phone in their orders, receive an estimate as to when the order will be ready, and then drive to the establishment to pick up their order.

The kitchen offers to the marketplace an explicit product, the pizza, and an implied service, fast food, no waiting. The customer's expectation is to obtain a good tasting pizza with a minimum of wasted time.

I had placed a phone order for the family's main course and proceeded to the store to pick up my order. Like most other customers, my family was waiting at home for their dinner. Everyone was hungry and expectations were high for a tasty meal, soon to be served.

At the store, the customer ahead of me in the service line had the same objective, to pick up dinner for the family, and the same expectations, that the order would be ready as promised. Unfortunately, his order could not be found. The customer's name was checked, the type of pizza was checked, the time the order was placed was checked. All to no avail.

Then the counter clerk who was working to solve the problem noticed an order slip on the floor by the telephone. It was the customer's order. The order had not been placed with the kitchen and the pizza had not been made. Although the customer was taking the news as pleasantly as possible, it was obvious that his expectations had not been met. This turn of events meant that his family's dinner would be delayed at least half an hour. It also meant that he would have to stand in the waiting area for that period of time.

At first glance, it appeared as if the employees were aware of and focused on delivery of the explicit product—pizzas. The kitchen staff and counter clerks were busy filling orders and no one knew how or why this customer's order literally slipped through the cracks.

It was also obvious that the customers were aware of and focused on the delivery of the implied service, that is, fulfilling customer expectations. Each customer had a look of embarrassed empathy for the customer with the lost order. Each customer felt a sense of exposure and vulnerability. Expectations had been set by the pizza kitchen only to be unfulfilled. A bond of trust was being broken and it affected every customer who observed it. There was no manager available to refer the problem to, and all the kitchen staff were giving it wide berth. The buck stopped at the counter clerk.

Once the situation had been clearly established, the counter clerk assumed a situational leadership role. Apologies were made, the cause of the problem was explained and the order was inserted into the front of the queue, to be made next. Understanding the need to reset the customer's bond of trust and expectations, the counter clerk announced that there would be no charge for the order.

The clerk had made a good faith effort to deliver on both the explicit and implied customer offerings. The clerk had communicated to all present that the customers, not the pizzas, were the reason the kitchen was in business. The customers saw this and accepted the gesture. Everyone understood that mistakes can happen. What was important was the way in which the customer's expectations were managed. From their reactions it was apparent that the bond of trust had been reestablished and the expectations maintained.

When it came my turn at the counter I asked the clerk if free pizzas were an authorized procedure in dealing with such a problem. The clerk informed me that there was no established procedure for such a situation but that each counter clerk had been instructed to use their best judgment to satisfy the customer. The employee may not have called it empowerment and I doubt there was a formal program in place. But what we all saw was an empowered employee assuming a situational leadership role.

Some Attributes of Empowerment

The example of the pizza employee demonstrates some attributes that are apparent wherever employees have been educated, enabled and empowered.

- They understand the real reason the company is in business and they take the initiative to overcome difficulties and move toward the business goals. The pizza clerk did not try to pass the responsibility to the manager or wait for someone to provide direction. The response was to assume a leadership role.
- They concentrate on solutions. Their profound knowledge and local wisdom combine with an understanding of the overall situation. This combination enables them to see and comprehend the right thing to do. Rather than pointing fingers and trying to identify who dropped the telephone order, the pizza clerk concentrated on solving the problem.
- They cooperate. They not only cooperate with each other and their suppliers but, perhaps more importantly, they cooperate with the customer.
- They tend to work with what they have. The pizza clerk used all the resources available to solve the problem and satisfy the customer. The customer was even offered the use of the business phone to call his home and advise the family of the delay.

Empowerment includes the requirement that those who are empowered must provide an output. With this observation we can use the Empowerment (E_3) and Responsibilities (R_3) elements of the partnership checklist to analyze the concept of empowerment.

The E_3 Management Practice: Empowerment

Empowerment is a concept and an activity. The challenge is to provide sufficient support, both conceptually and in reality, for it to become a useful part of an organization's culture.

The management practices outlined in the E_4-R_4 Partnership Checklist, those which educate, enable, and empower, clearly contribute to the actualization of empowerment as we defined it: The ability to make decisions, take action, and assume responsibility for the outcomes (concrete aspects), based on the authority and desire to do so (conceptual aspects).

Figure 8-1 illustrates the relationship between management practices, employee expectations, and the attainment of true empowerment throughout an organization.

The Education management practice is an action-oriented concrete process. The management organization provides the levels of education discussed in Chapter 5, and the employee partners use this new information, education, and intelligence to perform within their newly defined roles.

With the Education management practice, concrete steps can be taken to achieve results. The end result of this practice is a workforce of partners with knowledge and understanding that gives them the ability to make decisions.

The Enable management practice is also action-oriented. The management organization establishes the processes and provides the coaching and guidance discussed in Chapter 6, and the employees eliminate their fear through an understanding of their rights as partners. The Enable management practice has concrete steps that can be taken to achieve results. The outcome of this practice is a workforce of partners willing to take action.

The Empowerment management practice spans the gap between the conceptual and concrete aspects of empowerment. With the initial groundwork having been achieved through the Education and Enable management practices, the management organization's emphasis is primarily on the conceptual level. Here, through a social event or events full of ceremony and symbolism, the transfer of power and control is formally acknowledged by all.

This event must include certain conditions in order for the transfer of authority to be accepted and perceived as legitimate by the employees:

- The management organization must provide certain indications of sincerity.

Figure 8-1. Empowerment, practices, and expectations.

Empowerment	Practices and Expectations	
	Management Organization	**Employees**
Concrete Aspects		
• Decision-Making Ability	E_1–Educate	R_1–Roles
• Action-Taking Ability	E_2–Enable	R_2–Rights
• Assume Responsibility		R_3–Responsibilities
Conceptual Aspects		
• Transfer Authority	E_3–Empower	
• Desire to Participate		

- They must make their expectations known to all who are involved in the process.
- The employees must understand and accept their responsibilities.

Indications of Sincerity

There is perhaps no issue more fundamental to the success of empowerment than the issue of trust. How does an organization prove its sincerity? Obviously an organization cannot do this. However, management, acting as individuals, can provide specific assurances.

If the employees are lacking confidence in the endeavor, the management must build employee confidence by developing trust in the employees. Individuals have confidence in the things they trust. If employees trust the management they will have confidence in the empowerment process.

Honesty develops trust better than anything else. And one way to cultivate honesty in any organization is through a policy of openness and information sharing. For this reason, it can be quite beneficial to start the Education management practice prior to the Empowerment practice.

Confidence can also be developed by treating each individual with respect. Although many of the conceptual aspects of empowerment are somewhat abstract and can be known only second hand, respect is the result of a direct, face-to-face interaction. One individual treats another with respect and the effect is experienced on a physical level as well as an emotional level. Feeling and knowing that you are respected for yourself provides a sense of security, which supports participation and risk taking.

Many quality management programs have charters that include a statement on respect for the individual. Unfortunately, very few go beyond that to explain how to develop a sincere respect for each individual employee partner in the organization. Surely you can't agree with each individual's philosophy. Surely you can't be expected to accept everyone's idea of what a lifestyle should be. Aren't you entitled to your own opinion? And if so, how can you reconcile your opinions with respect for everyone?

Don't be misled by this thinking. From the standpoint of empowerment in the workplace, these are not the issues. In an organization with specific revenue, profit, expense, and cash objectives, "having a pulse" should be reason enough to receive friendly and sincere treatment. However, it is normally not sufficient to earn respect in the workplace.

Respect, in a business environment, is centered around the organization's values. The values help define what deserves respect in the context of the business endeavor. Any open organization striving for high performance and high involvement will respect and value people. But it will also place strong value on such attributes as effort, risk taking, and results. When each employee is provided with an understanding of the organization's values, they then have the guidelines by which to direct their behavior and performance.

In military organizations, respect is bestowed on the rank. Personal respect is different. Personal respect is not bestowed upon someone. Personal respect is earned. Performance and behavior that conform closely to the values of an organization result in respect being freely given by others who agree with those values.

Along with respect comes recognition. Recognition is one of the few concrete tools available that supports empowerment. In its basic form it is a manifestation of respect. An employee or group of employees perform in accordance with the values of the organization and, as a result, earn and receive respect in the form of recognition. This respect and recognition provide fulfillment to an individual's need for self-esteem.

The Attraction of Empowerment

Have you ever wondered why most people are so attracted to the concept of empowerment? Perhaps it is because, from a participant's standpoint, it is one of the few established processes through which they can earn social rewards. Figure 8-2 a development of Figure 3-6, illustrates how empowerment provides social rewards that fulfill the needs of social acceptance, self-esteem, and self-fulfillment.

Identifying Support Activities and Actions

Once the empowerment process has been initiated (normally this is signified by the social event), the management organization must follow up with the appropriate support activities. What is the appropriate support? The type and amount of support that is provided can be determined by the needs of the organization and the needs of the employees.

The organization's needs should be clearly spelled out in the vision, the mission statement, the business strategy, and the definition of empowerment. The employee's needs can be identified by matching the workplace environment to Figure 8-2.

A straightforward technique for selecting support activities is to identify the types of activities that lead to the desired outcomes of

Figure 8-2. The needs/rewards/empowerment relationships.

Reward Systems
(positive job attitudes)

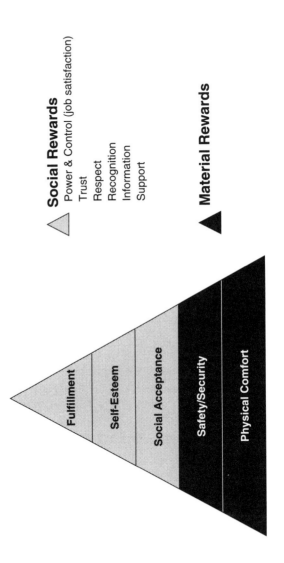

Fulfillment

Self-Esteem

Social Acceptance

Safety/Security

Physical Comfort

Social Rewards
Power & Control (job satisfaction)
Trust
Respect
Recognition
Information
Support

Material Rewards

empowerment as defined by the organization. Start by developing a list of desired outcomes.

Figure 8-3 is a good example of an outcome item list. List the item, then describe how it can be recognized. Your list may be longer or shorter, depending on the outcomes your organization is focused on. Once this list is developed, select an outcome from the list and itemize the actual examples of this that currently exist in the working environment. Then develop a list of ideas of activities or actions that could support this outcome within the organization.

Figure 8-4 is a good format for developing an understanding of what currently exists and what could, should, or would exist in the ideal situation. Performing this exercise in a group, using a brainstorming technique, has proved to be very effective in quickly and clearly identifying the appropriate support activities and actions necessary to foster success.

In most situations the list of ideas will greatly exceed the list of existing examples. This is only natural. However, those examples that do appear on the Existing Examples and Ideas List should be examined carefully. They will either be inappropriate and need to be revised to support the process of empowerment, or they will be the pillars on which to build employee empowerment.

In the example illustrated by Figure 8-4, senior management wants all employees to be more proactive in their daily efforts. This is described as an enhanced action-taking ability on the part of all employees. The organization has initiated a TQM process and everyone has been trained in team dynamics and a problem-solving process. A cross section of employees was invited to perform the Examples and Ideas exercise to identify what else could be done. Generating the ideas list provided visibility to two actions that, if combined, would contribute to the proper outcome: redesign the work process and involve employees in the work.

The consideration is to move from an assembly line process to a work cell process that greatly enhances the action-taking ability of all employees. Intuitively, it makes sense to include the people who are involved in performing the work in the redesign of the work process. However, if the management is sincere about developing an action-taking ability, the real opportunity is to assign responsibility for the redesign to the employees.

According to the cognitive scientists, it is difficult to become knowledgeable in a passive way. We have all experienced the numbing effect of sitting through a training day filled with lectures. On the other hand, using games and group interaction to stimulate thinking about new knowledge can be an exciting and rewarding event. The list of ideas suggests that a job rotation or cross-training system could

(text continues on page 204)

Figure 8-3. Empowerment outcomes list.

Empowerment Outcomes

Item List   **As Defined By:**

1. Action-taking ability: _____
2. Assumption of responsibility: _____
3. Attention to profitability: _____
4. Behavior as a partner: _____
5. Confidence: _____
6. Continuous improvement: _____
7. Decision-making ability: _____
8. Desire to participate: _____
9. Employee commitment: _____
10. Employee involvement: _____
11. Employee performance: _____
12. Exercise of authority: _____
13. Focus on customer satisfaction: _____
14. Focus on quality: _____
15. Information sharing: _____
16. Initiative: _____
17. Ownership of results: _____
18. Recognition for contribution: _____
19. Recognition for effort: _____
20. Respect: _____
21. Responsiveness to change: _____
22. Risk taking: _____
23. Shared feelings and emotions: _____
24. Situational leadership: _____
25. Trust: _____
26. Understanding of the business: _____
27. _____
28. _____
29. _____
30. _____
31. _____
32. _____

Figure 8-4. Existing examples and ideas list.

Existing Examples and Ideas Lists

Empowerment Outcome Item: Action-Taking Ability

(develop a list for each outcome item)

Existing Examples In The Work Environment:

1. Total quality management process
2. _____
3. _____
4. _____
5. _____
6. _____
7. _____
8. _____
9. _____
10. _____
11. _____

Ideas For Developing This Outcome In The Workplace:

1. Initiate a suggestion program driven by training in creative thinking
2. Organize work to involve front-line workers
3. Consider developing a job rotation system
4. Develop problem-solving opportunities: forums, teams, individuals
5. Develop an organization structure that supports empowerment
6. Initiate a cross-training program
7. Initiate an incentive pay plan
8. _____
9. _____
10. _____
11. _____
12.

enhance the knowledge, understanding, and skill levels of the employees, thus providing them with the intellectual abilities to take action.

Another idea was to develop an organizational structure that supports empowerment. An organization that is hierarchical tends to build a bureaucracy and is not conducive to individual initiative taking. Flat organizations, with few levels of management, place authority at the lowest level and support decentralized decision making.

The participants also felt that a focused suggestion program could do wonders for developing multiple empowerment outcomes. A suggestion program is the ancestor of empowerment and, as such, contains the essence of it. It is the original problem-solving forum. The idea is as old as the hills and yet it is still with us. Perhaps for that very reason it should be reexamined.

As a problem-solving forum, suggestion programs ask employees to understand why they are at work. They provide a structure to analyze surroundings and relationships, to develop better ways to reach work objectives, and to implement these changes.

Turning Creative Thinking Into Ideas and Action

Providing employees with a creative thinking workshop, in conjunction with a short-term, team-oriented suggestion program, is an excellent method of initiating empowerment.

By definition, a creative-thinking workshop opens minds to new ways of looking at things. The resulting ideas would "clean up" the work environment. The process shares information, improves communication, and focuses attention on profitability. What could be more empowering than asking employees for their ideas and then letting them act upon these ideas?

Management Expectations

Throughout this book we have seen how a set of expectations can determine the outcome of relationships. Customers whose expectations are met or exceeded tend to remain loyal: those whose expectations have not been met go elsewhere for their goods and services.

The same is true for the employer/employee partnership. Management must clearly communicate their expectations about empowerment to their employee partners. They must define empowerment to the employees in relevant and meaningful terms and they must describe an environment of empowered employee partners. They must share the vision of the company's future in terms that allow the employees to see themselves in this vision. Only when the employees can see how they contribute to the vision will it become meaningful and significant to them as individuals.

Most organizations that are developing an empowered workforce have certain expectations about the level of commitment they expect from each employee. Employees, on the other hand, have a need to know how much energy to contribute to the cause. This information will go a long way toward removing reluctance on the part of the employee population.

Some of the questions to be answered in the process are: What kind of performance expectations does management have? How is this performance defined and what does it look like? Perhaps more importantly, how will the results be measured? Performance measurement will always be a key issue in an organization that is moving to an open, information-sharing style.

A word of caution here. As an organization rushes toward an open, information-sharing environment staffed with employee partners, performance data will gain in significance. As this happens, it is important not to overlook the sharing of feelings and emotional information also. This will keep the organization headed in a people-oriented, humane direction.

Not only that, but research on creative thinking shows that the sharing of feelings and emotions develops an environment of safety, trust, and confidence that is necessary for the stimulation of creativity. In a marketplace that constantly demands new thinking, this concept of sharing feelings and emotional information is not to be overlooked.

Expectations of Participation

Of course, at the heart of the matter is the issue of participation and involvement. Any empowerment effort has involvement and participation as fundamental expectations. What has come to light during the research on this book is that each organization has its own idea of the degree to which the employees are allowed to make decisions and act. This tells us that senior management and human resources professionals must be prepared to define where and how employees can participate.

What kind of partners will they be? Full partners? Limited partners? Silent partners? Naturally they will be expected to participate in revenue generation, productivity improvement, and cost reduction processes. But will they be able to participate in personnel policies? Will they be involved in, say, the hiring process?

I/N Tek is a $1 billion dollar joint venture between Inland Steel and Japan's Nippon Steel. It is located near South Bend, Indiana, and is an advanced steel-finishing mill. Here the employees do the hiring. Job applicants are first tested for basic technical and social skills. Then they are interviewed by personnel, by the prospective manager, and by a worker from the team where they will be placed. Unless all three interviewers concur, the applicant is not offered a job.

Other organizations such as CP Industries, a manufacturer of pressurized gas tanks, in McKeesport, Pennsylvania, and Milliken & Co., one of the world's largest textile companies and recognized leader in research, technology, quality, and customer service, encourage employee participation in the hiring process. But these organizations are by far the exception. Most companies, concerned about the legal aspects of the hiring process, halt empowerment and the participation process at this point. Some are concerned that short-term thinking will prevail and the new hire will be approved just to obtain immediate help.

Certainly an open organization would agree that partners who are held responsible for the organization's bottom line should participate in the decisions that determine who joins the organization. In an open organization, the issue is an Education management practice issue. Partners who are involved in the interviewing and hiring process need to be aware of the legal requirements and be focused on the details of how the new hire would be an asset to the organization. Using this approach, the team assumes responsibility for the quality of its members.

What about the sacred cow of compensation? Partnerships require a different compensation philosophy than a hired-hand style of management. Will employee partners be allowed to participate in the development of the reward philosophy and the design of the pay plans? This topic has such significant impact that it is discussed in great detail in Chapter 9.

How much will employee partners be allowed to control the work process? Will they be encouraged to participate in problem-solving forums? Will they be allowed to schedule and control the work itself, to include process reengineering, scheduling and overtime of labor, production scheduling, and inventory planning?

Quad/Graphics, Inc. is in the business of printing magazines, catalogs, and commercial products. It is a multiplant operation with headquarters in Pewaukee, Wisconsin. It is one of the largest privately held printing companies in the United States, with over 6,500 employees. In an industry with an average annual sales growth rate of 10 percent, it has maintained an annual sales growth rate of 40–50 percent.

The company has developed an extraordinary workforce

through an extraordinary emphasis on the Education management practice. The company offers over one hundred courses to the employees. These include classroom and on-the-job training techniques. The courses emphasize both technical and personal development material and range in length from one day to ten weeks. There are four major categories:

1. Cultural
2. Technical
3. Human resources
4. Process management

The result of all this training is a workforce with the technical knowledge, decision-making skills, big picture overview, business focus, and communication skills that enable them to participate on a full partnership level.

For example, in the printing industry, a first press person is an hourly employee who runs the press and is responsible for the productivity and quality of the printed output. At Quad/Graphics, the first press person "owns" the press and "employs" the press crew. They are salaried partners who track and report daily production against schedule. They are responsible for product quality, customer satisfaction and cost control, among other things. They also have a say in hiring their press crew, scheduling and staffing the work shifts, and the performance management of their crew.

The extensive level of training is matched only by the extensive level of trust bestowed upon each employee. Each employee is trusted to learn his job and to make changes to improve it. As an ESOP company the employees are more than partners, they are owners. This concept is strongly reinforced and the employees are trusted to behave like owners. As a result of this, *Newsweek* magazine named the company Printer Of The Year eight times in a row.

A closer examination of the organization reveals that all this emphasis on education is in support of a more fundamental emphasis. The fundamental emphasis at Quad/Graphics is on employee responsibility.

The R_3 Employee Expectation: Responsibilities

Any management organization has certain expectations concerning the responsibilities of empowered employees. It expects them to think, behave, and perform like partners or owners. Among other things, it expects them to:

- Improve their personal performance.
- Improve their interpersonal relationships.
- Improve their effectiveness in group performance.
- Improve the success of the organization.

But, what factors contribute to employees assuming the responsibilities that define empowerment? From my experience, two factors emerge:

1. A clear understanding of the responsibilities
2. The ability to anchor one's focus

Initially, employees will expect to have their responsibilities clearly defined. Only then can they fulfill their role to assume responsibility. From an employee perspective, awareness and understanding of responsibilities provides a sense of security and stability. Their need for security and stability exists because empowered employees are personally at risk; they are individually accountable for the results of their decisions and actions.

I discussed the issue of responsibility and accountability with a colleague who, being a senior officer in a small business, was pursuing the concept of employee empowerment. After "empowering" the employees, he found a reluctance on their part to assume a decision-making role. Upon closer investigation, the employees revealed they were afraid of the effects that their decisions would have on the company. They were unsure of their responsibilities and expressed a need to understand what was expected of them. Could they really make decisions that would affect issues such as materials scheduling or customer satisfaction? If they did, what would the impact be on cost or net profit?

The second factor that contributes to employees assuming the responsibilities that define empowerment is the autonomy of empowerment itself. Empowered employees have no bosses in the traditional sense. They become their own authority. This presents a most difficult problem. Empowered employees must enforce their own discipline to stay on task always. They must police themselves. This accountability and discipline is not easy for the most seasoned professional. How then can employee partners do this?

The ability to anchor one's focus is the answer. Empowered employees can maintain self-discipline by anchoring their focus on their responsibilities. All issues, all discussions, all decisions, and all actions should lead back to the question, How does this relate to the responsibilities of an empowered employee partner to improve personal performance, face-to-face interactions, group outcomes, and the success of the organization?

I once worked for a company that found it necessary to reorganize a major division of its business. It planned to change the leadership, the reporting relationships, the market focus, and the business plan. It was a complete makeover. This division was driven by market share, and, with the proper products in place, an effective sales force was critical to its success.

Now, anyone who has ever been through a reorganization will tell you that the process tends to take the momentum out of an organization and can even have a negative effect on morale. One of the challenges that fell to me was to keep the momentum and morale of the sales force up during this period of change.

The answer was to keep them focused so intensely on their responsibilities that the changes, over which they had no control anyway, had no impact on their attitude or performance. This was accomplished through a short-term (three-month) high-intensity incentive program. Top quality merchandise and exotic travel vacations were offered for the type of selling performance that would exceed the business plan for this quarter. Videos, travel posters, four-color catalogs, and the issuance of daily lottery type pull-tab devices for performance were used to focus attention on the responsibilities defined in the sales agent role. The promotion was designed to create an atmosphere in which anyone could win anything at anytime, just by staying on task. The result was that the sales force virtually ignored the disruptive influence of the reorganization and, rather than falling behind, the division exceeded the sales quota for the quarter.

Certainly the rewards that were offered had a great deal to do with the success of the effort. However, the key to the program was the heavy promotional and communication campaign. A flood of attention-grabbing printed material placed daily emphasis on the activities needed to be a successful sales representative. The message was, "Carry out these responsibilities and you will be successful." And it worked.

A Technique for Defining and Aligning Responsibilities

The four management practices provide a good source from which to identify the categories, and elements within categories, that define employee partner responsibilities. Most open organizations incorporate the following categories. These are not the only categories, but they form a good basis for defining the elements for which empowered employees will need to assume responsibility.

- Data/information
- Communication

- Decision making/action taking
- Planning/organizing
- Evaluating/controlling
- Leadership
- Recognition/appreciation
- Personal development

Within these categories, it is possible to develop a list of elements your empowered employees will need to assume responsibility for, but if you develop the list, will the employee partners own it? Will your act of developing the list define the limitations of their empowerment? Perhaps a better approach is to have the employees participate in identifying and defining their responsibilities as they see them.

The air of empowerment acknowledges the fact that those who are involved in the decision-making process have a better understanding of the situation and are more committed to participation. This being the case, what process can be used to involve the employees in identifying and defining their responsibilities?

The real issue is not for employees to generate a list. The real issue is to get everyone *thinking* about "how to think about empowerment." To do this it's important to provide them with a technique for arriving at their own conclusion rather than providing them with the answer. This process of individual introspection, followed by group discussion, is a proven technique for establishing a thinking framework.

The process is conducted in the following general format. First, the group facilitator states a management expectation and then asks each employee to define, in her own terms, what responsibilities support the expectation. Figure 8-5 helps accomplish this. Each employee completes the form as indicated. The form is designed so that each employee mentally matches the management expectations to the employee responsibilities. This process presents an open-ended logic path. It encourages introspective thinking because the employee is encouraged to "finish the story."

This technique is oriented to the employee's perspective. It is designed to expand employee thinking about the concept of empowerment. Each employee develops her own definitions and mental images. The employees then discuss these concepts and learn from each other as they develop an understanding of their responsibilities.

Let's use the example, How Can I improve personal performance? One employee, thinking about the element of communication, may conclude she has a responsibility to collect and pass on performance information. Another employee may conclude he has a

Figure 8-5. The responsibility alignment form.

The Responsibility Alignment Form

How Can I Improve Personal Performance

(Insert appropriate management expectation)

- Improve personal performance
- Improve interpersonal interactions
- Improve effectiveness in group performance
- Improve the success of the organization

By Using:

- Data/information _____

  _____

- Communication _____

  _____

- Decision making/action taking _____

  _____

- Planning/organizing _____

  _____

- Evaluating/controlling _____

  _____

- Leadership _____

  _____

- Recognition/appreciation _____

  _____

- Personal development _____

  _____

responsibility to develop social skills that would enable better face-to-face interaction. A third employee may add the responsibility to establish a formal communications vehicle such as a company newsletter or an electronic bulletin board.

Applied to each category, group discussion of this diverse thinking will provide everyone with a better understanding of, and a commitment to assume, the responsibilities of an empowered employee.

It is important to note that this exercise has no preestablished correct answers. The objective of the exercise is to start each employee thinking about his responsibilities as an empowered employee partner. This exercise will initiate a thought process that each individual can repeat on a personal basis, each time he encounters a situation in which he can exercise his empowerment. It is a tool that helps each employee develop a personal experience base which, as it grows, will be the source of improved problem-solving skills and higher quality decisions.

Empowerment and Teamwork

In today's organizations, teamwork has proved to be quite effective and very desirable. Perhaps the ultimate team is the one that is made up of empowered individuals acting together. This concept is often referred to as a self-managed or self-directed work group or, even more advanced, self-managed work groups.

The self-directed work group concept, although not for every organization, is a logical evolution for empowerment. Research indicates that over 50 percent of the Fortune 500 companies have some form of self-directed work groups.[2] These work groups normally consist of multiskilled employees who assume responsibility for an entire process and the operational activities that support it. As compared to traditional teams, self-directed work groups have more resources available to them by virtue of their empowerment. Leadership is shared and team members rotate among job tasks. Often these tasks include upstream and downstream functions such as planning and scheduling work flow, inventory, manpower staffing, customer satisfaction, establishing budgets, and participation in new product development. In addition, if they are a self-managed work group, they may be responsible for handling personnel issues such as scheduling vacations, performance reviews, member selection, and pay decisions.

Empowerment and Performance Management

Empowered employees, especially self-managed work groups, perform entirely different roles and functions than do traditional employees. Therefore, it stands to reason that in this environment the process by which performance is evaluated will need to be adjusted to reflect these differences.

A performance management system is a path of communication that defines performance expectations and then compares actual performance against these expectations. Intended or not, in most companies, this path is parallel to the other formal channels of communication. To support the organization the values and expectations defined by the performance management system must match and support all other messages about values and performance that the organization communicates.

First and foremost, the performance management system criteria must support and reinforce the leadership's vision, mission, and performance expectations. In an environment based on the four management practices this is relatively straightforward because the practices that educate, enable, and empower employees clearly define performance expectations.

Occasionally there will be a disconnect between these messages. An example is the organization that asks its employees to become empowered team members and then evaluates them on individual performance. Sounds silly, but it happens. When performance evaluations are linked to compensation, such as where annual increases are determined by the evaluation rating, the evaluation system will overpower all other messages. If pay is tied to individual performance ratings the criteria will become dominant in determining individual behavior. Remember, "What gets rewarded gets repeated."

A New View of Performance Management

Organizations that develop an open, partner-oriented, high-performance work culture tend to view performance evaluation as an opportunity for recognition, development, and performance improvement. As such, they change from a once-a-year event to an ongoing process of feedback and development.

The key to achieving effective feedback and development is the ability of each individual to communicate clearly and openly, using a common performance language through a common education.

Because companies that implement the E_4-R_4 Partnership Checklist share information in an open environment, all employees can be involved in the development of mutually agreed upon performance objectives. These organizations tend to value behavioral skills in addition to technical skills. They include these elements in their evaluation systems. Baseline criteria that support the business objectives is developed for both categories. These goals tend to stratify on four levels:

1. Company goals
2. Team goals
3. Individual performance goals
4. Career/development goals

An addition to this list might be to include personal goals as an informal fifth tier. Associating success of the business with achievement of personal goals can be a very strong reinforcement to the partner relationship.

Performance feedback in the form of results is measured by the employee and compared against the baseline criteria. These performance results are shared openly and discussed in a timely manner with the supervisor/coach. Action planning is jointly developed to correct for any off-plan results. It is a whole different method of managing the work process.

Empowerment and
High Quality Performance Evaluation

The American Production and Inventory Control Society (APICS) estimates the costs associated with inferior quality are between 20 to 25 percent of the cost of goods sold. This cost estimate does not include the associated costs of order processing errors, wrong shipments, delays or partial shipments, invoicing errors, and poor product documentation.

Empowered employees are responsible for quality. In an organization based on the four management practices, they are educated to look for every opportunity for incremental improvement and have the responsibility to stop production rather than produce a bad product. They understand the needs of the customers and have the right and responsibility to revise procedures rather than provide poor customer service. They are educated and able to improve the accuracy of the organization's data.

But what is the cost of poor quality in leadership or peer performance on teamwork, morale, employee commitment, and communication? Does it follow that they have the responsibility to help improve the quality of the performance of their peers and leaders by evaluating their performance? Several forward thinking organizations are investigating different ways of involving employees in the performance evaluation process. GTE Directories is one of those companies.

GTE Directories, located in Dallas, Texas, is a Malcolm Baldrige Quality Award winner. They have self-directed work teams in several areas and are moving toward a self-managed team concept where teams have responsibility for coaching, counseling, hiring, firing, and pay. In several situations the company has 270-degree evaluations, where performance input is received from the customer, peers, and key constituents.

When David Rawles was vice-president of human resources he championed the development of self-directed and self-managed work groups. He is now vice-president of manufacturing with at least 25 percent of the 550 manufacturing employees in the process of transitioning to chartered self-managed work teams. A coordinating council guides the direction of these teams. The committee provides aid in policy-related issues. According to Rawles, "We don't want to rewrite the company policies just for the teams, but we will allow procedures to be customized, within reason, by the teams. There are specific laws and GTE policies that must be followed pertaining to performance appraisals. We want to provide latitude to the process but there also needs to be some structure." In the case of GTE, the latitude allows self-directed teams to provide recommendations of how to administer performance appraisals. Although not exactly team-based appraisals, the ability of employees to be involved in the design process is a significant departure from the traditional approach and results in a process that is more meaningful and constructive to the organization and the individual.

The 360-Degree Evaluation

The 360-degree performance evaluation technique is one approach to providing empowered employees with a tool to improve the quality of leadership and peer performance in their group. It is a relatively straightforward technique. The employee, in this example the supervisor, is evaluated by her manager, a selection of her peers, and a selection of the employees whom she supports in her role as facilitator/mentor. Many organizations that utilize the 360-degree appraisal also include their internal or external customer. After all, if the customer isn't satisfied not much else matters.

Each employee level (subordinate, peer, and supervisor, in traditional terminology) performs an evaluation using criteria that are important to goal attainment on that level. For example, a selection of employees who are supported by a supervisor/facilitator/mentor would evaluate this employee based on criteria that support their empowerment. Often this evaluation is on a sliding scale.

The objective is to provide qualitative feedback that will enable the individual to receive positive reinforcement in areas of high quality performance, and to take very targeted action in areas where she needs to enhance her effectiveness.

Figure 8-6 provides a good idea of the style of evaluation and the type of questions that are part of the 360-degree evaluation process. Each performance category has several questions that define the meaning of that category to that level. The questions present a sliding scale that can be graphed to present a performance management profile.

Each level has its own unique perspective and its own cumulative score. Thus the employee being evaluated receives a clear understanding of the behaviors and skills necessary to be a completely effective partner in an open, business-focused environment. The criteria will vary from level to level and from company to company, but the concept remains the same.

Performance Management Is Work Management

Looking at performance management from this perspective changes the nature of how work is managed. Management of the work process becomes a continuous cycle. The interaction takes place on an informal basis every time employee partners get together. An informal 360-degree performance evaluation occurs as they work together to define objectives, establish goals, monitor progress, evaluate results, and formulate action for improvement. Often the employee is responsible for making the needed changes, sometimes the subordinate, peer, or supervisor is responsible to resolve issues outside the realm of influence of the employee. Either way, the focus is always on the overall results of the organization and how the individual performance contributes to them.

How will the person whose performance is being evaluated feel about the process? Initially this approach could be perceived as threatening. In fact, a great deal of participative design work is necessary for this approach to be successful. However, in an organization

Figure 8-6. The upward evaluation example.

Category: Communication

Questions:
1. When communicating with employee partners, my facilitator/coach normally

   1   2   3   4   5   6

Provides minimal   Allows access to the
information   information source

Category: Planning/Organizing

Questions:
1. When planning a project, my facilitator/coach

   1   2   3   4   5   6

Allows minimal   Turns the process
participation   over to the team

Note: Normally there will be from three to five questions under each category.

committed to an open, educated, partner-oriented work culture the results are well worth the effort. A process that looks at performance from multiple perspectives improves the accuracy of the performance evaluation data and provides a better understanding of where improvements can be made.

Moving away from traditional performance evaluation sounds like a lot of work. Is it worth it? Anyone who is involved in the process of enabling and empowering employees will tell you that it is neither quick nor easy. It's a bit like turning the Queen Mary. For that reason, it is important to take advantage of every opportunity to involve employees in the development of tools that support the process. The development and implementation of tools such as the 360-degree performance evaluation is one of those opportunities that should be seriously considered.

The Ripple Effect

Empowerment has a profound ripple effect on every aspect of an organization's culture. The American Express Travel Related Services Company provides us with a good example of how performance management issues ripple into the issue of job description. Randy Simon is a vice-president at American Express Travel Related Services, an organization that is going through a cultural change process focused on enhancing customer satisfaction, employee satisfaction, and shareholder value. While she was associated with the compensation group, it addressed the issue of job definition and performance management. One of the actions it initiated is a pilot program that focuses on competencies. During a personal interview, Ms. Simon told me:

> We decided to look at positions from the perspective of roles rather than jobs. We wanted to reward the proper skills, competencies, and thinking. Focusing on roles rather than job descriptions provides greater flexibility for the individual and for the organization. People can move much more easily from one project to another and from one area to another. This helps the organization to place resources where they are needed and enables employees to develop different skill sets. In this way we are not constantly reevaluating the job.

The pilot program looks at the various aspects of each role. Then the skills and competencies needed to fill those roles are defined.

Going forward, future plans are for employees to participate in developing their own personal capabilities profile. This includes cataloging their skills and areas of proficiency and knowledge. Every employee will conduct a self-assessment using analysis instruments designed specifically for this purpose.

Once an employee's profile has been established, they will be able to pull up the role specifications, compare them to their profile, and create a personal development plan to close any gaps that may exist. American Express appears to have developed a technique that links personal development goals to overall performance goals.

Empowerment and Future Staffing

In response to the urgency of developing a sustainable competitive edge, many organizations are downsizing. They are not only divesting themselves of various business units, but they are also reducing the staffing levels in the business units they retain.

In the future, this perspective on labor availability may change. As the baby boom generation nears retirement, demand for goods and services will continue to increase but the U.S. Department of Labor projects the pool of qualified labor will decrease. So it stands to reason that competition for the labor pool will increase. As qualified talent becomes scarce, compensation prices for this talent will increase. Looking to the future, the decision to "make-or-buy" is quite clear. Either spend the time and energy now to make your qualified employees and facilitator/mentors of tomorrow, or spend the excessive cost it will take to buy them in the future.

Companies with a management philosophy similar to that represented by the E_4-R_4 Partnership Checklist will not be caught in the qualified labor shortage squeeze. They will have developed their labor pool into a partnership of highly desirable, highly qualified workers. Rather than seeking employees they will be a potential source of employees. Their employees will be desired by other organizations that are experiencing a shortage of qualified employees. They will offer them material enticements to join their organization and some will depart, as they should.

However, intuitive and anecdotal data indicate that employee partners will stay with an organization if they are involved in the success of the business, if they have a clear line-of-sight, if they participate in a quality of work-life that cannot be duplicated, and if they share as partners in the success of the organization.

Notes

1. Shirley A. Richard, "Empowering Employees: A Case Study on Improving Customer Service," *Compensation and Benefits Management*, Vol. 7, No. 4. Fall 1991, pp. 47–50.
2. Loren Ankarlo, *Implementing Self-Directed Work Teams*, Boulder, Colo.: Career Track Publications, 1993.

9

E_4-Engage:
The Management Practice
R_4-Rewards:
The Employee Expectation

"The key to growth is quite simple . . . it is creative people
with money."

—George Guilder

In this chapter and in Chapter 10 we demonstrate how the last element of this checklist utilizes reward systems to engage the employee's desire to participate. We examine how reward systems work to
hold the entire change management process together and propel it
forward. In doing so, we will develop a perspective of the E_4-R_4 Partnership Checklist as a system that provides complete satisfaction to
workplace needs and expectations.

Management's Challenge:
Securing Active Participation

The Partnership Checklist represents a change management architecture that transforms employees from hired hands into partners. If the
managers and human resources professionals are pursuing a linear
implementation of these practices they will already have shared information and educated all employees. They will have designed and
initiated processes that enable employees to participate and become

involved. And they will have conducted the appropriate social events to empower everyone.

The final element in the process is to secure the active (rather than passive) attention and efforts of the employee population. The challenge to managers and human resources professionals is to create an incentive for employees to pursue the interests of the organization and the team.

Employees will be concerned about the risk/reward relationship. During the process of partnering, employees have been asked to assume new roles, accept new rights, shoulder new responsibilities, and take new risks, all with a focus on improving the operating margin and the long-term competitive position of the company. Their question will be, Now that I have agreed to accept the risk of changing from an employee to a partner, what will my rewards be? Remember, this is a major shift in how employees view their relationship with the organization. They need substantial encouragement and support to go from one state of mind to another. The most obvious approach to providing this encouragement involves linking the fulfillment of employee social and material needs to the achievement of the team and organization's objectives.[1]

In order to engage them in the process and realize these gains, it is necessary to treat them as partners in all ways. They need to share in the information that partners receive. They need to share in the goal setting and decision making that partners participate in. And they need to share in the rewards of their efforts. Figure 9-1 illustrates how the reward systems complete the relationship.

Why the Four Management Practices Work

In the context of the Partnership Checklist, rewards can be defined as "that which provides satisfaction." On a personal level, rewards indicate effectiveness. They tell us how well our efforts produce the results we are striving for, the satisfaction we seek. If we do not receive social and material satisfaction to the degree that we are anticipating, it indicates that our performance is not as effective as it needs to be.

From a management perspective social and material reward systems are a source of employee motivation. From an employee's perspective, social and material reward systems are a source of satisfaction. Figure 9-2 depicts the fundamental reasons why a combination of the four management practices is so successful in connecting employees with the organization. These management practices act as a system of rewards that provides a high degree of interlinked social

Figure 9-1. Empowerment, practices, and expectations completed.

Empowerment	Practices and Expectations	
	Management Organization	**Employees**
Concrete Aspects		
• Decision-Making Ability	E$_1$–Educate	R$_1$–Roles
• Action-Taking Ability	E$_2$–Enable	R$_2$–Rights
• Assume Responsibility		R$_3$–Responsibilities
Conceptual Aspects		
• Transfer Authority	E$_3$–Empower	
• Desire to Participate	**E$_4$–Engage**	**R$_4$–Rewards**

Figure 9-2. Why reward systems work.

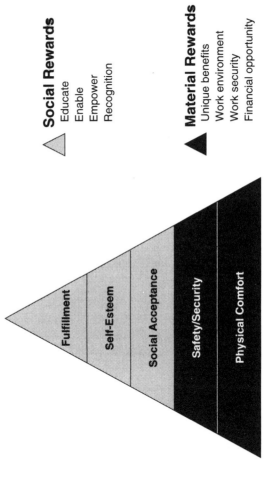

Reward Systems
(positive job attitudes)

Fulfillment

Self-Esteem

Social Acceptance

Safety/Security

Physical Comfort

△ **Social Rewards**
Educate
Enable
Empower
Recognition

▲ **Material Rewards**
Unique benefits
Work environment
Work security
Financial opportunity

and material satisfaction to everyone. The first three elements of the Partnership Checklist offer social rewards that are a source of emotional or intrinsic satisfaction.

In this system, employees receive feedback on how their personal performance affects the company's profitability and cash flow. This feedback of performance information provides social rewards in the form of positive reinforcement and reinforces their right as partners to receive performance information.

For example, what is the satisfaction to the accounting staff for training the rest of the company in the fundamentals of how financial performance is tracked and reported? In an open workplace that values education this becomes an opportunity to gain respect from their partners, to gain exposure to the rest of the organization, and to provide visibility and recognition for the type of work the "bean counters" are involved in.

In addition, it can be fun for them. Almost everyone enjoys sharing insights into their area of expertise. Aside from these social satisfiers, they receive tangible benefits in the form of faster reporting and improved data accuracy from those who are the source of the data, once they understand its value and use.

Social rewards contribute to a feeling of job satisfaction and create positive job attitudes. The ability to see the outcomes of efforts and to make adjustments as needed is rewarding because it provides a sense of control and stability in a changing world.

When material rewards are linked to operational indicators or financial results, the connection of the individual to the company is complete. In this situation, employees receive feedback on how their personal performance affects their material wealth. They see a clear link between their standard of living and the company's profitability and cash flow. The company's well-being becomes their well-being and they connect with the same connection that all partners have, through a sense of shared destiny.

Figure 9-3 illustrates some systems that more progressive companies have established to provide motivation and satisfaction.

Who Cares About the Company?

One challenge in developing the partnership is to get employees to care about the company on both an intellectual and an emotional level. How can you get employees to care about the company? The answer is straightforward: First, they have to know the company cares about them.

Competition requires technological and social change. Manage-

Figure 9-3. Reward systems and sample elements.

Social
- Skill development
- Job redesign
- Involvement processes
- Quality management
- Continuous improvement
- Education
- Empowerment
- Information sharing
- Performance feedback

Material
- Equity ownership
- Base compensation
- Incentive pay
- Benefits

Combination
- Skill-based pay
- Competency-based pay
- Suggestion systems

ment's expectation is that employees will accept and embrace this change. The employees, on the other hand, have a concern for their social and financial well-being as it relates to change in the workplace. This is both an intellectual and emotional concern. If they embrace change will it destroy them? They have seen the negative effects of change in the past and are wary of the outcomes. The answer is to acknowledge these concerns and offer satisfaction as part of the social contract of employment.

In an open, high-involvement culture, the social and physical working environment becomes significantly more positive. Each of the four management practices address an aspect of employee well-being. Demonstrating concern for the employee's well-being generates a reciprocal concern on the part of each employee for the well-being of the company.

The Partnership Checklist represents, in a sense, a self-generating satisfaction system. The process generates the means to provide satisfaction and promote a sense of partnership. As partners, employees care about each other and care about the organization in which they work.

How the Four Management Practices Provide Satisfaction

Figure 9-4 illustrates the primary relationships between the four management practices and three basic categories of needs that each individual strives to satisfy: intellectual, emotional, and physical. As the model indicates, the Educate management practice provides satisfaction primarily on an intellectual level as people learn how to assume their role as partners. The Enable management practice provides satisfaction primarily on the emotional and physical levels as people assume their rights as partners and begin to interact together and take action.

The Empower management practice provides satisfaction primarily on the intellectual and emotional levels as people assume their responsibilities as partners and begin to think and feel they have control in their environment. Uniquely, the Engage management practice provides satisfaction to all three levels of need as employee partners receive intellectual, emotional, and physical rewards.

The fact that the Engage practice has a significant impact on all three levels is not to say that one practice is more important than another. The Partnership Checklist represents a holistic design in which all elements have equal importance. For example, how would you like to be responsible for cost reduction or productivity improvement without understanding what it is based on? How would you like to have the accountability of a partner without receiving any of the material rewards?

Figure 9-4 illustrates how the lack of even one element—Educate, Enable, Empower, or Engage—dramatically decreases the degree of overall satisfaction provided by the system.

This Is My Money

P. T. Barnum said, "Money is a terrible master, but an excellent servant." Although the first three management practices provide substantial intrinsic and social rewards, logic and experience tell us that the only real way to completely transform employees into partners is to enable them to view the company's money as if it were their own. For that reason, the Engage management practice places an emphasis on the material aspect of rewards.

Figure 9-4. The satisfaction system.

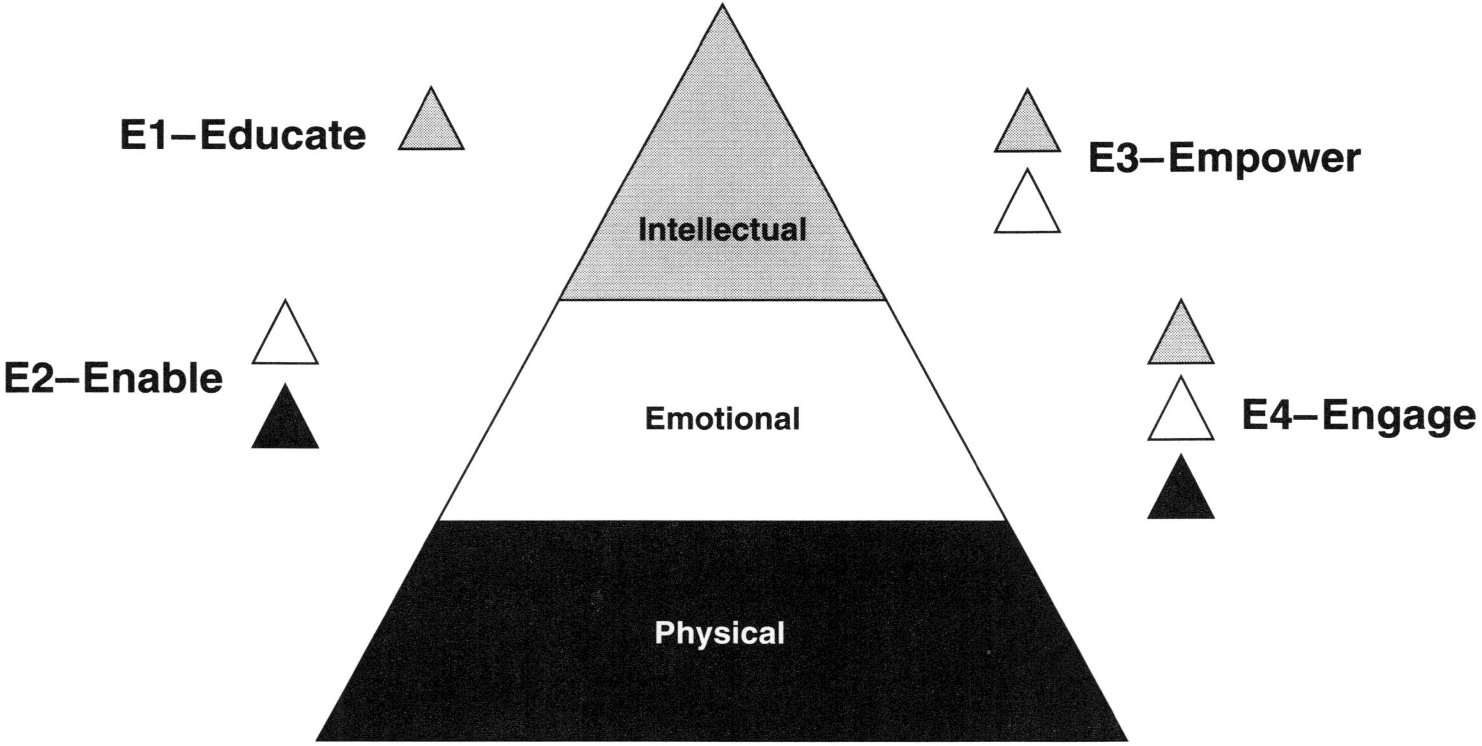

Not so long ago it was difficult to find information on incentive pay. Now the media is full of stories about organizations that are considering it if not actively applying it. Pay is an excellent communications tool because of the attention placed on it by all employees. As such, it is being used as a tool for organization development. It is being used to align the work culture with the business strategy.

Each year the American Compensation Association (ACA) conducts a salary budget survey of U.S. and Canadian firms. The data for the 1994–95 survey was provided by a broad cross section of industries comprised of 3,307 U.S. firms and 332 Canadian firms. Figure 9-5 illustrates the results of this survey and provides a good picture of the trend toward the use of variable pay.

The Economic Research Institute notes in its January 1995 newsletter that compensation consultants report the most business ever in this area. "Billed more in the first six months of 1994 than in all of 1993—and are billing more hours in the last six months than the first . . . Benefit planning, except for cost control, is on hold. Compensation is getting the attention."[2] The trend is obviously toward using pay as a tool to develop a partnership with all employees.

However, a few argue against the use of material reward as a technique for building partnerships. They suggest instead that employees be "paid fairly." Certainly everyone agrees that employees should be paid fairly. But in today's economy the old fixed-wage thinking does nothing to develop a partnership with the employees.

Survival and success in today's economy require that employees be treated as business partners. As partners they should share the risk of business downturns and share the rewards of business growth. A "fair" fixed wage could be an excessive expense during an extended economic downturn. It could cause the company to reduce the work force or, even worse, go out of business. Where is the fairness in that?

On the other hand, if a portion of the labor cost is variable and linked to the performance of the company, then individual discretionary spending can flex in partnership with the fortunes of the company. Not being able to purchase the new computer for the home or upgrade the family car this year is much preferable to standing in the unemployment line.

These few contrarians also suggest, once this "fair wage" has been established, to do everything possible to get the employees to forget about pay. That may be an effective approach for cultures with a more esoteric philosophy on life, but the Western world lives in a consumer-oriented society.

Our economy is driven by the ongoing introduction of new products and services. As a result, we are constantly forced to reeval-

Figure 9-5. Variable pay.

This is a new column added to the Salary Budget Survey this year. Variable Pay is defined as the amount established by management as a percentage of payroll to be granted as variable pay during the year. Included in this calculation are individual incentive awards, special individual recognition awards, group/team awards, organization-wide awards, and scheduled lump-sum awards. Excluded are any awards intended only for management/executive level employees.

VARIABLE PAY ACTUAL 1994	NATIONAL		EASTERN		CENTRAL		SOUTHERN		WESTERN		CANADIAN	
	No.Cos.	%	No.Cos.	%	No.Cos.	%	No.Cos.	%	No.Cos.	%	No.Cos.	%
Non-exempt	383	3.2	108	2.8	94	3.8	68	3.5	113	3.0	52	3.2
Exempt	429	4.3	118	4.0	113	4.7	73	4.4	125	4.1	63	5.8
Officers/Executives	350	10.1	98	9.7	94	9.5	60	10.5	98	10.7	54	10.4

VARIABLE PAY PROJECTED 1995	NATIONAL		EASTERN		CENTRAL		SOUTHERN		WESTERN		CANADIAN	
	No.Cos.	%	No.Cos.	%	No.Cos.	%	No.Cos.	%	No.Cos.	%	No.Cos.	%
Non-exempt	353	3.4	97	3.0	100	3.7	57	3.8	101	3.2	38	2.8
Exempt	393	4.4	104	4.1	113	4.8	65	4.6	111	4.3	48	5.3
Officers/Executives	320	9.7	82	9.2	89	9.1	61	11.2	88	9.9	40	10.4

uate how we spend our limited income. This brings to mind the fact that it is limited. How many people do you know who do not have some form of personal budget? The importance of pay to our lifestyle makes it almost impossible to forget.

Information sharing and understanding is an integral part of building an employee partnership. If employees are educated in business finance and use this knowledge to improve the company's profitability, they will naturally seek to share in the fruits of their efforts.

How strong can a partnership be if we focus employee attention on the bottom line and then do not share the financial growth that is created as a result of this new awareness. How long will employees participate? If pay is not included in the partnering process, the process will not work.

It has been suggested that incentives demean the individual, that they place the power of favoritism in the hands of a few or that they aren't fair, or don't work. These are problems caused by plan design and may have been true during the rapid (and still growing) experimental stage of variable compensation plan design. Yes, piecework does tend to emphasize individual effort over teamwork. Poorly defined performance criteria or discretionary incentives do tend to provide supervisors with the challenge of fairness. Poor plan design can focus employees on the wrong objectives. However, these are not the issues or elements of incentive plans that are designed to reward all employee partners for growing the company. If a company wishes to see cooperative, team-based activities, the rewards (and the process of setting them) must reflect this. If a company wishes to reduce the distinctions between "line" and "management," then reward systems must reflect this.

In addition to the fact that it will raise your standard of living, pay is an excellent communications tool because of the attention placed on it by all. Rather than try to forget it, the more progressive organizations are using it as a tool for organization development, to align the work culture with the business strategy.

You Get What You Pay For

In Western business you tend to get what you pay for. If you provide social payment, in the form of training, recognition, and a comfortable workplace, you get a social focus in the form of satisfied, happy workers. But you don't necessarily get an aggressive, competitive, organization. If you provide financial payment in the form of incentive compensation linked to the company's economic performance, you get a financial focus in the form of productive, cost efficient employees. Obviously, the answer is to properly use the appropriate mix of both social and financial rewards.

Perhaps a more pertinent discussion is one about the changing responsibilities of the compensation professional. It appears that this role has expanded to include the design and development of satisfaction systems—systems that link the fulfillment of employee social and material needs to the achievement of team and organizational objectives.

Belief System vs. Tangible Assets

If compensation is not linked to the cultural change process and performance results, then the organization is driven solely by a belief system. This creates the difficulty of engaging everyone in the same belief system and leads to disagreement about what is the right belief system. Figure 9-6 illustrates these relationships. At one extreme is the concept of piecework incentive. At the other extreme is the concept of "transparent compensation" where the system is based on a belief system. In the middle are the four management practices. By providing a full array of social and material rewards they have a greater universal appeal and engage more of the population in the partnership process.

Fairness and Partnership

Properly designed, material reward systems help build deep, solid business partnerships among all stakeholders and customers. For that reason it is important to understand the driving forces behind an effective design. Behavioral psychologists will tell you that any reward (social or material) needs to be viewed by the recipient as:

- Positive
- Immediate
- Certain

In other words, the offering must be attractive, desirable, and satisfy a need. The reward will be most effective if provided as rapidly as possible after the performance, and there should be no other conditions attached to the reward other than successful completion of the performance. These are the clinical elements that should be considered in the design of any effective reward system.

In addition, from a business standpoint and in the context of developing an employee partnership, material reward systems should also be:

Figure 9-6. Greater universal appeal.

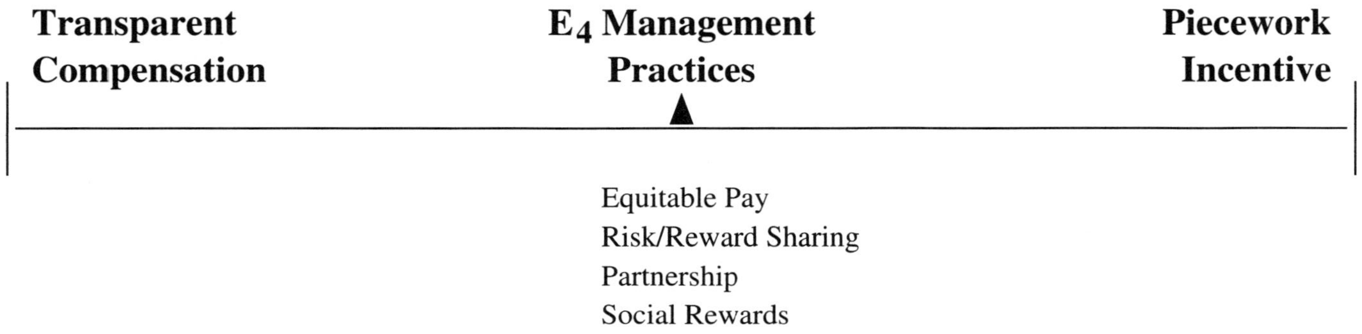

Transparent Compensation	E₄ Management Practices	Piecework Incentive
	Equitable Pay	
	Risk/Reward Sharing	
	Partnership	
	Social Rewards	

- Fast
- Flexible
- Fair

The whole purpose of a material reward system is to develop a partnership that supports the business objectives. They should be fast, not only in the immediate delivery of the reward but also in their ability to respond quickly to changing business conditions.

In today's economy a company's key performance factors can change rapidly. Success will be determined by the employees' ability to respond to these changes. Reward systems should be flexible enough in their design and positioning so they can reward the changes in behavior and performance that occur as employee partners change their focus. For example, if a company chooses to enter a new marketplace, the need may be to focus on obtaining market share. In this case, activities that achieve growth will be valued over other activities. Once market share is achieved, the need may be to rapidly refocus performance toward profitability. The emphasis will shift from activities that achieve growth to activities that increase margins and reduce costs. Reward systems should be flexible enough to support these changes.

Reward systems must be fair. Obviously the participants must be able to affect the performance criteria. But in addition, the reward system must be designed to focus employee attention on how to make the pie bigger rather than how to split up the pie. This is the subtle difference between a material reward system for partners and a material reward system for employees. In a traditional company, management makes the decisions that determine the profitability of the company. In this situation, competition is for a share of those results. In an open, partner-oriented work environment, employees have a significant ability to make decisions and affect results. In this situation, competition is focused outward, toward making "our" pie bigger.

By their very nature, material reward systems are thought of as serious, controlled, and meticulously planned in great detail. This certainly is true for plans linked to base pay. However, this seriousness can cause us to lose perspective of the partner/reward relationship. The following example provides a good example of a material reward system that is fast, flexible, fair, and contains a high degree of social rewards also.

Kirk Malcki, president of Pegasus Personal Fitness Centers in Dallas, Texas, employs fifteen physical fitness trainers. Each trainer has weekly and monthly performance goals they are focused on. Malcki asks the trainers to make their own list of rewards they would like to receive for achieving these goals. The rewards range in value from $25 to $200. The result of this process is a list of personalized rewards that range from time off to rock concert tickets. Each individual has been acknowledged and involved in defining the needs they want satisfied.

Short- and Long-Term Rewards

A reward system for partners is based on the organization's success. This success should be considered on both a short-term and long-term basis. Systems that reward short-term success tend to focus on current activities, such as performance to plan, productivity, cost reduction, and profitability. These systems tend to provide material reward, in the form of cash, on a monthly, quarterly, or annual basis. The payment made is linked to the improvement received during the measurement period.

However, employee partners perform activities and make contributions that have long-term impact on the success of the organization also. Examples of these activities are the identification of new customer needs, product development, service design, new market penetration, and the development of strategic skills and talent.

Systems that reward and encourage these types of contributions are more long term. They tend to be equity-based rewards that reflect the benefit to the company that accrues from these strategic decisions and actions. Examples of equity-based rewards are stock bonuses, stock options, simulated equity such as phantom stock or stock appreciation rights, or employee stock ownership, where employees gradually purchase stock in the company with the results of their efforts.

These long-term equity-based rewards are already an accepted method of compensating senior management. It stands to reason that if an organization is going to ask its employees to make an intellectual and physical contribution as partners it should provide a share in both the short- and long-term benefits that result from that contribution. Only when a satisfaction system includes both short- and long-term reward elements will it be perceived as fair by the employees. And only then will they perceive themselves as partners.

How to Create Involvement, Motivation, Satisfaction, and Commitment

Most pay systems consist of material rewards that are designed to attract, retain, and motivate employees. They are extrinsic satisfiers that guide performance and reinforce the business results that generate economic value. A review of twenty-seven studies on profit sharing and productivity showed that profit sharing was positively related to productivity. Perhaps more significantly, the profit sharing effects did not appear to be dependent on the simultaneous use of other practices.[3]

It appears as if variable pay plans generate motivation that results in a commitment to business objectives. However, a recent study of 663 companies that utilize variable pay indicates that they may do little to attract and retain employees.[4]

An environment based on the Partnership Checklist criteria not only offers material rewards, it also develops a culture that offers social satisfiers that retain employees. Education in business finance, information sharing, and processes that support goal setting, problem solving, and decision making offer involvement, motivation, and personal satisfaction to employees. These intrinsic satisfiers guide work behavior and reinforce the employee interactions that make up an effective organization.

Worried about attracting qualified employees in a competitive labor environment? An open, partner-oriented culture is a strong competitive attraction for new employees interested in establishing a business partnership.

Rewards Demonstrate That Financial Knowledge Is Valuable— or the Price Is Right

Reward systems are no longer just pay delivery systems. They are manifestations of the company culture. They reinforce and define it.

The Clay and Bailey Manufacturing Company is a Kansas City, Missouri–based manufacturer of vents and valves associated with liquid or powder containment. It is also a foundry that produces gray iron castings for the construction industry. The company has been in business since 1913. It employs 110 people, most of whom belong to the United Steel Workers union. Ron Borst is the president and CEO of Clay and Bailey and talks to us about how he is developing employee interest in company profitability. "Competition is stiff in our businesses and we are constantly looking for ways to reduce our costs. In the past, there was a confrontational relationship between management and organized labor. About two and one half years ago we started to develop a more cooperative environment together."

Union representatives were included in the planning and decision-making process as everyone worked together to change the culture. An example of this partnering is their TQM effort, which is called TQ-We.

"The union thought it would send a better message if we replaced the word 'management' with the word 'we.'" Explains Borst "After 35 years of adversarial relations, something like this provides good visibility to our cultural change effort."

Continuous improvement teams (CIT) were formed. Each week, teams of employees meet on company time for 45 minutes to discuss quality, safety, and cost issues. To lead the process a CIT steering committee was formed. The committee consists of all foremen, managers, and four union officials.

Of the organization, 98 percent participates on the CIT teams and all team members have gone through ten 2-hour training sessions. These sessions familiarized everyone with the concepts of TQM, statistical process control, teamwork, and leadership.

Borst wants all employees to become more involved in the costs of doing business and to share in the dollars that are saved. He started with safety, initiating a bonus program that focused on injury reduction. From there he implemented "Attendance Bingo" where teams and individuals earn cash awards based on improved attendance. Borst says, "We identified the value to the company of a reduction in absenteeism. Then we developed a process to share those savings with the employees."

All this was in preparation for moving toward an open-book environment. "Our employees can have a significant impact on costs and profitability. It is important for them to make this connection between their daily activities and the profitability of the company." Borst tells us. "The challenge is to get the point across subtly, without preaching. You won't get them all, but those with whom you do connect can make a difference and lead the way."

As part of the connection process Borst created his own version of "The Price Is Right." Each month, he displays three workplace items in the CIT meeting room. Information accompanies the items and explains what they are and how they are used. Employees are asked to guess the price of each item.

The items remain on display for one week while employees submit their estimates and, in some cases, research the cost. The individuals and the teams who come within ten percent of the total cost of the three items receive a cash bonus from Borst. At the end of the week the costs are displayed next to the items along with the names of the winners.

Borst says,

> This money comes right out of my pocket. It is my personal cash and I am glad to pay it. I see the costs of goods and operating expenses. Each month I pick three items I know they can have an impact on. For example, we use corrosion-proof bolts in the manufacture of our vents and valves. They

look just like ordinary bolts but they each cost $8.60. One day while I was walking through the facility I saw several lying on the floor, so I included a bolt as one of the items for that month.

Borst continues,

We spend thousands of dollars each month on gas for the foundry furnaces. Last winter I gave them the average cost for a summer month and asked them to estimate what the gas bill for February was. I wanted to make the point of how expensive it was to heat the facility. The nearest guess was off by 60 percent!

About the purpose of the program Borst says,

This program is an opportunity to get a message across. It is educational to them and it is educational to us because it shows us how little they know about the profit and cost elements of the business. If they can measure the events around them in dollars, they will have a much better understanding. For example, when they see a casting on the floor, I want them to see it as a $5 bill laying there.

We have quarterly team leader meetings where the team leaders present the team's favorite improvement project to the steering committee. I report on the financials during these meetings. I talk about revenue, cost, efficiencies, and inventory control, and I can see a lot of blank stares about the room. We are moving toward a self-directed work team concept. In order to successfully achieve this it is necessary for everyone to understand these concepts.

I want people to understand how they can impact the financial health of the company. In doing so, they can provide a competitive edge that will help us continue to grow.

The next logical step is to develop customized training for all members of the CIT steering committee on how to read an income statement and balance sheet. After a beta test with the steering committee, the training would be used to develop a line-of-sight capability for the rest of the organization.

Material Reward System Categories

Material reward systems come in four basic categories: benefits, recognition, base pay, and incentive (variable) pay. Every category consists of a variety of structures, each with their own strengths and weaknesses. In order to implement an effective Engage management practice it is necessary to understand the differences and choose a category that matches the company's need for organizational effectiveness and economic value. We will provide a brief overview of benefits, recognition, and base pay, and focus the majority of our attention on incentive pay.

Benefits

Long overlooked by employees, benefits are changing in response to changing employee needs. Many organizations now offer a menu of benefits from which to choose. In this way, each employee can design a benefits package that satisfies his or her unique needs.

In addition to traditional financial-based satisfiers such as retirement, savings, and health-related benefits, companies are now offering benefits that satisfy time-based needs such as child care, elder care, and flextime, and personal-based needs such as continuing education and fitness spas.

Recognition

Recognition systems support an organization's needs to communicate values and develop a companywide sense of unity. To achieve this, they tend to focus on providing social satisfaction. Recognition is normally a social event during which the values of an organization are communicated and the recipient is established as a role model. It can range from formal ceremonies to a personal "thank you" in acknowledgment for the contribution of time and effort.

Recognition creates a pleasing environment and is often used as a vehicle that creates fun in the workplace. Many programs use symbolic "trophies" such as a ceramic pig, or an old bowling trophy, or even a frayed segment of rope, to place a significant contribution in the context of a congenial atmosphere where it can be discussed openly by all. In a company that emphasizes recognition it is not uncommon to find multiple programs in use, ranging from an honorable mention in the company newspaper, to a certificate for two to dinner, to a personal card from the company president.

In general, recognition is an after-the-fact show of appreciation for one's contribution. It is a method of saying "thank you." As such, it is a useful tool for developing a company's culture. A recent survey by the William M. Mercer firm reported that two thirds of the three thousand companies surveyed used special recognition awards.

Recognition can help move employees to a higher level of

involvement. I once worked for a company in which the recognition plan ranged from employee-of-the-month to membership on the president's council. Whereas being recognized as an employee-of-the-month provided social recognition, participation on the president's council enabled the employees to speak directly with the president about matters of policy, product, or anything else that was on their mind. Such an opportunity developed a high level of involvement not only on the part of the council members, but also on the part of their colleagues who wanted their opinions voiced.

Base Pay

One major tradition in base pay has been the concept of job-based pay, where the amount of pay is a function of the job content and its value to the company. Base pay is rapidly breaking from this tradition. One of the directions it seems to be moving is toward a market-based pay, where the base value of the job is determined by the marketplace. This trend is modified by several extenuating factors, not the least of which are labor availability, competition, labor need, and economic capabilities. Some companies will pay above "market" to fill certain positions if these positions are critical to the organization's success. Some companies will not pay the market price for employees either because it is a matter of management philosophy or for economic reasons.

Base pay provides the employees with the foundation for financial stability and security. It is the basis around which they establish their economic budget. But it is only one element of the relationship between pay and partnership.

Pay and Partnership

There are two critical points to consider when viewing the relationship of pay to partnership. These points are:

1. What is the total cash compensation offered by the company?
2. What portion of that compensation is shared risk?

Total cash compensation is exactly that—the total combination of base pay and incentive pay that is targeted (and budgeted) to be awarded to employees in conjunction with attainment of a targeted level of performance.

Where a company sets its total cash compensation level will have a significant impact on the degree of employee partnership that is developed. If, all other things being equal, employees are offered a total level of pay that is below what the market is offering for similar skills, capabilities, and job-related activities they will naturally think and feel they are being exploited. If, on the other hand, they are offered a level of pay that is above the market, they will think and feel they are being included in the income generation process as valuable partners.

Shared Rewards, Shared Risk

Companies that have entered into a partnership with their employees demonstrate this partnership by sharing the risks and the rewards of the business with them. One approach is to establish the base pay at below market levels but provide an opportunity to earn additional income resulting in a total cash compensation package that exceeds the market. In this scenario, a company may set base pay at the 90th percentile of the market for all positions. In addition to base pay the company provides the opportunity to increase this pay on an individual basis as new and valuable skills are acquired by the employee. Such a plan has been termed *pay-for-skill* or *skill-based pay*. This pay concept has also been applied to the acquisition of knowledge and the acquisition of competencies.

For example, the All In One company produces a product that requires a variety of skills such as reading engineering diagrams, machining parts, entering data into a computer, and performing statistical process control activities. Rather than hire employees for each of these activities, they have decided to pay the machine operator for each of these skills acquired. A fully skilled operator will be at the top of the pay range and receive a total pay that is above the market for machine operators. However, the company has kept total labor costs (pay and benefits) lower with this approach than if they had used a traditional pay approach and hired a larger staff at a lower per person wage. Pay for skills, knowledge, or competency has the potential to develop an organizational flexibility that could provide a competitive edge. However, if this flexibility is not needed, or if these skills or talents are not utilized, this plan could result in higher labor costs and prove to be a competitive disadvantage.

In an open, educated, business-focused work environment in which incentive pay is linked to company performance, employees tend to acquire new skills and knowledge because they see the connection between their pay and the financial results of the company. The skills, knowledge, and competencies are viewed as another tool to enhance the success of the company and increase their standard of living.

Incentive (Variable) Pay

Incentive pay systems primarily support a company's need for improved economic value while addressing the material needs of employees. In general they are a performance contract that is established before the fact. They offer the potential to earn a reward for a pre-established level of performance or achievement.

In most organizations these plans are in addition to base pay and offer the opportunity to receive above-market pay for above average performance. A good risk/reward partnership scenario is one in which a company's base pay position is below market, with an incentive opportunity that brings total pay to a level above market. For example, base pay is 90 percent of the market but the total targeted pay opportunity, tied to specific performance criteria, is 120 percent of the market.

In this design, the employee partner is "risking" the below-market portion of his pay (the 10 percent he could conceivably get from a company that pays market levels) for the opportunity to share in the above-market portion of the incentive (the 20 percent of market pay he will receive if the company reaches preestablished performance objectives).

This approach makes sense from the perspective of establishing a risk/reward partnership, but a difficulty exists in convincing the employee population to accept a base pay that is less than what the market is offering. Much of the concern with this type of risk/reward sharing centers around the employees' perception of their ability to affect the outcome and earn the incentive portion.

Employees in an environment created by the four management practices are already partners and understand the risks and rewards inherent in business. They will be much more receptive to this approach because of their level of business education, their line-of-sight capabilities, and their participation in the goal-setting process.

Degree of Risk Sharing and Partnership

The degree of risk/reward sharing that a company should apply to a variable pay plan is a function of three elements. Each of these elements should be considered when developing the relationship of risk to reward. They are:

1. The degree of business partnership the company wants to establish with the employees
2. The degree of risk the employees can assume
3. The degree the employees can affect the outcome

Sales environments often have highly leveraged plans, where 30 percent to 50 percent of a sales employee's pay could be determined by their performance. In this type of plan there is a high degree of risk/reward partnership. The employees are normally risk-oriented and comfortable in an environment in which they determine their own level of income based on their ability to impact the results.

Some nonsales environments may have a very low risk/reward leverage, where base pay is at market level and the incentive opportunity is in the range of 2–6 percent of base pay. In this situation, if the company achieves the preestablished performance targets, the employees receive a total cash compensation of 102–106 percent of the market.

These organizations may be experimenting with incentive pay, viewing the incentive as a compensation expense to be contained rather than a self-funding investment that pays off when results exceed plan. Or they may be in a market in which outside forces, such as the price of raw materials or capital investment, have a far greater impact on profitability than the employees can have.

GE Fanuc pays well in excess of local community wages for similar positions. They also have a profit-sharing plan that recently paid 2.9 percent of base pay to all employees. In this situation, 2.9 percent of base pay equates to approximately a week's pay. One has to wonder if an additional week's take-home pay is sufficient to establish a solid partnership in the minds of all employees. In this case, perhaps the above area wages and other rewards and recognition programs establish the partnership, and the year-end profit sharing simply reinforces this. In general, the greater the overall opportunity to earn rewards based on performance and results, the greater the partnership link will be, all other things being equal.

Types of Incentive Plans

Incentive pay plans are as diversified as the companies that use them. The details are endless, but certain types of plans have been identified:

- Profit sharing
- Annual bonus
- Gainsharing
- Small group incentives
- Individual incentives
- Key contributors
- Equity ownership

Profit Sharing

Profit sharing is perhaps one of the more widely used types of all-employee incentive plans. It is based on sharing a portion of the company's profits with the employees. A good example is the company that places 50 percent of all profits above a certain threshold into a pool to be distributed among the employees equally or based on their percentage of the total payroll. Or the company that places 12 percent of all pretax profits into a pool. At the end of the year, the pool is shared with all employees as a percentage of their base compensation.

Profit sharing communicates to all employees that the purpose of the company is to make money and, if it is successful in doing so, all employees will share in the rewards. It is perhaps the ultimate demonstration of the concept of partnership.

Unfortunately, in the past, profit sharing has been less than effective in creating the link between employee performance and rewards. In traditionally managed companies, most employees either did not understand how their daily activities could affect profit, did not trust the numbers being reported, or had little opportunity to make a difference. In addition, profit-sharing companies normally pay out the incentive once a year, after the annual profits have been calculated. The fact that this type of plan offers reward that is neither immediate nor certain detracts from its motivational capabilities.

Rejuvenating the Profit-Sharing Design

The focus that a culture based on the Partnership Checklist criteria places on profit may put a new face on the profit-sharing design. In such a culture, all employees understand their relationship between profit and daily activities. All information is available and understood. There is no secrecy or doubt about the data. All employee partners are empowered and enabled to make decisions and act to affect profit.

Wainwright Industries in St. Peters, Missouri, pays out 15 percent of profits to all associates (employees). Each associate in the organization receives exactly the same share. Wainwright makes the link between profit and performance by including profit and net income measures as part of the "Key Quality Indicators" they track closely. Each associate understands how their performance can impact these indicators. The only real drawback is the issue of an annual payout.

If the timing could be shortened to a quarterly measure, then profit sharing could prove to be quite motivational.

Annual Bonus

Annual bonus does not really belong under the heading of incentive pay. Yes, it is pay and, yes, it is paid out if the company meets certain business objectives. But these plans are usually arbitrary and poorly defined. The exception to this is the plan that mimics profit sharing but with other financial or operational indicators. Either way, the annual bonus lacks many of the critical elements that link pay to performance and results. The traditional annual bonus is more like a recognition plan, where monies are made available for distribution to all employees if the company "has had a good year."

Fastener Industries has a bonus plan that is based on yearly profits and determined at the discretion of the board of directors. The unique twist is that this cash bonus is awarded on a semiannual basis, in mid-June and mid-December. This timing may have a significant effect on the motivational impact of this plan. June starts the summer vacation period, when additional cash is always welcome, and December brings with it the joy, and expense, of gift giving.

Gainsharing

Gainsharing gets closer to an ideal motivational design. In this type of incentive plan, various indicators are included in a formula that determines the amount of incentive pay based on the organization's or facility's results. Normally, employees either receive an equal amount of incentive pay or they receive an amount as a percent of base pay.

Receiving an equal cash amount is effective in communicating a sense of equal partnership and shared destiny. Receiving a percent of base pay tends to communicate that (theoretically) different levels of pay equal to different levels of responsibility and the ability to affect results. The approach used is a function of the organization's culture and compensation philosophy. Employees in an open, educated, partner-oriented environment will understand either approach.

Unlike profit sharing, which normally is a companywide plan, gainsharing plans are usually based on performance of a division, facility, or plant. The criteria for such plans typically include operational indicators such as productivity, cost, quality, safety, and customer satisfaction. An example is the Eaton Corporation employees at the Belmond, Iowa facility, who receive incentive pay for staying below a certain established percentage of the costs that they are able to control. This pay is calculated as a percentage of their total earnings.

The payouts for such plans are usually more frequent than those of profit sharing, sometimes being calculated and issued on a monthly basis. The use of operational indicators and the increase in timely payout of rewards significantly improves the motivational impact of this plan.

Learn How to Earn

Some organizations use gainsharing plans to introduce basic business finance training. They establish the gainsharing formula and then use financial education to teach employees how they can increase their incentive pay. Employees in an environment based on the Partnership Checklist criteria will have a solid line-of-sight between their daily activities and the operational indicators and, as a result, will be able to make a significant positive impact on results.

Small Group Incentives

Small group incentives get even closer to a direct link between performance and reward. Like gainsharing, operational indicators are included in a formula that determines the amount of incentive pay. Normally, these plans have from three to five performance objectives and pay based on the group performance. They stimulate improvement by rewarding employees for performance over which they have direct control.

Small group incentives can be powerful stimulators of performance. However, without proper consideration, the design's emphasis on group performance could result in an overall expense to the company. For example, if one of the small group objectives is productivity, it may overproduce and flood the downstream group with product. The negative impact on inventory cost, material use and movement, and storage costs certainly do not contribute to operating income.

Many organizations are reluctant to use small group incentive plan designs, perhaps because of the difficulty in establishing the teams and their measurements. It may also be because they are concerned about the potential disruptive element of such a design. Although important, these concerns should not prevent the use of such a strong motivational tool.

Whenever I design a small group incentive plan for a client, it is usually because they want the strongest performance/reward link possible. As part of the design, I also recommend a large group element to keep the motivation in balance. Figure 9-7 illustrates this point. Using a small group/large group plan, employees are focused on the few key performance elements they can directly affect. In this case, three operational measures, each equally weighted, total 75 percent of the incentive opportunity. The other 25 percent of the team's earning opportunity is linked to a financial measure that indicates the overall health of the organization.

In an open, educated organization that uses small group incentive plans, employees will have a clear line-of-sight from their daily activities to their group's operational indicators and how these affect the company's financial indicators.

Individual and Key Contributor Incentives

Individual incentives and key contributor incentives move away from the concept of teamwork and partnership. Individual incentives are most often used in a sales environment in which employees are viewed as stand-alone individual contributors. Even this idea is losing favor. Sales is being viewed as a team activity, with the product design and sales support groups sharing in the results of the selling effort.

Key contributor incentives are rewards provided to individuals, usually on an annual basis. They can be issues in recognition for an exceptional individual contribution, such as single-handedly saving an account or creating a new product. More often than not they are used as a retention technique by issuing some form of equity instrument, such as phantom stock, stock options, or actual stock, that has a vesting schedule attached to it. They may still be useful for this purpose but, unless rewards are some form of equity, key contributor plans may have the same effect as an annual bonus or recognition award.

In a partnership environment careful consideration should be given to the negative effects on the culture of singling out individuals with bonuses either to recognize their performance or to keep them with the company. A partnership environment that issues rewards based on individual performance sends a conflicting and confusing message. A partnership environment should provide every employee with all the necessary intrinsic and extrinsic rewards they need without singling out individuals for special treatment.

Equity Ownership

Companies that provide their employee partners with opportunities to own stock move beyond the partnership phase. This approach

Figure 9-7. Small group/large group incentive pay design.

Incentive Design Element	Measurement	% of Incentive Opportunity
Small group	**Operational**	
	1. Productivity	25
	2. Schedule	25
	3. Quality	25
Large group	**Financial**	
	4. Operating income	25

could be considered the ultimate objective of an open, educated, partner-oriented environment—a company of owners.

Most companies provide the opportunity for their employees to purchase stock through some form of savings vehicle such as a 401(k) plan, or a discounted stock purchase plan. Stock can also be used in an incentive plan, such as when it is included as an option in a profit-sharing plan or bonus plan.

In a profit-sharing plan, the employee has the opportunity to purchase shares of stock with the money earned through a profit-sharing plan. In a bonus plan, stock, instead of cash, is awarded to the employee.

Restricted Stock Bonus Plans

Plans that make the issuance of stock contingent upon some event or activity are called *restricted stock bonus plans*. These plans are used to stimulate performance or retain key employees. For example, a restricted stock plan can be designed to pay out only when certain performance goals have been achieved, such as if the company meets a certain ROA growth rate or certain profitability level.

Until now, these plans have been used mainly on the executive level. I am aware of very few companies that are using restricted stock bonus plans with their employees, perhaps because in a normal company culture, this type of reward system is neither positive, immediate, nor certain. In more traditional cultures, the motivational impact of such a design could be lost on employees below the executive level because they are unable to understand the complexity and value of such a plan.

Equity programs have a real potential to connect the employee with the company. Unfortunately, the data show that most employees do not clearly understand the potential value that exists in owning company stock. As a result, many employees choose not to participate.

Stock Options

A stock option gives employees the right to purchase shares of company stock at a fixed price, during a certain period of time. This type of design offers a share of the future success of the company. If the value of the stock goes up between the time the option was awarded and the time the option to purchase expires, the employee receives the benefit of the increase in value.

I recently worked on an assignment for a Fortune 500 company that was interested in establishing more accountability on the frontline manager level. As part of this development, the managers had to understand the key business issues embodied in financial statements. They had to develop a line-of-sight capability from their activities to the income statement and balance sheet.

The project was to develop a one-day workshop that would provide financial education on two levels. The first level developed a basic understanding of financial statements. The second level developed an understanding of how their day-to-day business decisions affected the bottom line.

Key managers in the training department were responsible for achieving this objective. In working with them I became aware of the fact that the company had recently initiated an all-employee stock option plan.

Each employee had been awarded an option to purchase several hundred shares of company stock at some point in the future. The price was fixed at the price per share on the day of issuance. If the stock price increased, the employees would realize the difference in the form of a bonus payment. For example, if the price of the stock was fixed at $65 per share and increased in price to $85 per share at the time the options matured, an employee could "exercise" the option by paying $65 per share for stock worth $85, for a gain of $20 per share. If the employee had an option to purchase several hundred shares the total gain would be significant.

Any good financial planner will tell you that the right thing to do is to have a balanced portfolio of wage income and capital income. Obviously, senior management saw this as a strong incentive for all employees to become more engaged in the company, linking their performance to the company's performance and to their personal income.

Unfortunately, the employees didn't see it the same way. The human resources department wasn't prepared for the number of calls they received from employees who wanted to return their stock option information package because they "couldn't afford to or didn't want to buy any stock."

Obviously a large portion of the employee population did not own stock and had no idea how a stock option worked. Because they were not educated or experienced about stocks they were unable to appreciate the reward that was being offered to them. An effort had been made to engage them prior to ensuring they had the proper education to understand the offer, but there was too much emphasis on the Engage management practice without enough emphasis on the Educate management practice.

The solution was obvious and fortuitous—use the one-day financial education workshop to make the link between earnings per share and the value of their stock option. What had been developed as a frontline management workshop was now being considered as an educational tool for all employees.

Employee Stock Ownership Plans

An ESOP is similar to a profit-sharing plan. Based on the performance of the company, it contributes to the plan each year. This contribution is used to purchase company stock, which is allocated to the employees based on some predetermined formula.

Each year the employee's account grows, based on the annual contributions and the growth of the value of the stock that is currently held. Normally, employees receive the vested portion of their account when they retire or when they leave the company.

Although such a plan can move employees into an ownership position, it also contains several drawbacks that need to be addressed.

For ESOPs to be an effective motivator, the company culture must create and support an employee ownership mentality. The Partnership Checklist criteria is an ideal tool for developing such a mentality.

Rethinking Incentive Designs

The application of the four management practices greatly enhances the types of incentive designs that can be used to engage all employees. Compensation professionals are well advised to reevaluate incentive designs in light of these practices. Perhaps these practices will enhance the motivational element of profit sharing. Perhaps equity plans can be used on all levels to stimulate employee partnership.

In an open, educated environment, employees understand the financial relationships behind the stock price. They understand how their performance can affect earnings and they understand the relationship between stock price and earnings per share. Such a company can effectively use equity-based instruments such as stock, restricted stock bonus plans, stock options, or stock appreciation rights (SARs) to develop an ownership mentality on the part of each employee.

In the next chapter, we will examine the process of identifying the appropriate reward system for your organization.

Notes

1. Thomas J. McCoy, *Compensation and Motivation: Maximizing Employee Performance With Behavior-Based Incentive Plans*, New York: AMACOM, 1993.
2. *ERI Update.* Economic Research Notes To Subscribers, vol. 25, January 1995, Economic Research Institute, Redmond, Washington.
3. *High Performance Work Practices and Firm Performance*, U.S. Department of Labor, Washington, DC, August 1993, p. 33.
4. Jerry L. McAdams, CCP, Elizabeth J. Hawk, CCP, *Organizational Performance & Rewards, 663 Experiences In Making The Link*, Scottsdale, Ariz.: American Compensation Association, Consortium for Alternative Reward Strategies Research, 1994, p. 37.

10

Incentive Compensation Plans: Choosing the Right Reward System for Your Organization

Incentive pay plans have evolved in conjunction with the movement to empower and involve employees. Occasionally they have led the way. But more often they have followed after an initial approach of team building, TQM, or some other employee involvement process.

The effectiveness of these reward systems at improving the company's profitability and competitive position is still being evaluated. Compensation professionals and senior management analyze the results in an effort to identify what works and why. Conclusions as to the effectiveness and applicability of a given design type (profit sharing, gainsharing, etc.) are being formulated as a result of these studies.

A note of caution is appropriate here. For the most part, the participants of these plans have been a traditional employee population. This population is currently going through the throes of change, where their roles, rights, and responsibilities are being redefined. This is a young, ongoing process, and progress is being made. However, change is slow and difficult. If you ask most line employees in companies that have change efforts in place, they will say that the fundamental relationships are slow to change and do not change as dramatically as one would be led to believe.

Human resources professionals need to be aware that the effectiveness of one type of incentive pay design with today's employee population might not be the same with that employee population next year. As an organization progresses through the implementation of the four management practices the effectiveness of various reward structures will change. For example, self-directed work team members are much more knowledgeable about the business and their role than the average employee. For them, an incentive compensation plan with higher level measures, such as Return On Equity or long-term equity-based rewards, may be much more effective than monthly cash payouts based on operational measures.

The point to keep in mind during the incentive plan design phase is that where the employee population is along the maturity continuum will have a significant impact on the effectiveness of a specific incentive plan design. First introduced in Chapter 3, Figure 10-1, the relationship continuum displays this concept. The upper half of this figure depicts the organizational maturity continuum.

Getting Started: The Compensation Philosophy

Prior to any design work, it is necessary to define the company's philosophy toward compensation in general. The compensation philosophy is a statement of values and beliefs on which all compensation decisions are based. Developing a compensation philosophy is critical to the creation of an open organization. It sets the expectations about how pay will be used by the organization. Setting these expectations will help define roles, rights, responsibilities, and rewards and will remove any preestablished or false expectations about compensation.

A compensation philosophy defines the purpose of the compensation system. It should reflect the culture and focus on the business issues. In an environment based on the Partnership Checklist criteria it might look something like this:

• Our compensation philosophy will be linked to and support our company culture and our business strategy.

• We view compensation as an investment used to encourage and support behaviors that achieve our business objectives. Examples of these behaviors are: involvement and participation, performance improvement, individual improvement, teamwork, problem solving, decision making, goal setting.

• We will maintain a compensation plan that provides employee satisfaction with pay by providing compensation that is aggressively competitive with the industries and employers with whom we compete for human resources.

Figure 10-1. The relationship continuum.

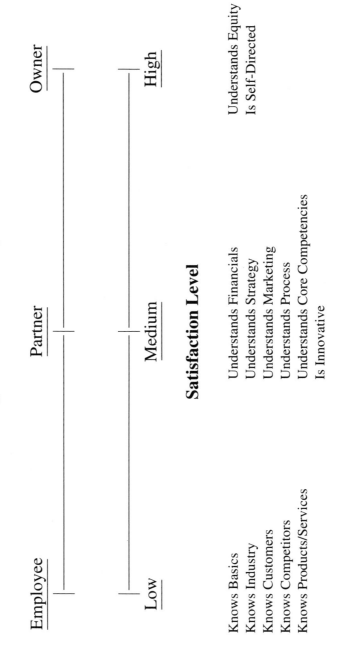

Organizational Maturity

Employee   Partner   Owner

Low   Medium   High

Satisfaction Level

Knows Basics
Knows Industry
Knows Customers
Knows Competitors
Knows Products/Services

Understands Financials
Understands Strategy
Understands Marketing
Understands Process
Understands Core Competencies
Is Innovative

Understands Equity
Is Self-Directed

- We will be open in our compensation communications as to:
  —General pay principles
  —Specific pay mechanisms
  —Competitive positioning
  —Salary administration issues
  —Purpose of performance appraisal systems
  —Mix of cash, benefits, perks, etc.
  —Rights and responsibilities
- We intend to provide our employees with an employment opportunity that can be more financially and socially rewarding than our competition. Making the most of that opportunity is dependent on the employee's contribution.
- We will provide compensation that is responsive to and reflective of the quality of performance of both our employees and the company.
- Compensation will be used to develop the partnership between all employees by sharing both the risk and the rewards of the business in a responsible manner.
- In managing our compensation system we will look at total compensation: base pay, incentive pay, benefits, and recognition.
- Our compensation system will help our employees understand our business by:
  —Cultivating in each employee an understanding of the industry and our business
  —Acting as a focal source of information as to the organization's key performance indicators and our performance against plan

Once the compensation philosophy has been developed it provides a general direction to the design of specific pay plans. What follows is a proven approach to the design of an incentive compensation plan. This approach is a linear catalog of events that take place during the development process. Because of their level of experience or need, many organizations enter into the development process at a more advanced stage. However, those with less experience or with a more conservative management style will want to start at the beginning.

The Reward System Design Charter

The Steering Committee's Role

Normally, senior management forms a steering committee to provide direction and guidance and a design committee to research and develop the actual plans. One of the key activities of the steering committee is to develop the Reward System Design Charter.

The design charter is the road map that guides the design committee during the development process. Without the charter, the design committee might invest significant time and effort in the development of a plan that would not be accepted by the steering committee.

During the creation of the design charter the steering committee members develop an understanding of their responsibilities. They exhibit their commitment to the process. They define core values of the organization and they develop the compensation philosophy that supports the business strategy and company culture.

The charter defines the responsibilities of the design committee. It defines the parameters of the design effort and the design process. It also outlines the review and approval process the reward system design will undergo. This document, although somewhat difficult to develop, provides the expectations and guidelines necessary for the design team can use to produce an acceptable result.

An Example of a Reward System Design Charter

The following is an example of various key elements and their associated details that could be included in the Reward System Design Charter:

- Vision: Mental Image of a Future World
- Mission (organization's purpose)
- Strategy to get there: the point of difference
    High-quality, low-cost, innovative products, customer service, environment. Based on the Partnership Checklist criteria.

- Corporate values (what is valued and therefore eligible for reward)
    Customers, employees, community, products, financial results, culture, ethics.

- Management philosophy (how we treat people and why)
    Innovative vs. stable, educated vs. in-the-dark, enabled vs. isolated, empowered vs. order taker, open vs. closed, team vs. individual, partner vs. hired hand, fair treatment, diversity, meaningful work, continuous learning and renewal, balancing stakeholders.

- Operating philosophy

> Minimize investment, ROA, volume emphasis, growth vs. harvest, develop market vs. penetrate existing market, acquisition vs. retention.

- Compensation components for consideration
  Sharing vs. zero sum, team vs. individual, lead change or lag change or concurrent with change, centralized vs. decentralized, risk vs. security, performance-reward linkage, market vs. internal equity, purpose: attract, retain, motivate, improve results, support teamwork, improve quality of workforce. Autocratic vs. democratic, market position, mix of total compensation, purpose of performance appraisal.

- Defining the design process.
  Wide participation vs. narrow participation.

- Defining the roles and responsibilities of design team (and consultant) (this authorizes the design team to proceed).

- Defining the strategic objectives the reward system will affect and the benefits it will generate by completing the following statements:
  Our objectives are . . .
  By doing this we will . . .
  The benefits to the organization are . . .
  The benefits to the employees are . . .

- Defining the scope and constraints of the design committee.
  Areas to be addressed and areas not to be addressed.

- Compensation budget and financial viability test.
  Degree of self-funding, break-even threshold.

- Timetable.
- Milestones.

The Design Committee

Reward systems are made up of core values, a process, and a structure. The core values are normally defined in the charter. The process and structure of the reward systems are normally developed by the design committee. The design committee, often comprised of a cross section of employees, is responsible for providing a process to integrate *satisfaction systems* (material and social reward systems) into the business strategy and the human resource initiatives. This process can be totally inclusive by addressing incentive compensation linked to performance, recognition systems that reinforce the organization's values, work processes that support teamwork, and employee development that results in qualified partners.

If the charter emphasizes a focus just on incentive compensation, the design committee is responsible for researching the various types of plans, evaluating how their design elements relate to the organization's culture and strategy, and developing a plan that is recommended to the steering committee.

Comparing Profiles: Partner Profile vs. Current Employee Profile

One of the key steps in developing an incentive plan is to identify the current level of employee understanding and expectations. Normally this is done with an employee survey and, although several good commercial instruments are available, many organizations customize their own.

A good approach is to develop a partner profile based on the elements of the E_4-R_4 Partnership Checklist. You can start by defining the critical attitudes, behaviors, skills, and understanding an employee partner needs in order to be proficient in the company. These critical elements can then be used in a survey to identify how closely the employee population conforms to the "ideal" partner.

A company moving toward an open, partner-oriented, high-performance culture may want to divide the survey into segments that align with the four management practices. For example, a survey may consist of cultural, business, operation, and finance sections. The questions in each section should focus on the types of attitudes, behaviors, and understanding that exist in the organization.

For example, questions under the cultural segment may deal with how well the employees understand the processes that enable them to participate and become involved, or how effective they think these processes are, or how active they are within these processes. Other questions may focus on issues such as: Is there a team mentality? To what degree is there group and individual problem solving? Are communications open and accessible? To what extent does participation and respect exist in the workplace?

Still other questions may be focused on how empowered the employees perceive themselves to be. Is there trust that permits risk taking? To what extent are all employees involved in goal setting and decision making?

Under the business segment questions may explore how well the employees understand the business strategy and their role in achieving specific goals. How well do they understand the industry and the company's position in it? To what degree are they aware of the competitive pressures, economic influences, and other big picture issues?

Under the financial segment questions may probe how well the employees understand how the company makes a profit and generates cash. How often do they receive financial information? To what degree do they understand it? How much information do they receive? How much do they need? Do they participate in the collection of this data? Do they participate in goal setting as it relates to the data? How much performance feedback do they receive? How often? Do they understand when the company is doing well, and why?

The result of the survey is a profile of where the employee population is along the maturity continuum. This profile can be compared to the profile of a partner based on the Partnership Checklist. The differences will point out opportunities for development and education.

Defining Incentive Plan Objectives

Another step in the process of developing an incentive plan is to define the objectives of the plan. The design committee, guided by the charter, defines why the plan is being established. Is it to drive performance? Is it to establish a closer performance/reward linkage? Is it to foster teamwork? Is it to reinforce the partnership? Is it focused on long term or short term? Who will participate? What are the restrictions? How will the incentive plan fit into the overall compensation strategy, strategic business plan, and the other human resources initiatives?

The elements of the partner profile, the results of the employee profile, and the defined objectives of the plan are three tools that can be used by senior management and human resources professionals to help define and select the appropriate reward system.

Six Key Incentive Plan Elements

Six key elements must be present in the structure of an incentive plan design for it to be effective as a tool to build a partnership and engage employees in the business. These key elements must be properly balanced to bring about the desired result, namely, increased efficiency and effectiveness that creates increased profit for the company and increased income for the employee partners.

These six elements are couched in the perspective of the employee. We know the perspective of management; it is concerned with ROI and minimizing expenses. Experience has taught us that a plan designed using only the management perspective has little chance of success.

The logic is clear. If a plan is designed to engage employees in a partnership relationship then the employee's perspective must be incorporated in the design. Figure 10-2 illustrates these six elements:

1. Motivational design
2. Personal commitment
3. Management support
4. Training
5. Service/material support
6. Positive reinforcement

The purpose of an incentive plan is to build a partnership that engages all employees in the business. In order to do this effectively it is important to understand the key elements of any successful plan. Only then can we design a plan that meets the participants' needs and works effectively in the environment.

Motivational Design

Three questions that address the employee's perspective fit under this category. The first is Do I understand what is expected of me? Perhaps most fundamental to any design is the necessity that the employees understand what is expected of them. Simply offering an attractive incentive, say 25 percent of base pay for improving profit, is not enough. In order to fully participate, each employee must understand the specific activities she can perform that will earn her the incentive. The value of a line-of-sight capability fits in here. With a comprehensive line-of-sight provided by the Education management practice, each employee can develop a detailed understanding of what is expected of her.

The second question a participant will have is, Can I do it? Participants must be able to affect the outcome by their actions for an incentive plan to be effective. For example, if employees are offered an incentive for increasing profit but have no opportunity to participate in problem solving or decision making, they will not feel they can affect the result. Or, if they have no understanding or access to the numbers that go into calculating profit they will not have confidence in the accuracy or honesty of the numbers and will feel they cannot affect the outcome. With the appropriate application of Enable and Empower management practices, employees will know they can affect the outcome and achieve the objectives.

The third question, Is it worth it to me?, focuses on how attrac-

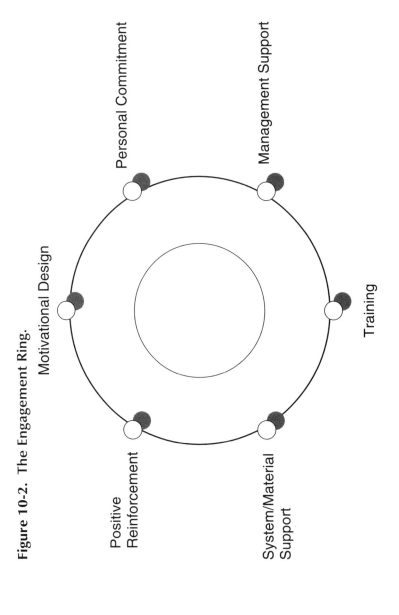

Figure 10-2. The Engagement Ring.

tive the incentive offering is—not to the plan designer or the chief financial officer, but to the participant. Implicit in this question are the issues of What type and How much. What type of reward will be perceived as most attractive to the participants? Cash? Merchandise? Travel? Time off? Training? Equity? Personal or professional growth opportunities? Paid professional memberships? The answer may differ for each employee.

Bob Bromley, Roy Harrison, and Dennis Spratt are professional financial consultants with offices in Kansas City, Kansas. Among other services, they offer investment vehicles, such as custom trusts, insurance policies, and investments that provide long-term capital protection. This approach has been widely used on the executive level as a form of incentive, however, in the past it has not been made available to the general employee population, apparently for several reasons. In a traditional organization, the general employee population has not had the opportunity to participate in incentive compensation.

In the organizations that provide incentive opportunity it was clear that the benefits of a mechanism for long-term capital protection and growth were not perceived to be as valuable as the opportunity to earn additional cash. The offering was not an effective motivator because it was not perceived as positive, immediate, or certain.

On the other hand, employee partners in an open organization are educated in business finance. Eventually they reach a point where they understand economic concepts such as the impact of inflation and taxes on the profitability of the company. They develop a level of economic understanding where they can act creatively to minimize the negative effect of these elements on profit and retained earnings. For example, they will understand that purchasing raw material in large quantities may be beneficial in times of high inflation, when prices of raw material rise rapidly. They will understand that too much cash not being properly invested will lose value. They understand the lease versus purchase decisions made to take advantage of certain tax opportunities.

Once the Education management practice raises them to this level of understanding (and it does not take long), they will easily transfer this understanding to their personal financial situation. They will want to apply their business knowledge to the protection and growth of their personal net worth. At this point, investment vehicles that provide long-term capital protection may become their reward option of choice. Harrison, Spratt, and I are actively investigating the motivational value of this approach.

Open, educated, partner-oriented work environments will change the business landscape as significantly as desktop computers have done. This is an excellent example of the need to rethink the basics when developing human resources systems for an such a work culture.

Personal Commitment: I See Me Succeed

Behavioral psychologists will tell you that the most attractive types of rewards are those chosen by the recipient. An obvious statement, but beneath the surface is a truth that should not be overlooked. Choosing a reward requires that the individual create a mental image of himself with the reward. This concept, called *visualization,* is used extensively in Olympic and professional sports. Visualization is the creation of a mental picture of a future event. It requires the subconscious mind to accept as fact that the individual has already achieved success and earned the reward.

Having established the powerful value of visualization, how can it possibly be incorporated in the incentive plan? Here creativity enters into the design process. Some organizations enable a cross section of the employee population to participate in identifying and choosing the rewards to be offered. Thus a series of rewards are established that are attractive to the participants and are something they can actively envision themselves obtaining.

Some organizations, like Herman Miller, the Zeeland, Michigan–based manufacturer of office furniture, use cash but allow employees to purchase things like vacation time with the incentive earnings. Other organizations establish a "token" society in which incentive is paid in points that can be redeemed for merchandise or travel. One company I am aware of allows each employee to choose from a menu of cash compensation. Participants can choose all base pay and no incentive, some base pay with some incentive pay, or a little base pay with a lot of incentive opportunity.

Companies have established mortgage banks where families can save for a home. At our stage of family development, the ability to earn college tuition credits for the children would be a valuable incentive.

Perhaps the best advice for choosing the most effective reward is to consider the employee sociographics and demographics. As the employee population ages, their material needs change. A young workforce may want a higher risk/reward ratio in the incentive payout design. Or they may want aggressive investment vehicles that can enable them to build wealth. An older workforce may want a lower risk leverage, less aggressive investment vehicles, and more resources focused on medical and retirement vehicles. For that reason, many compensation professionals think that once it is established, a material reward plan should be overhauled every five years or so to make sure it remains attractive to the participants. I am of the opinion that incentive plans should be monitored constantly and evaluated at least annually.

Two questions that address the employee's perspective fit under the category of personal commitment. The first is, Did I have the opportunity to participate in the goal setting? The team building process has documented the fact that commitment to the attainment of a goal is a function of how involved the participants were in establishing the goal. That supports the findings of behavioral scientists who tell us that participation in goal setting develops a sense of ownership.

Common sense and personal experience show us that the people being asked to achieve the goals have a good idea of what is realistic and attainable. They understand what can be done with the available resources and how to do it. My experience as director of incentives for a Fortune 500 company proved to me that teams who are allowed to set their own performance goals tend to establish higher goals than their management would have established. If we want to generate commitment to goals, they need to be the goals of the people being asked to achieve them. If employees have an opportunity to participate in goal setting, they will feel more like partners and be more committed to overcoming obstacles and achieving the objectives.

The second question under personal commitment is, What has caused me to envision myself succeeding in this venture? Again we see the value of visualization. If, as a partner, I participated in goal setting, I will have had the opportunity to voice my concerns and recommendations. To do this I will have had to develop a mental picture of the activities required to achieve the goals. I will have visualized myself in the process, achieving the goals.

Management Support

Two questions that address the employee's perspective fit under the management support category. The first is, Is my manager committed to the program? If so, why? and the second is Will he/she encourage and facilitate my success?

Early in his employment, each employee learns the unwritten rule of long-term survival/employment: Do what the boss wants done and support what the boss wants supported. The converse of this rule is: If the boss isn't interested in it, you won't get much support. Based on these personal experiences, each employee will look to his immediate boss for affirmation that the incentive program is something to actively participate in. Perhaps the best reassurance is to see the supervisor included in the same, or a similar, incentive plan.

Obviously, if the plan is designed correctly, it will attractively link performance to rewards. This being the case, the supervisor will be committed to the program for personal as well as business reasons. In an open, partner-oriented environment that utilizes a concept called *tiered linkage*, the coach/facilitator's incentive payout is linked in part to how well his/her team performs. Tiered linkage reassures all employees that, as partners, everyone earns rewards based on group performance. Tiered linkage reassures them that others in the organization will benefit from their contribution and therefore, will encourage and facilitate their success.

Training

Two questions that address the employee's perspective under the training category are: Do I have the skills and knowledge to accomplish the task? and What actions must I take to be successful?

If employee partners are asked to achieve certain goals they will need the skills and knowledge necessary to achieve the objectives. The Education management practice specifically addresses this issue. A more subtle issue is an understanding of the actions within a process that are necessary to be successful. Here the role of leadership and the sharing of personal experience becomes important.

In an environment based on the Partnership Checklist criteria, each employee understands the importance of sharing her personal experience in a way that educates others in how to be successful. During team meetings, employees share their understanding of the mechanics of the process and their perceptions of how to affect the key performance indicators. The experienced pipe fitter, rather than using his tricks of the trade to make himself perform above the group, needs to share the shortcuts and other observations born of experience so that the group can improve their performance. The experienced customer service representative shares her knowledge of stress management and administrative procedures to make the department more effective.

This information sharing is really experience sharing and comes from level four education. It is the sharing of local wisdom. It is a critical element of the social environment that communicates what actions must be taken to achieve maximum success. By effectively cultivating this sharing of wisdom a company makes a quantum leap in its competitive position.

Service/Material Support

Two questions that address the employee's perspective fit under this category. They are:

1. Am I provided with the support (service or material) that is necessary for me to achieve my objectives?
2. Am I providing the support necessary for my customers to be effective and successful?

In a sales environment the answer to the first question might take the form of a supply of valid sales leads from the marketing department to the sales representative. Or it could be a sales promotion that encouraged the customer to partner with the company.

In an operations environment the answer to the second question could take the form of a commitment to ensure a clean and effective handoff of the product or service being supplied to an internal customer. An example would be ensuring the recipient was aware of the urgent nature of the document that was placed in the in-box rather than allowing it to be covered, unnoticed, by additional incoming mail.

Positive Reinforcement

Two questions that address the employee's perspective fit under this category. They are:

1. Do I receive timely performance feedback that encourages me?
2. Do detailed and accurate performance reports indicate where the effort is succeeding and where it needs assistance?

For an incentive program to be effective it must provide continuing information on performance. Performance feedback is a form of positive reinforcement that provides social reward that, in and of itself, is worth striving for. In addition, if rewards are contingent upon performance, then the participants will want their performance to be as effective as possible. Feedback on the effectiveness of performance, for example, how closely the performance came to achieving the goal, contains vital information needed for improvement. Performance without this timely and accurate information is like bowling with a curtain in front of the pins or golfing without keeping score. Actions are performed but it is impossible to determine the need for improvement and the direction the change should take.

Using Incentives to Support Change

During the discussion about the use of incentives, the question often arises about when and how to use them. Should an incentive plan be installed at the beginning of the cultural change process, to lead the process and help pull participation?

The upside to this approach is that each employee will have a clear vested interest in the success of the change process. This interest goes a long way toward reducing resistance and increasing active participation in the process. The downside to this approach is that employees may not understand how they can affect the results. Or, the systems and processes may be in such a state as to thwart their efforts at performance improvement. For example, an employee whose pay is linked to productivity and quality will quickly become frustrated if he can't receive materials on a timely basis or if the process he is using cannot be maintained within quality specifications.

Another approach is to initiate incentive pay after the change management process has been implemented. The upside to this approach is that the systems and processes will be aligned for performance. The downside is that employees may perceive only the negative elements of the change process as it is implemented. Reorganization, downsizing, and uncertainty can lower morale, create cynicism, and develop resistance to the change process.

A third approach is to initiate incentive pay concurrent with the change management process. The upside of this approach is that employees see they are partners who will share in the gains that result from change. The downside is the difficulty explaining this type of pay plan if downsizing must take place.

Incentive Plan Design Elements and the Four Management Practices

When to introduce incentive pay into the change process is a function of how senior management perceives its usefulness, for example, will pay be most helpful and provide the greatest return if it leads, lags, or is concurrent with the company culture?

One way to help answer that question is to compare the key design elements of an incentive pay design with the key elements necessary for change to an open, business-focused culture. This comparison will indicate the major areas of support that incentives can contribute to the change management process.

Figure 10-3 matches the six key design elements of an incentive pay design with the E_4 management practices to show where the areas of major linkage and support exist. Note that the key incentive

Figure 10-3. Incentive plan design elements and the E₄ management practices.

E₄ Practices	Six Key Incentive Elements					
	Motivational Design	Personal Commitment	Management Support	Training and Education	Support	Positive Reinforcement
Educate	Understand What Is Expected			Possess Proper Skill and Knowledge		
Enable	Able to Do It	Participate in Goal Setting	Encourage and Facilitate	Know Actions to Take	Provided With Needed Resources	Timely and Accurate Performance Data
Empower	Allowed to Do It	Participate in Goal Setting			Take the Necessary Actions	
Engage	Worth It to Me	Envision Success				Timely Performance Feedback

element of motivational design has a major influence on all four management practices. In addition, note that each of the six key incentive elements influences the Enable management practice.

The Self-Funding Budget

Part of the creative challenge in designing a motivational plan is to present an offering that the participants view as being attractive while remaining within the budget.

Most incentive plans are based on a self-funding design. They tend to start the payout at some threshold level that supports the business plan. In other words, employees earn base pay for performance up to the threshold level, and above threshold they begin earning incentive rewards.

The financial viability of a plan is determined by where the payout threshold is established. One of my clients established the payout threshold at 95 percent of business plan. This was to offset a base pay that was 10 percent below market. In the company made business plan, the employees received a 10 percent incentive payout which brought them to market level.

The financial viability of a plan is also determined by the percent of gain above threshold that will be shared with the participants. So what percent is a good share? The current data range from 2.5 percent to 20 percent. The specific split is a function of the company's attitude toward partnering and its degree of understanding of the principles of behavioral psychology.

Praxair is a Danbury, Connecticut based firm that is an international producer of industrial gases. The industry is capital intensive, with most of the labor costs incurred in the distribution. The company has a base pay rate set at 95 percent of the market rate and it offers an incentive opportunity of 15 percent tied to return on capital. Each year the Return on Capital Threshold is established and a payout schedule is developed.

One unique element of the plan is the way the reward is perceived by the employees. The incentive payout is expressed in Days Pay. Each quarter the results are calculated and expressed in terms of numbers of days of pay that were earned as a result of the plan. Looking at this plan with a reverse perspective, it could be an indicator of the size of a "phantom workforce" that would be needed (but was not utilized) to achieve the same results under normal or planned performance levels. According to Tony Annoni, director of international human resources, "The end-of-quarter score of days earned is eagerly awaited by all employees."

Annoni goes on to say,

We share with our employees all the financial information that is released to the public. In addition, the business objectives are well understood by everyone. In conjunction with this information sharing, the incentive plan helps create a higher level of understanding about the business. The underlying message is that every employee's effort counts. Because costs impact profit, which impacts return on capital, everyone takes an interest in the operation of the business. It also reminds us how customer relations and outside economic events can impact the company and thereby, each employee's individual compensation level.

The Reward System Selector™ Process: Choosing the Right Reward System

In addition to deciding when to implement an incentive pay plan, the design committee will need to decide the appropriate reward system design. A design committee that is starting from zero will normally, through research, develop an understanding of the seven more prevalent incentive pay plans discussed in Chapter 9. Often they will benchmark companies who successfully use a specific design. This education and benchmarking process provides them with insight as to the strengths and weaknesses of each design that enables them to choose the appropriate design and customize it for the specific needs of the company and the employees.

One good approach to matching reward system type to the organization and the employees is to utilize what I have termed the Reward System Selector process. This process involves the use of the Reward System Selector worksheets in a workshop conducted by a facilitator who is knowledgeable in the field of incentive compensation.

The five worksheets used in the Reward System Selector process are:

1. The Design Element Worksheet
2. The Organization's Culture Elements Worksheet
3. The Organization's Needs Worksheet
4. The Employees' Needs Worksheet
5. The Reward System Selector Summary Worksheet

Workshop Overview

The following is a brief overview of the Reward System Selector workshop. While the specifics of each organization will differ, examples of major categories and other details are provided in the worksheets as thought starters.

The first step in the workshop is to complete Figure 10-4, the Design Element worksheet. At this point, members of the design committee list their knowledge of the key elements, the strengths, and the weaknesses of each reward system. Next they complete Figure 10-5, the Organization's Culture worksheet. This worksheet collects a list of the existing and desired cultural elements of the company. Then they complete Figure 10-6, the Organization's Needs worksheet. This worksheet collects a list of the organizational development needs (intrinsic) and the economic value needs (extrinsic) of the company. Next the committee completes Figure 10-7, the Employees' Needs worksheet—a list of the intrinsic and extrinsic needs of the employees that can be addressed in the workplace, by the company.

Finally the information on the first four worksheets is distilled onto Figure 10-8, the Reward System Selector Summary worksheet. During this process the design team discusses where each element from the worksheets should be placed on the summary sheet. For example, if the Organization's Culture worksheet lists open communication as an element, this element would be placed in the column next to the type of design or designs that support that element.

Specific questions asked during the summary process should lead the group in building a line-of-sight between the reward systems and the needs of the organization and the employees. Examples of questions are: Where is the linkage between the needs of the employees and the organization? If it doesn't exist, where should it be? What is needed to make the linkage? Which reward system addresses this linkage most effectively? Do reward systems in the organization currently make this linkage?

The outcome of the Reward System Selector process looks similar to Figure 10-2, where some boxes will be filled with information and others will be empty. This outcome provides a clear picture of which types of designs will:

- Be compatible with or support the organization's culture.
- Fulfill different types of organizational needs.
- Fulfill different types of employee needs.
- Link the fulfillment of employee needs to the achievement of business objectives.

(text continues on page 278)

Figure 10-4. The Design Element Worksheet.

Reward System Selector		
Type of Design	**Positive Attributes/Strengths**	**Limitations/Weaknesses**
Profit Sharing		
Annual Bonus		
Gainsharing		
Small Group		
Individual		
Key Contributor		
Equity Ownership		

Figure 10-5. The Organization's Culture Worksheet.

Organization's Culture		
Major Categories	**Current Elements**	**Desired Elements**
Demographics		
Vision		
Values		
Leadership Philosophy		
Compensation Philosophy		
Communication Philosophy		
Participation Philosophy		
Empowerment Philosophy		
Operating Philosophy		

Figure 10-6. The Organization's Needs Worksheet.

Organization's Needs		
Intrinsic Categories	**Current Elements**	**Desired Elements**
Educate		
Enable		
Empower		
Engage		
Unity		
Management Skills		
Superior Execution		
Flexibility		
Extrinsic Categories	**Current Elements**	**Desired Elements**
Business Plan		
Key Financial Measures		
Key Operational Measures		
Budgets		
Investor Expectations		

Figure 10-7. The Employee's Needs Worksheet.

Employees' Needs		
Intrinsic Categories	**Current Elements**	**Desired Elements**
Roles		
Rights		
Responsibilities		
Focus		
Positive Reinforcement		
Empowerment		
Participation		
Extrinsic Categories	**Current Elements**	**Desired Elements**
Rewards		
What Pay		
Why Pay		
How Pay		

Figure 10-8. The Reward System Selector Summary Worksheet.

Reward System Selector™ Summary Worksheet

Type Of Design	Organization's Culture	Organization's Needs		Employees' Needs	
		Intrinsic	Extrinsic	Intrinsic	Extrinsic
1. Profit Sharing					
2. Annual Bonus					
3. Gainsharing					
4. Small Group					
5. Individual					
6. Key Contributors					
7. Equity Ownership					

Line-Of-Sight, Expectations, and the Creation of a Satisfaction System

Dissatisfaction is the result of unfulfilled expectations. As we have seen, the Partnership Checklist identifies four key expectations that employees have. Part of management's responsibility is to help set and meet these employee partners' expectations.

Communications from senior management is critical to setting expectations. A good outline for setting expectations consists of communicating to all employees the following information:

- The mission: the main reason for the organization's existence.
- The objectives: the goals that, when achieved, will fulfill the mission.
- The strategy: a plan of action for reaching the objectives.
- The rewards: how the benefits of success will be shared.
- Management's expectations of employee performance: clear expectations build self-confidence, which leads to success, which leads to self-esteem.

Here the value of a good line-of-sight capability comes into play.

Providing employees who have line-of-sight capability with a clear understanding of the performance expected of them and their roles and goals enables them to relate their activities to the business strategy. It enables them to use their local wisdom to focus their activities in support of this strategy. They will make decisions, develop tactics, and take action that move the organization toward its business goals.

A line-of-sight capability develops flexibility within an organization. It provides awareness of customer needs and an understanding of how to adapt individual performance to the customers' changing interests.

If we associate a comprehensive Line-Of-Sight Linkage Tree with the relationships between the needs and rewards that are identified through the Reward System Selector process, we have all the information necessary to create an effective and efficient *satisfaction system.*

A long line-of-sight has the unique ability to connect the individual to the organization. Line-of-sight provides information to employee partners on the connection between their daily activities and the company's performance, between their pay and the economic health of the company.

The ultimate extension of a line-of-sight is the connection of company objectives to personal needs, where the attainment of one leads to the fulfillment of the other. A company that is based on the four management practices and that uses material rewards, creates a satisfaction system that offers fulfillment of social and material needs based on behavior and performance. Such a model contains all the elements essential to a lasting partnership.

The Performance-To-Reward Linkage Tool

Remember the Variance Tracking Form discussed in Chapter 6? We said we would discuss how reward systems link to that tool, and now we will.

Figure 10-9 illustrates how a slight modification to the variance tracking form can develop a direct line-of-sight link between performance and rewards. By adding a row to the form for incentive pay, the link between pay and performance is clearly stated. This clearly displays the impact a negative variance has on pay. It also clearly displays the impact on pay of improvement efforts to regain and exceed plan.

In this example, incentive pay only begins when performance meets plan. The employee estimates the weekly incentive earned at plan ($100 incentive forecast). The form provides visibility to the negative impact of performance variance ($0 incentive earned), and to the forecast effect on incentive pay of improvement efforts. If the actual performance meets the forecast performance for weeks 2 and 3, the employee will be back on schedule and have week 4 to earn above-plan incentive pay.

In this example we only used one performance objective to show the line-of-sight linkage between pay and performance. In a real plan, there would be multiple objectives, each with its own performance table.

* * *

In the end, an employee partnership can only be developed if the people decide for themselves to participate in the effort. And they will do so only if they see the potential for their needs to be met by partnering with the organization.

The four management practices provide a process that helps employees make the transition from a job mentality to a career mentality. They create a satisfaction system that offers the opportunity of ownership and partnership: ownership of a career and partnership in a company.

In any successful organization, every employee has to be committed to the business process if it is to exist past the first change of

Figure 10-9. The performance-to-reward linkage tool.

Department: _____

Team: _____

Partner: _____

Date: _____

Project: _____

Performance	Week 1	Week 2	Week 3	Week 4	Month Total
Plan	150	150	150	150	600
Forecast	150	162	163		
Cumulative Forecasted Variance		–13	0		
Incentive Forecast	$100	$ 0	$300	$100	$400
Actual	125	162			
Cumulative Actual Variance	–25	–13			
Incentive Earned	$ 0	$ 0			

direction caused by the economy. This commitment comes from the partnership developed by the four management practices—partnership in the design of the business process and partnership in the results.

The four management practices create a sustained culture that can weather the storms of economic change and emerge from each one stronger, faster, and more intelligent than the competition. The companies that implement these management practices will be winners in the new economy.

Bibliography

Adises, Ichak. *Corporate Lifecycles.* Englewood Cliffs, N.J.: Prentice-Hall, 1988.

Ankario, Loren. *Implementing Self-Directed Work Teams.* Boulder, Colo.: Career Track Publications, 1992.

Boyd, Charles. *Individual Commitment and Organizational Change.* New York: Quorum Books, 1992.

Case, John. *Open-Book Management: The Coming Business Revolution.* New York: HarperCollins, 1994.

Connellan, Thomas. *How to Grow People Into Self-Starters.* Ann Arbor, Mich.: The Achievement Institute, 1988.

Denison, Daniel. *Corporate Culture and Organizational Effectiveness.* New York: John Wiley & Sons, 1990.

Fox, Emmet. *Around the Year With Emmet Fox.* New York: Harper & Row, 1979.

French, Wendell L., and Cecil H. Bell, Jr. *Organizational Development: Behavioral Science Interventions for Organizational Improvement.* Englewood Cliffs, N.J.: Prentice-Hall, 1990.

Lawler, Edward E. III. *Pay and Organization Development.* Reading, Mass.: Addison-Wesley, 1983.

———. *Strategic Pay: Aligning Organizational Strategies and Pay Systems.* San Francisco: Jossey-Bass, 1990.

———. *The Ultimate Advantage: Creating the High-Involvement Organization.* San Francisco: Jossey-Bass, 1992.

McCoy, Thomas J. *Compensation and Motivation: Maximizing Employee Performance With Behavior-Based Incentive Plan.* New York: AMACOM, 1992.

Montgomery, Cynthia A., and Michael E. Porter. *Strategy: Seeking and Securing Competitive Advantages.* Boston: HBS Press, 1991.

Naisbitt, John. *Global Paradox.* New York: William Morrow & Co., 1994.

Porter, Michael E. *Competitive Advantage: Creating and Sustaining Superior Performance.* New York: The Free Press, 1987.

Schank, Roger, with Peter Childers. *The Creative Attitude: Learning to Ask and Answer the Right Questions.* New York: Macmillan, 1988.

Stack, Jack. *The Great Game of Business.* New York: Currency Books, 1992.

Watson, David L., and Roland G. Tharp. *Self-Directed Behavior: Self-Modification for Personal Adjustment.* Monterey, Calif.: Brooks/Cole Publishing, 1981.

Index